Women, Mysticism, and Hysteria
in Fin-de-Siècle Spain

Women, Mysticism, and Hysteria in Fin-de-Siècle Spain

JENNIFER SMITH

Vanderbilt University Press
Nashville

Cover image: *Lectura* (c.1901–1902; Reading) by Julio Romero de Torres. Courtesy of Museo Nacional Centro de Arte Reina Sofia (Reina Sofia National Museum and Center for the Arts).

Library of Congress Cataloging-in-Publication Data
Names: Smith, Jennifer, 1970 November 13– author.
Title: Women, mysticism, and hysteria in fin-de-siècle Spain / Jennifer Smith
Description: Nashville : Vanderbilt University Press, [2021] | Includes bibliographical references and index
Identifiers: LCCN 2020056887 (print) | LCCN 202005 (ebook) | ISBN 9780826501875 (hardcover) | ISBN 9780826501868 (paperback) | ISBN 9780826501882 (epub) | ISBN 9780826501899 (pdf)
Subjects: Women—Spain—Social conditions—19th century | Women—Spain—Social conditions—20th century | Mysticism—Spain—History | Women mystics—Spain—History | Hysteria—Social aspects—Spain—History | Feminism—Spain—History.
Classification: LCC HQ1692 .S596 2021 (print) | LCC HQ1692 (ebook) | DDC 305.40946—dc23
LC record available at https://lccn.loc.gov/2020056887
LC ebook record available at https://lccn.loc.gov/2020056888

CONTENTS

ACKNOWLEDGMENTS

I WOULD LIKE to express my deepest gratitude to Denise DuPont, Véronique Maisier, Nicholas Wolters, and the outside readers for Vanderbilt University Press, for generously offering their time and expertise to read earlier drafts of the book and give insightful feedback. I would like to thank Catherine Jagoe for her help in the early stages of this project when she generously shared many of her materials with me. Thanks to Lourdes Albuixech and Véronique Maisier for their assistance with translations from Spanish and French, and Francisco Vázquez García for sharing an electronic copy of one of his books when the university libraries in the US were shut down due to COVID.

Thanks go to *Revista de Estudios Hispánicos* and *Decimonónica* for permissions to reprint previously published material. Financial support for early research for this project came from the Program for Cultural Cooperation between Spain's Ministry of Education, Culture and Sports and United States Universities and from the Timothy J. Rogers Fellowship Foundation. The time needed to complete this project was made possible by sabbatical leave granted by Southern Illinois University, Carbondale.

Finally, I would also like to thank my husband, Shawn, and daughter, Francesca, for their love and support.

INTRODUCTION

ON JANUARY 23, 1836, Doña María de los Dolores Quiroga, more commonly known as Sor Patrocinio, was detained and charged with faking divine favors in order to aid in the subversion of the state by Prince Don Carlos and his followers.[1] Medical doctors came to the aid of the prosecution in an attempt to demonstrate that Sor Patrocinio's stigmata were self-inflicted and had been cured.[2] The court found her guilty and ordered her to leave Madrid and reside in the Convento de Concepcionistas (Conceptionist Convent) in Talavera de la Reina.[3] Despite, or perhaps because of, the court's judgment against the Spanish nun, her fame increased within the religious sectors of Spanish society, as word of her divine favors spread throughout the country. On September 24 of 1844, not quite a year after Isabel II was crowned queen of Spain at the age of fourteen, a royal decree ended Sor Patrocinio's exile, and the Spanish nun returned to Madrid.[4] Shortly thereafter, she played a pivotal role in the arrangement of the marriage of Isabel II to Francisco de Asís, and came to occupy a position of privilege in the royal court. However, the controversy surrounding Sor Patrocinio followed her throughout her life: she was subjected to an assassination attempt in 1849, a kidnapping attempt in 1866, and was forced to go into exile on several occasions. In 1877, several years after having escaped to France following the liberal victory in the Revolution of 1868, Sor Patrocinio was allowed to return to Spain, where she would remain until her death at age ninety-two, on January 27, 1904. The understanding of Sor Patrocinio's mysticism and divine favors as either authentic or feigned represents the divide between, on the one hand, the Catholic segments of society that supported the modern-day saint in the hopes that she would strengthen a Church that was under fierce political attack, and on the other hand, the secular scientists, doctors, and liberals who wanted to weaken the political power of the Church.

Although fraud was the main charge brought against mystics in cases such as Sor Patrocinio's, what civil authorities really sought was to discredit these women and weaken what they perceived to be a political threat.[5] In Sor Patrocinio's case, her close relationship with Isabel II led progressive liberals to view her as the mastermind behind Isabel II's political alliance with the more conservative Partido Liberal Moderado (Moderate Liberal Party).[6] Though few cases of mysticism were brought to the civil courts in nineteenth-century Europe, those that were garnered widespread attention from the public, who tended to view the cases as trials of the supernatural.[7] The prosecution in these cases employed two main strategies: translating mystical phenomena into criminal acts—in Sor Patrocinio's case this meant charges of fraud (faking her stigmata) and attempted subversion of state (visions of Don Carlos)—and destroying the mystics' reputation through expert testimony by medical doctors.[8] Sometimes defendants were exonerated but declared hysterical, which meant acquittal still carried the stigma of a medical diagnosis.[9] Indeed, Jan Goldstein, in her study "The Hysteria Diagnosis and Politics of Anticlericalism in Late Nineteenth-Century France," argues that the large increase in the diagnosing of religious experiences as hysteria in late nineteenth-century France was "consonant with the frenetic crusade for laicization which marked republican politics in this era."[10] This leads Goldstein to conclude that hysteria was a political construct used by liberals to strengthen their own power and to undermine the Catholic Church.[11] Janet Beizer goes farther to assert that "fastened onto the hysteric's almost totemic form is the anxiety of an age."[12]

The Republican press, largely through satire and caricature, also played a pivotal role in discrediting such women. According to Andrea Graus, "Anticlerical and Republican caricature used [Sor Patrocinio's] image to warn of the dangers of the clergy ruling the state. She [. . .] became an icon of absolutism and the struggles

¿Quién quiere sebo?

FIGURE 1. "¿Quién quiere sebo?" (1868; Who wants some lard?) by SEM from the collection *Los Borbones en pelota* (1868; The Bourbon dynasty in the nude). http://bdh.bne.es/bnesearch/detalle/bdh0000180846. Courtesy of the Biblioteca Nacional de España (The National Library of Spain).

the liberal regime had to face."[13] One of the various images of Sor Patrocinio that Graus analyzes is the nun's depiction in *Los Borbones en pelota* (The Bourbon dynasty in the nude), a collection of satirical and pornographic watercolor paintings signed SEM.[14] While the Queen herself is the protagonist of the collection, appearing forty-seven times, Sor Patrocinio is also depicted nineteen times, often engaging in "deviant" sexual activities such as lesbian activity, masturbation, and group sex.[15] Figure 1 shows Sor Patrocinio engaging in a sexual act with the queen in her bed, with a severed penis on the floor beside them. Graus argues that this image not only serves to degrade both women but also shows the nun's influence over the queen: "by lying on top of Isabel, the nun is taking control over Spain."[16] Lou Charnon-Deutsch notes that the severed organ on the floor next to Sor Patrocinio and the queen also serves "as a warning about the castrating power of powerful women."[17] Particularly relevant to my study here is that this image serves as a pictorial example of the way female mystics were discredited through their explicit sexualization in medical and literary texts of the time.

Indeed, the specific aim of this book is to show that the reinterpretation of female mysticism as hysteria and nymphomania in late nineteenth- and early twentieth-century Spain was part of a larger project to suppress the growing female emancipation movement by sexualizing the female subject. I argue that we see this phenomenon in medical, social, and literary texts, and that despite many liberals' hostility toward the Church, the techniques secular doctors and intellectuals employed to discredit female mystics have striking similarities to the ways the Spanish Inquisition reinterpreted female mysticism as sexual deviance and demonic possession in order to discredit powerful women. I also argue that we can better understand mysticism's subversive potential in terms of the patriarchal order by examining the writings of Emilia Pardo Bazán. The only woman author studied here, Pardo Bazán, unlike her male counterparts, rejected the hysteria diagnosis and promoted mysticism as a path for women's personal development and self-realization.

The first two chapters are historical in scope and explore the cultural fascination with mysticism and hysteria in women primarily in medical, social, and philosophical writings of the time. The first chapter contextualizes the topic by exploring Spanish medical discourses on women to reveal how the hysteria and nymphomania diagnoses, as well as the increased social pressures on couples to produce more offspring, sought to pathologize religious chastity and women who pursued a life and career outside the domestic sphere. In addition to demonstrating how the hysterization of the female body operated in Spain in the nineteenth century, this chapter shows how two other Foucauldian strategies not specifically concerned with women—the psychiatrization of perverse pleasure (in the form of nymphomania, masturbation, and female same-sex desire) and the socialization of procreative behavior—were also involved in the construction of a female subject "naturally" unable to assume the same rights and freedoms as men. This investigation also reveals European, and specifically Spanish, precedents for

Sigmund Freud's theory of female sexuality. It becomes clear that Freud's idea that normal women only find pleasure in sexual acts that lead to reproduction was merely a unique reconfiguration of a variety of nineteenth-century medical assertions.

Drawing parallels between the early modern period and the late nineteenth century, Chapter 2 argues that nineteenth-century doctors and intellectuals attempted to discredit mysticism in order to undermine one of the few existing models of female emancipation. Indeed, prominent figures such as Santa Teresa de Jesús continued to attract the attention and admiration of the general public at the turn of the century. Yet, by reinterpreting religious ecstasy as disease or sexual deviance, many doctors and intellectuals were able to impose their restrictive conceptions of female identity that insisted women's biology confined their sphere of influence to the home. This chapter looks at texts such as Ramón León Mainez's *Teresa de Jesús ante la crítica* (1880; Teresa de Jesús, in the face of criticism), Eduardo Zamacois's medical treatise *El misticismo y las perturbaciones del sistema nervioso* (1893; Mysticism and disturbances of the nervous system), and the 1907 Spanish translation of Auguste Armand Marie's *Mysticisme et folie* (Mysticism and insanity), among many others, in order to show how authors such as these practiced retrospective medicine. In other words, just as the counter-reformation Church had often interpreted mystical rapture in women as sexual deviance and demonic possession, these authors diagnosed past manifestations of female mysticism as hysteria and nymphomania, diseases directly related to female sexuality.

In Chapter 3 I connect my cultural analysis to a trilogy of novels written by radical naturalist Eduardo López Bago. Combining naturalist determinism and sexually explicit topics, López Bago created novels that gave fictional representations to popular medical discourses of the day. Although his works are not as well-known as those of canonical authors such as Leopoldo Alas, Emilia Pardo Bazán, and Benito Pérez Galdós, and although López Bago was brought to court for pornography charges (of which he was ultimately acquitted), his novels were immensely popular, indicating their influence on the reading public of his day. The particular focus of this chapter is López Bago's *Cura* trilogy which includes *El cura*

(1885; The priest), *El confesionario* (1885; The confessional) and *La monja* (1886; The nun). These works give fictional representation to late nineteenth-century discourses on female sexuality and specifically to the (re)interpretation of female mysticism as hysteria and nymphomania. The purpose therefore is to show how these texts serve as a relatively faithful reproduction of the medical discourses analyzed in Chapters 1 and 2.

Chapter 4 compares the *Cura* trilogy with Leopoldo Alas's literary masterpiece *La Regenta* (1884–85, The regent's wife). It argues that the narrator of *La Regenta*, although subtler in approach, also uses Ana's mystical experiences as a coded sign for her hysteria. This analysis distinguishes itself from other critics' work by studying Ana's hysteria in relation to specific Spanish discourses at the time, rather than to the theories of Freud, whose work was little known in Spain until the 1920s,[18] or to the much more contemporary psychoanalytical theories of Jacques Lacan and Luce Irigaray. Instead, I build on Noël Valis's pivotal essay "Hysteria and Historical Context in *La Regenta*," in order to place Alas's representation of mysticism and hysteria in a wider contemporary social context. This context includes *La Regenta*'s dialog with López Bago's trilogy which was written at essentially the same time. Moreover, I engage with Denise DuPont's work on Alas's own views on mysticism and more specifically on Santa Teresa in order to explore the degree to which Alas personally viewed mystical experiences, particularly in women, as a sign of hysteria.

Chapter 5 explores the ways the well-known feminist author Emilia Pardo Bazán broke sharply with these cultural trends by dismissing the diagnosis of hysteria as a negative cultural construct imposed on women, and by embracing mysticism as a viable path for women's self-realization. In certain essays and short stories, she rejects the notion of the female body as saturated with sexuality and inherently pathological, and points to social and political causes for the frequent manifestation of "disease" in women as well as to the blatant misogyny informing the practice of medicine in her day. Moreover, embracing the mystical idea that self-realization led to personal autonomy, Pardo Bazán argued that the freedom to defy institutional authority was a privilege earned through education, discipline, and self-realization, as seen in the case of the mystics. This belief explains Pardo Bazán's presentation of mysticism as a viable path for personal emancipation, her interest in female hagiography, and her decision to deal with the theme of female mysticism in her last novel, *Dulce dueño* (1911; Sweet master). This chapter, then, simultaneously explores Pardo Bazán's critiques of the hysteria diagnosis as well as her belief that mystical theology provided the philosophical basis for female emancipation. The inclusion of the writings of a female author who defied the cultural trends of the time in the last chapter reveals a competing narrative and begs the question, To what degree did Pardo Bazán's alternative perspective influence changing views on the question of women, hysteria, and mysticism?

This project specifically dialogs Denise DuPont's *Writing Teresa: The Saint from Ávila at the Fin-de-siglo* (2011) and Kathy Bacon's *Negotiating Sainthood: Distinction,* Cursilería, *and Saintliness in Spanish Novels* (2007). It is distinct, however, in its specific focus on mysticism and hysteria as a general cultural phenomenon discussed in medical, literary, and cultural texts. In its approach it is much closer to Cristina Mazzoni's *Saint Hysteria: Neurosis, Mysticism, and Gender in European Culture* (1996). However, while *Saint Hysteria* focuses entirely on Italy and France, my study deals specifically with Spain and studies the understandings of mysticism and hysteria through the writings of Spanish authors, intellectuals, and doctors. In short, my investigation distinguishes itself in its attention to the peculiar circumstances and details of Spanish interpretations of mysticism at the turn of the century and therefore comprises the first book-length study on the fin-de-siècle debate on mysticism and hysteria in Spain in relation to women.

The theoretical approach employed is best described as Foucauldian and feminist, although the ideas of Thomas Laqueur are also of pivotal importance here, as in any discussion of the history of conceptions of sexuality. Considering the sometimes-tense relationship between feminism and Foucault, and the continued debates surrounding Foucault and Laqueur's portrayal of the evolution of thinking on sexuality, a few words seem in order on these matters. Feminist critiques of Foucault often highlight the influential French philosopher's seeming gender blindness.[19] Dominique D. Fisher notes, for example, that Foucault's *History of Sexuality* "addresses women peripherally, dedicating only a few pages to the hysterization of women's bodies and to a brief reading of the Lapcourt incident."[20] However, Fisher goes on to show how feminist critics such as Sandra Bartkey and Judith Butler have effectively used Foucault's ideas on power articulated in the *History of Sexuality* to dismantle essentialist ideas about gender.[21] Similarly, Angela King argues that lacunae in Foucault's work in regard to women "can be fruitfully exposed, explored and remedied."[22] This book takes up this task by showing the unique ways in which specific sexual discourses on women affirm, negate, or expand on Foucault's theories.

There is also the question of the degree to which Foucault and Laqueur's ideas are translatable to the Spanish context. Richard Cleminson and Francisco Vázquez García, leading scholars in the history of sexuality in Spain, stress the importance of not merely applying the ideas of such thinkers without studying specifics, and of noting that Spain did not simply copy ideas from other European countries, but dialogued with them and modified them.[23] Still, they also acknowledge that "any examination of the practices and representations which occurred around sexually ambiguous persons in modern Spain must necessarily draw on the work of Michel Foucault and Thomas Laqueur."[24] In accordance with this line of thinking, my own analyses, while drawing on Foucault and Laqueur, rely heavily on the specifics of Spanish discourses themselves. Indeed, my discussions of hysteria, nymphomania, and female same sex-desire have the specific aim of bringing the Spanish context more into focus. While scholars like Catherine Jagoe were pioneers in bringing medical discourses on female sexuality to a much wider reading public,[25] here I aim to build on this work by examining lesser studied topics, such as medical discourses on mysticism and female same-sex desire, and lesser studied texts, such as Eduardo Zamacois's *El misticismo y las perturbaciones del sistema nervioso* (1893) or V. Suárez Casañ's *El amor lesbio* (1892?; Lesbian love).

When applying the ideas of Foucault and Laqueur, there is also the matter of liberalism's later development in Spain and whether that makes the Spanish case different. In this regard, it is important to remember that despite economic lags in industrialization and in the development of a large middle class, cultural practices that accompanied the rise of liberalism in the West firmly took hold in nineteenth-century Spain.[26] This is clearly evident in the growth of the Spanish hygiene movement and its close ties with liberalism and legal medicine. In Spain, as in other European nations, liberalism was a movement overwhelmingly led by white, upper-middle-class men who sought to maintain traditional social hierarchies despite liberalism's assertion that all individuals were deserving of the same rights.[27] In his book *Monlau, Rubio, Giné: Curar y gobernar: Medicina y liberalismo en la España del siglo XIX* (2003; Monlau, Rubio, Giné: Cure and govern: Medicine and liberalism in nineteenth-century Spain), Ricardo Campos-Marín underscores the ties between doctors' liberal political affiliations and their medical work. Although some dabbled with more radical political ideologies, they were generally conservative in their views about women and the working classes and were committed to finding in nature and science reasons for rationalizing the marginalization of such groups. For example, Campos-Marín notes the conservative views of the famous Catalan hygienist Felipe Monlau not only on questions of gender, but also on social class.[28] Despite Monlau's writings on the poor working conditions of industrialized laborers, he insisted on the naturalness of inequality and the social hierarchy, on the sanctity of free enterprise, and even on the workers' intrinsic wickedness.[29] Thus, while Spain's transition to liberalism and modernity was most certainly more uneven than in neighboring countries, the liberal medical agenda of Spanish doctors shared the aim of keeping women, working classes, and other marginalized groups in their place, even when it varied, to some degree, in implementation.

While the categories of sex and class were used in ways we would understand them today, the category of *raza* is more unclear. According to Joshua Goode, in turn-of-the-century Spain, the latter term was malleable and used to refer to the people of the Spanish nation as a romanticized "spiritual entity, with its citizenship partaking of an inborn collective soul."[30] The embrace of Spain's multiethnic past through theories of racial fusion and hybridity, while seemingly more inclusive, served to "forge a naturalistic and scientific sense of unity in a Spain increasingly seen as fractured by region, class, and political ideology."[31] This understanding of the Spanish "race" combined with the desire to socially engineer a stronger society led to the racialization of all "degenerate" groups that were believed to threaten the nation. According to Ricardo Campos Marín, José Martínez Pérez, and Rafael Huertas García-Alejo, each individual was defined by the degree to which s/he conformed to the biological collective referred to as the *raza*.[32] Those who did not, because they were working-class, were sexually promiscuous, suffered from tuberculosis, etc., were a threat to the Spanish political body and conceived of as a pathogenic Other. Citing Foucault, Richard Cleminson and Teresa Fuentes Peris remind us how these theories of racial degeneration worked hand in hand with the "science" of perversions, the focus of my study here.[33] Indeed, in *La invención del racismo* (The invention of racism), Francisco Vázquez García argues that modern racism in Spain emerged out of this liberal biopolitcal regime, which sought to eliminate obstacles to the new social order.[34] Building on the work of the British sociologist Zygmut Bauman, Vázquez García asserts that racism in modern Spain was not about returning to pre-modern prejudices, but rather about the development of a new mode of social engineering tied to Modernity.[35]

While the issues of race, class, and disability receive less explicit attention here, they are intertwined with the topic at hand. According to Bridget Aldaraca, the exaltation of the Angel in the House was aimed precisely at "an aspiring bourgeoisie whose principle concern [was] to draw a sharp line between itself and the lower classes."[36] This domestic ideal inherently precluded women forced to work outside of the home out of necessity. Doctors and hygienists overwhelmingly condemned the practice of allowing women to work in factories and shops on the grounds that it was a threat to the woman, her children, and the future of the Spanish "race" as a whole, thereby invoking fears of degeneration.[37] Moreover, the revered chastity of the idealized angelic wife and mother was contrasted with the salacious sexual appetites attributed to lower-class women. This is seen most clearly in *La Regenta* (analyzed in Chapter 3) where the latter group of women are portrayed as natural sexual deviants. Unlike their upper-middle-class counterparts, they don't struggle with their conscience about transgressing social norms on female chastity. In fact, it is upper-middle-class women's worries about their own fall in social status that lead them to redirect their sexual desires through spiritual pursuits. We see this struggle in the *Cura* trilogy with Gertrudis, in *La Regenta* with Ana, and with Lina in *Dulce dueño*. In all works, fear of degeneration and class descension looms large in the female protagonists' reservations about acting on their own sexual desires.

The question of race and disability are also related to the extent that racism is understood as part of the modern Spanish nation-building project and that hysteria is understood as a *discapacidad* (disability), even though this term was not used at the time.[38] If in fact the objective of the liberal-medical regime was to retain traditional hierarchies by pathologizing socially undesirable groups, the hysteria diagnosis itself was part of this social engineering project. In "Criphystemologies: What Disability Theory Needs to Know about Hysteria," Anna Mollow asserts that hysteria is an undocumented disability, like post-traumatic stress disorder today, and is therefore frequently absent in key texts on disability studies.[39] Turning her attention to this omission, Mollow reminds us that hysterics suffered from the same stigma of sufferers of documented disabilities while simultaneously having their suffering dismissed as "all in their head."[40] In this way Mollow reminds us that the construction of hysteria was very much entwined in power relations in the same ways documented disabilities were.

While my approach here is most certainly feminist, it does not rely solely on the ideas of any particular theorist. It builds on a range of diverse feminist studies on hysteria (Beizer, Cixous, Goldstein, Hunter, Irigaray, Maines, Mitchell, Showalter, Smith-Rosenberg) and theories that began to dismantle the idea that biological sex, unlike gender, is fixed. Judith Butler, of course, was pivotal in dismantling the sex/gender distinction. In *Bodies That Matter: On the Discursive Limits of Sex*, Butler argues that to claim sex is a social and linguistic construct is not to deny the existence of a material body outside of language, but rather it is to recognize there is no understanding of that body that is not in some way a construct of the knowledge and culture that interpret it. In other words, "there is no reference to a pure body which is not at the same time a further formation of that body."[41] Along this line of thinking, the present study takes as its point of departure the premise that all conceptions of the material body and one's biological sex are cultural and linguistic constructs rather than material realities.

There is also the question of how to read literary texts in relation to other discourses, here specifically, in relation to medical texts and the views of literary authors. The branch of cultural studies influenced by new historicism advocates for the study of the reciprocal relationship between literature and history.[42] The purpose is to study both how literary texts influence culture and vice versa.[43] In this vein, this study seeks to put literary discourses within a larger dialog, while acknowledging at all times the instability of the narrative constructed. This approach is facilitated by the fact that, as Catherine Jagoe points out, in nineteenth-century Spain the boundary between literature and science was not as clearly demarcated as it is today.[44] Many authors of the time, like Eduardo López Bago and Eduardo Zamacois, both studied here, were medical doctors and authors of literary works. Moreover, as medical texts were intended for a broad audience of nonspecialists, they were written in a literary style, while literary texts, imbued with the culture of the day, frequently employed scientific language.[45] Yet, as all texts, and all language for that matter, are larger than the minds and social contexts that produce them, the aim of this analysis is to highlight one prominent discursive dialog among many.

Finally, a word on the selection of texts seems in order. My purpose here is to show a specific dialog between medical texts and literary works that portray female mysticism as sublimated sexual desire and disease. I analyze in detail lesser-studied Spanish medical texts on the subject as well as literary texts that clearly reproduce or refute the ideas presented in such works. Eduardo López Bago's *Cura* trilogy is particularly illustrative because of its unambiguously faithful reproduction of many of the medical ideas examined. Similarly, *La Regenta* has been selected as a point of comparison with López Bago's work both for its striking similarities in its sexualization of mysticism and for its philosophical and stylistic differences in its treatment of the subject. Pardo Bazán is then brought into the dialog because her essays, short stories, and last novel, *Dulce dueño*, specifically refute ideas put forth by López Bago and Alas. While Benito Pérez Galdós, one of the great writers of the period, also dealt with female mysticism in works such as *La fontana de oro* (1870; The fountain of gold), *La familia de León Roch* (1878; The family of Leon Roach), *La loca de la casa* (1892; The madwoman of the house), and *Halma* (1895), his treatment of false mysticism in women is generally less explicitly involved in the sexualization of the mystical experience.[46] Alas himself noted that while Galdós also took an interest in exploring questions of false mysticism in women, these explorations were less focused on these women's intimate, personal experiences of religion.[47] While there is certainly more work to be done on this topic in relation to Galdós and other authors, this study is not meant to be exhaustive but rather illustrative of one particular metanarrative in medical and literary texts of the day.

1 Women and the Deployment of Sexuality in Nineteenth-Century Spain

IN NINETEENTH-CENTURY SPAIN, as in many other European countries of the time, medicine and hygiene became predominant forms of managing the population.[1] The term *medicina legal* (legal medicine) was used to refer to a legal system in which medicine served as the guiding light in the formation of laws. Two early treatises on the subject were Ramón López Mateos's *Pensamiento sobre la razón de las leyes* (1810; Thinking on the reason of laws) and Francisco Fabra Soldevilla's *Filosofía de la legislación natural* (1830; The philosophy of natural legislation).[2] These authors, both doctors, argued that medical knowledge of human nature should provide the fundamental principles for all legislation.[3] Doctors began playing a larger role in social reform and politics and the term hygiene (*higiene*) was now frequently invoked in the name of social improvement. The two branches of hygiene, public hygiene and private hygiene, worked hand in hand to ensure the protection, growth, and health of both the individual and the community; it is therefore not surprising that hygienists dealt extensively with issues of gender and sexuality. The new national concern with the health of the populace brought about the first manuals on hygiene in the 1840s, the creation of university professorships of Higiene Pública y Privada (Public and private hygiene) in 1843, the Dirección General de Beneficencia y Sanidad (General organization of welfare and health) in 1847, and the Ley General de Sanidad (The general law of health) of 1855.[4] This was also accompanied by the emergence of systems of collecting and analyzing national statistics on the population toward the end of the century.[5]

Intellectuals of the time were very of aware of hygiene's new role as a technique of social control. For example, the nineteenth-century doctor Francisco Méndez Álvaro, an important figure in the establishment of the Sociedad Española de Higiene (Spanish society of hygiene), argued that hygiene must assume the role formerly played by religion as the primary defender of society.[6] And the medical doctor and author of the *Curso elemental de higiene privada y pública* (1871; Elementary course on public and private hygiene), Juan Giné y Partagás (1836–1903), argued that hygiene was more effective at policing the nation than the Civil Guard.[7] So, while those involved in the dissemination of a national hygiene were aware of its regulating effect on the population, they presented it as a progressive social force, as an objective science that sought every individual's well-being and that offered a preferable alternative to the rigid doctrines of the Catholic Church and the physically oppressive practices of the national police (la Guardia Civil). In this way, hygiene was able to partially disguise its reactionary elements and newly gained power over its subjects and make them more palatable to the public.

As the hygiene movement was generally concerned with affirming a conventional and bourgeois social order, it focused much attention on keeping women in the domestic sphere. According to Thomas Laqueur, the ideas of the French Revolution and the rise of liberalism in late eighteenth-century Europe made it increasingly difficult to argue against female emancipation since liberal theory asserted that all human beings were naturally free.[8] On what grounds, therefore, could traditional patriarchal society continue to deny women the same rights as men? The solution was found in "nature."[9] Doctors and scientists would now argue that women's nature determined their subordinate position in society. Or, in the words of the famous Catalan hygienist Pedro Felipe Monlau (1808–1871), women could not be freed because they were restricted by the "yoke" (*yugo*) of their natural constitutions.[10]

Laqueur explains that the proponents of liberalism in the modern era used new scientific interpretations of female sexuality to deny women the very rights they themselves were fighting for, and they did so based on a change in the conception of the two sexes that took place toward the end of the eighteenth century.[11] According to Laqueur, from the time of the Greeks up until the eighteenth century, the difference between the sexes was viewed as a hierarchical one (4–5). The female was merely an inverted, less-fully developed, and inferior male (4). The womb was an inverted penis, the ovaries were inverted testes, and the uterus was equated with the male scrotum (4). However, Laqueur argues that by the end of the eighteenth century, the old hierarchical model of homologies between the sexes was substituted for a new model that polarized the sexes and stressed their absolute difference (5). This polarization of the sexes, which began with a reexamination and redefinition of the female sexual organs, extended to all aspects of the individual's existence (5).

Laqueur's theories have had several detractors who have argued that there was never one prevailing view on sexual differentiation. Scholars such as Joan Cadden, and Lorraine Daston and Katherine Park, for example, have asserted that a wide variety of views were always in circulation.[12] Although this debate is far from over, Catherine Jagoe has effectively shown that there is enough evidence in the Spanish medical discourses of the time to substantiate the prevalence of the transition from the one sex model to the two sex model in nineteenth-century Spain.[13] To be sure, most nineteenth-century medical texts on women insisted on differentiating the male from the female in both physique and character.[14] Nineteenth-century Spanish doctors agree that women are smaller and weaker than men and that they are controlled by their reproductive organs. More importantly, women are viewed as hypersensitive; their emotional side dominates over their intellect and they are therefore naturally better suited for loving and nurturing a family than for intellectual tasks or active participation in society.[15]

It is apparent that, as Laqueur argues, the view of the female as "not inferior" but "different" did not, in any way, help to liberate women. This polarization of the sexes merely affirmed that women, as men's opposite, should not be allowed to enjoy the same freedoms. In fact, in a speech he gave to the Real Academia de Medicina (The royal academy of medicine), Andrés del Busto y López (1832–1899), also known as the Marquis del Busto, goes so far as to argue that laws need to be written on the books that protect women from such freedoms, which he refers to as "las quimeras y las utopias de los que, queriendo confundir su destino con el del hombre, la quieren ocupar en la gestión de los negocios públicos y en el gobierno de los pueblos" (the preposterous ideas and utopias of those who, wanting to confuse [a woman's] destiny with that of a man's, want [women] to be involved in the management of public business and in the government of nations).[16] The passive, maternal, nurturing woman was therefore supposed to restrict herself to the domestic sphere while her opposite, the active, social, intellectual male, was supposed to move about society freely.

It was also argued that the various upheavals that nature imposed on the female body, mainly menstruation, pregnancy, childbirth, lactation, and menopause, made a woman unable to perform outside the home. Other medical experts claimed that the household, composed of the union of man and woman, was one organic whole, and therefore counted as only one free subject, whose "head," the husband/father, exercised its lawful right to vote and participate in civil society.[17] This prohibition on female participation in society was reinforced by medical texts that described the pathologies of women who did not fulfill their prescribed role. For example, learning was seen as antagonistic to woman's role as procreator. It was argued that if a woman became interested in learning at an early age, her genitalia and reproductive organs would not develop correctly, and she would very likely be infertile as an adult.[18] The well-known doctor and hygienist Ángel Pulido Fernández (1852–1932) tells the women readers of his *Bosquejos medico-sociales para la mujer* (1876; Socio-medical advice for women) that mental activities could lead to insanity.[19] And Monlau makes the argument that fertilization is facilitated by the couple's possessing opposite characteristics and that in cases where the husband

and wife practice the same profession, the woman will not be able to conceive.[20]

The reaffirmation of the domestic role of women was particularly restricting in the nineteenth century as capitalism and industrialization established the home as a strictly private sphere. Unlike in agricultural communities, where a large part of production continued to take place in the home, with industrialization and the rise of urban living, the role of the home in the marketplace was reduced strictly to consumption. However, it should be pointed out that this domestication of women applied primarily to middle-class women since many lower-class women were forced to work outside the home out of economic necessity. For example, as Raymond Carr notes, by the turn of the century one third of the workforce in the province of Barcelona was composed of women.[21] On the opposite side of the class spectrum, wealthy women who had the time, money, and freedom to enjoy a life outside of the home through various social activities were often portrayed as frivolous and selfish for not conforming to the domestic ideal.

In the first volume of *The History of Sexuality*, Michel Foucault devises the concept of the deployment of sexuality to describe the social pressures in the nineteenth century to define oneself in terms of one's sexual behavior.[22] Foucault, refuting the notion that the nineteenth century was a period in which sex was silenced, argues that this period actually saw an explosion of discourses on sexuality and that the individual was constantly being incited to define oneself in the terms of this new sexual knowledge. Foucault outlines four specific strategies of the deployment of sexuality: hysterization of women's bodies, pathologization of children's sex, socialization of procreative behavior, and psychiatrization of perverse pleasure.[23] A study of nineteenth-century medical discourses on women reveals how the hysterization of women's bodies, as well as the socialization of procreative behavior and the psychiatrization of perverse pleasure, constructed a female subject "naturally" unable to assume the rights of male citizens.[24] Thus in addition to demonstrating how the hysterization of the female body operated in Spain in the nineteenth century, this chapter also addresses feminist critiques of Foucault's lack of concern with women by showing how two Foucauldian strategies not originally concerned with women were also involved in the construction of the female subject in the nineteenth century.

While there has been an increasing body of work produced in the last decades on sexuality in modern Spain,[25] this is the first study to examine in detail the specific ways in which these three Foucauldian technologies apply to the predicament of nineteenth-century Spanish women.[26] Furthermore, this investigation also explores in detail European, and specifically Spanish, precedents of Sigmund Freud's theory of female sexuality.[27] It becomes clear that Freud's idea that normal women only find pleasure in sexual acts that lead to reproduction was merely a unique reconfiguration of a variety of nineteenth-century medical assertions. Finally, this chapter lays the groundwork for the examination of the sexualization of female mysticism in fin-de-siècle Spanish literature and culture examined in the subsequent chapters.

Hysterization of the Female Body

The hysterization of the female body involved the view of the female body as "thoroughly saturated with sexuality" and, therefore, inherently pathological and hysterical.[28] This made woman one of nineteenth-century doctors' preferred objects of study. From the time a woman reached puberty until the time she completed menopause, her entire being was seen as dominated by the natural drives of her reproductive organs. Nervous disorders such as hysteria were attributed to wandering wombs and ovaries that were not being employed in the service of reproduction. When such disorders appeared in apparently normal women, that is, married, childbearing women, the inherent pathology of the female body was assumed to be the cause.

The result was that all women, married and unmarried, sexually active or chaste, with or without children, could be controlled by medical discourses that insisted that the female body was naturally "hysterical," and therefore in constant need of medical supervision and treatment. Most Spanish medical texts on women at the time begin by enumerating the differences between the sexes and take advantage of the opportunity to emphasize women's highly excitable and irritable nature. For example, Baltasar de Viguera, author of the four-volume *Fisiología y patología de la mujer* (1827; The physiology and pathology of women), claims that a female's excitability is the essential defining characteristic of her sex: "La muy fina escitabilidad de todos los organos . . . es cabalmente lo que constituye el caracter específico del bello sexo." (The keen excitability of all of the organs . . . is exactly what constitutes the specific character of the fair sex).[29] Women's excitability is quickly related to their sexuality and predisposition to nervous disorders since it was believed that the female sexual organs, the womb in particular, were directly connected to the central nervous system and, therefore, responsible for hysteria in women.[30] For example Felipe Monlau, in the second edition of his best-selling *Higiene del matrimonio, o, El libro de los casados* (1858) argues that "en la matriz retumban indefectiblemente *todas las afecciones* fisicas y morales de la mujer" (emphasis mine; *All the* physical and moral *diseases* of women unfailingly resound in the womb).[31] And Viguera insists that the womb plays a dominant role over all the other organs in the female's body: "todos los organos y funciones de su economia existen en bastante manera subordinados a las imperiosas simpatías del útero, tanto en el estado fisiologico como en el patologico" (all of the organs and their functions remain subordinated to the imperative demands of the uterus, both in the physiological and pathological states).[32] At one point, Viguera even expresses his awe at the tyrannical power of the womb and exclaims, "¡qué de exaltaciones, trastornos, conmociones é irregularidades nerviosas, no se irradian á veces de este mismo aparato visceral, ostentando su alta prepotencia, y desquiciando el órden físico y moral con escenas tan singulares que sorprenden y admiran al mismo tiempo!" (what exaltations, disorders, nervous commotions and irregularities, do not irradiate at times from this same organ, showing off its absolute dominance, and upsetting the physical and moral order with scenes so unique that they produce shock and awe at the same time!).[33] This view of the womb as an organ that not only dominates woman, but also makes her body inherently hysterical because of its temperamental nature, saturates the female subject with her sexuality.

This hysterization of the female body was further achieved by the medical assertion that natural periods in a woman's life were also pathologies in and of themselves. Puberty, menstruation, pregnancy, childbirth, breastfeeding, and menopause were all viewed as disorders that needed medical supervision and treatment. For example, the medical hygienist Ángel Pulido Fernández believed that menstruation, pregnancy, birth, and breastfeeding caused insanity in women.[34] According to arguments like those of Dr. Pulido Fernández, even a healthy woman who followed the "natural" path of marriage and procreation could still easily slip into insanity during at least a fourth of her lifetime. Since the female body was seen as inherently diseased, the nineteenth-century woman was prone to illness even if she strictly followed the dictates of the new national hygiene.

Despite the large number of female ailments that were receiving attention by the nineteenth-century medical community, hysteria was one of the most studied female illnesses of the time.[35] Yet the origins of hysteria date much further back. According to Mark S. Micale, hysteria can be traced back to the ancient Egyptians and Greeks who viewed it as a female disease that resulted from a womb that began to wander throughout the female body.[36] However, despite the disease's long history, it was not until the nineteenth century that hysteria became a main focus of medical science.[37] This period witnessed a proliferation of scientific discourses on the subject, and an abundance of theories arose on the origins and causes of the disease.[38] The most prominent of all the nineteenth-century physicians working with hysteria was the French doctor Jean-Marie Charcot, who became famous for his *leçons du mardi* (Tuesday lessons) at the Salpêtrière hospital where he would hypnotize and induce hysterical fits in his patients before an audience.[39] Although Charcot subscribed to the neurological model of the disease, arguing that a lesion in the brain produced hysteria, in many ways he merely consolidated the idea of hysteria as a female disease specifically related to the female sexual organs.[40] The vast majority of Charcot's patients were women, and by placing these female hysterics on public display he helped to solidify the image of the hysterical woman.[41] Moreover, Charcot often would induce and arrest hysterical fits in women by manipulating their ovaries, which seemed to reaffirm those theories that assumed a direct link between hysteria and the female reproductive organs.[42]

The signs of hysteria included a large and very diverse group of behaviors and symptoms. However, probably the most characteristic sign of the disease was the hysterical attack that was said to resemble an epileptic seizure. Charcot, who claimed to be able to induce and control such fits through hypnotism, analyzed and divided the attacks into various stages: "a period of epileptiform agitation, a period of *grands mouvements* (including the famous arched back position), a period of passional attitudes, and a period of delirious withdrawal."[43] However, other typical symptoms of hysteria were paralysis, the inability to walk or stand, numbness in areas of the skin or parts of the body, blindness, deafness, the inability to speak, digestive disorders, and menstrual problems.[44] Furthermore, another school of thought arose on hysteria during the nineteenth century which elaborated the idea of the "hysterical temperament." According to these doctors, hysteria was less a physiological disease than a character disorder. A woman with a "hysterical temperament" was highly emotional and tended to engage in unconventional, defiant, and/or lewd behavior.[45] According to Catherine Jagoe, a woman could be diagnosed as a hysteric for simply being arrogant or rebellious.[46] Thus, the symptomatology of hysteria was expanded to include unseemly and/or defiant behavior in women.[47]

Despite the abundance of theories in the nineteenth century that viewed hysteria as a neurological disorder, Spanish doctors in general continued to support theories that viewed hysteria as a disease of the female sexual organs.[48] In 1876, the Sociedad Ginecológica Española (Spanish Gynecological Society) held a formal session on hysteria in which four of the five doctors that spoke agreed that the seat of hysteria was the female reproductive organs.[49] Thus in

Spain, even in the second half of the nineteenth century, it appears that the understanding of hysteria as a disease tied to female sexuality was still the dominant theory. In general, these doctors agreed that hysteria mainly attacked women, and specifically women who were deprived of sexual intercourse or who overindulged in sexual behavior.[50] Women were said to be particularly vulnerable to the disease during puberty when they first experienced the instinct for procreation.[51] As far as treatment was concerned, these doctors, though they condemned it, recognized the use of genital massage to produce orgasm in the hysterical woman. They preferred the use of medication, electrotherapy, and hydrotherapy in the form of douches, baths, and showers.[52]

While these discourses on hysteria were constructing a completely sexualized female subject, at the same time a series of parallel discourses were asserting that women were void of sexual feelings. With the discovery of spontaneous ovulation and the realization that female orgasm was not a necessary part of reproduction came a de-emphasis on female pleasure.[53] Many doctors asserted that women's sexual desire was not as strong as men's, and that a woman had less difficulty abstaining from sex. For example, in *Fisiología de la noche de bodas: Misterios del lecho conyugal* (1892; Physiology of the wedding night: Mysteries of the marriage bed), Amancio Peratoner states that "no poseyendo la mujer excitantes interiores, sient[e] menos que el hombre la fogosidad de la carne" (not having internal arousal, [women] feel less than men the passion of the flesh),[54] while Monlau claims that a respectable group of doctors has concluded that "el instinto genesico es mas imperioso en el hombre que en la mujer, y que en todas las especies animales el sexo masculino es mas ardiente que el femenino" (the reproductive instinct is stronger in men than in women, and in all the animal species the male is more passionate than the female).[55] Doctors began to affirm that women ardently desired conception and childbirth rather than sexual pleasure. This new passionless woman, reinforced through social discourses idealizing the *ángel del hogar* (angel in the house), formed an ideal of femininity against which the highly sexualized hysterical woman would be contrasted.

Although contradictory, these two female constructs appear to have worked together to uphold conventional conceptions of femininity: when women fell short of this ideal, and they almost always did, they could be diagnosed as hysterics and subjected to medical intervention. In this way these opposed sets of discourses worked together to police female behavior.

Socialization of Procreative Behavior

Foucault's concept of the socialization of procreative behavior refers to an orientation of the sexual practices of the married couple toward concerns of the state. Under this system, couples learn to control and regulate their sexuality so that they can contribute to the increase of healthy bodies, when the state is in need, or to the reduction of the number of offspring in times of overpopulation.[56] The idea of procreation as a service to the state is repeated again and again in the various nineteenth-century hygiene manuals. For example, Peratoner asserts that marriage is "un acto que toca las mas altas consideraciones sociales" (an act the relates to the highest social considerations).[57] Juan Giné y Partagas repeats the same idea in his *Curso elemental de higiene privada y pública* when he claims that "el objeto del matrimonio es á la vez higiénico, moral y social" (the purpose of marriage is at once hygienic, moral, and social).[58]

Foucault refers to the normative heterosexual couple who put their sexuality in the service of the state as the "Malthusian couple."[59] Thomas Robert Malthus, an English economist whose *Essay on the Principle of Population*, originally published in 1798 and then expanded and republished five times during his lifetime, was very influential on the thought of nineteenth-century European politicians.[60] Malthus, claiming that population, if left unchecked, would far surpass the amount of food produced, argued that crime, disease, war, and vice were necessary to keep the population under control.[61] In his 1803 edition, the English economist added moral restraint to this list, by which he meant the delaying of marriage until one had enough money to support a family: "It is clearly the duty of each individual not to marry till he has a prospect of supporting his children."[62] According to Malthus, without these limits, overpopulation would destroy any given society.

Despite the influence of Malthus's essay on nineteenth-century thought, European governments generally disregarded his main argument that overpopulation threatened to undermine any given society. Malthus was seen as a pessimist, and his fears about over-population were viewed as unsubstantiated. Governments through-out Europe actually undertook active campaigns to increase their populations because they believed more people meant more eco-nomic capital and military strength.[63] Esteban Rodríguez Ocaña shows that the Spanish government actually began to view the health and number of the population in specific monetary terms: "Enlazamos así con el componente económico del análisis higiénico. La vida humana llega a medirse en términos monetarios y la población total se representa como el capital colectivo del Estado, atendiendo al precio del trabajo o de la producción. A partir de ahí era posible calcular el coste de la muerte y el de la enfermedad" (In this way we connect the economic component with our analysis of the hygiene movement. Human life comes to be measured in monetary terms and the total population is represented as collec-tive capital of the State, taking into account the cost of labor and production. From then on it was possible to calculate the actual cost of death and illness).[64]

Hygienists took it upon themselves to argue against Malthusian fears about overpopulation. Pulido Fernández, for example, asserts that "los que creen que el mundo está suficientemente poblado, se equivocan de medio a medio. Es mas, la higiene solicita su aumento" (Those who believe the world is sufficiently populated are completely wrong. Moreover, hygiene asks for an increase).[65] Felipe Monlau takes up several pages of his *Higiene del matrimonio* to refute Malthus's theory directly, arguing that the population has never reached the levels that Malthus anticipates, that is, levels at which there were more people than food to feed them.[66] Stress-ing that the health of the state was dependent on a large popula-tion, Monlau encourages the government to take action to promote population growth. He suggests laws that would prevent the marriage of couples who would not be able to produce offspring (253). For example, he believes that people who are infertile should not be allowed to marry and that every woman should have the diameter of her pelvis measured before marriage in order to prove that it is large enough for giving birth (31–32). Moreover, unlike Viguera and other doctors who felt that marriage was the best cure for hysteria, Monlau strongly discourages marriage in such cases since he believes that hysterical women are often infertile (235). He also speaks out against marriages where there is a wide gap in age between the man and the woman, since these marriages are rarely fecund (58).

For nineteenth-century hygienists, celibacy itself is a disease. Monlau suggests that the government fight against what he refers to as "el cáncer del celibato por eleccion" (57; the cancer of voluntary celibacy). However, unlike other hygienists of the time, who felt that nymphomania and satyriasis (the male form of nymphomania) ran rampant throughout the convents and monasteries, Monlau does make an exception for chastity in the case of clergy, as well as in the case of soldiers during wartime (50–53). Yet, in all other cases Monlau condemns celibacy and infertility as an indication of low moral character and asserts that people who choose to remain single are reprehensible (228–30).[67] Similarly, Giné y Partagas claims that insanity and criminality are much more prevalent among single people,[68] while Peratoner attributes a long list of illnesses to celibacy.[69] However, as a positive incentive for marriage, these hygiene manuals generally include detailed statistics that "prove" that married people are healthier and that they live longer. According to Peratoner: "Por cada 78 casados que llegan á los 42 años, solo se cuentan 40 célibes que alcancen dicha edad" (For every seventy-eight married people that reach the age of forty-two, only forty celibate people reach that age).[70]

As part of this technique of the socialization of procreative behavior, doctors also sought to pathologize all sexual practices a married couple might engage in that did not serve the ultimate goal of increasing and improving the population. That is why, as Foucault states, birth control practices became a specific target of medical pathologization.[71] Although contraceptive methods in the nineteenth century were not very advanced, at least by today's standards, they did exist and were widely practiced. The most common was *coitus interruptus*, although a very primitive condom also existed.[72] Other couples tried to avoid conception by not engaging in intercourse during the time the woman was most fertile.[73] Despite the existence and practice of these birth control practices, the hygienists led a campaign in which they asserted that contraception, or conjugal onanism (*onanismo conyugal*), as these doctors called it, was a crime against nature and responsible for the abundance of illnesses that were beginning to manifest themselves in society. V. Suárez Casañ, for example, claimed that incomplete intercourse caused insanity,[74] and according to Monlau, it was the number one cause of hysteria in married women.[75]

The hygienists' sexual prescriptions were intended not only to regulate the size of the population, but also to improve it. In his *Enciclopedia médica popular* (1894; Popular medical encyclopedia), Suárez Casañ bemoans the fact that society pays more attention to perfecting the various breeds and species of animals than it does to perfecting the human species and argues that this has resulted in the spread of syphilis, insanity, alcoholism, nervous disorders, and tuberculosis.[76] Along the same lines, Monlau regrets that, despite medicine's understanding of hereditary transmission, the government does not establish laws, besides those against incest, to bring about "la regeneracion física de la especie humana" (the physical regeneration of the human species).[77] However, the speech that Alfonso XII gave at the inauguration of La Sociedad Española de Higiene (Spanish Society of Hygiene) on April 23, 1882, shows that the state was indeed already considering hygiene as a means of improving the Spanish race: "se trata de mejorar la sociedad, procurando en lo posible acrecentar la superioridad de nuestra raza, con lo que podríamos contar con soldados y trabajadores más útiles e inteligentes, consiguiendo con ello contribuir al desarrollo y engrandecimiento de nuestra industria y agricultura" (it is about improving society, insuring to the extent possible an increase in the superiority of our race, with which we could count on more able and intelligent soldiers and workers, thereby contributing to the advancement and expansion of our industry and agriculture).[78]

Although the threat of the spread of disease along with the state's need to have a strong army and labor force compelled hygienists to become concerned with the health of the lower classes, for the most part, the bourgeoisie practiced this eugenics plan on itself.[79] In other words, even though the lower classes were not to remain immune to state plans to improve the population, the bourgeoisie was particularly interested in establishing its own biological and physical superiority through the health of its own body.[80] According to Foucault, just as the nobility had sought to distinguish itself through its body, symbolized by its blood, the nineteenth-century middle class looked to set itself apart through the health and vigor of its body and through the offspring that body produced (124). The lower classes were the Other, the infirm part of the population against which the bourgeoisie sought to distinguish itself (123–24).

The implementation of state plans to improve the quality of the population worked hand in hand with nineteenth-century theories of degeneration that attributed the decline of a people not only to hereditary factors, but also to factors under individuals' control, such as their behavior. According to many nineteenth-century medical doctors, acquired diseases or character deficits could be passed on to one's offspring. For example, both Monlau and Peratoner argued that married couples who overindulged in sexual activities would produce deformed children.[81] And, Suárez Casañ states that "el mal modo de vivir es también una de las causas más comunes de la debilidad de los hijos" (a bad lifestyle is also one of the main causes of the frailty of children).[82] Therefore, one's behavior and lifestyle, if not in accordance with the precepts of hygiene, could lead to one's own degeneration as well as to that of one's offspring. In this way one's actions and moral character were directly linked to the health or decline not only of one's immediate family but also of one's "race."

So how did these strategies of the socialization of procreative behavior come to bear upon women? Most obviously, woman's "natural" role as procreator also became her social duty. Reproduction was now both a natural and a social imperative reinforced by proscriptions on all sexual behavior outside of marriage and on all practices that did not directly lead to reproduction. While the natural and social obligation to be both a wife and mother restricted women to the home, even more restricting were those theories that related female behavior to degeneracy. Since it was believed that the child's body was in complete organic communication with the mother's, particularly during pregnancy and breast-feeding, the emotional state, behavior, and moral character of the mother, both during and after pregnancy, was believed to affect the child. A woman's thoughts alone, if they were not of a moral nature, were believed to cause severe deformities in the child. For example, Suárez Casañ asserts that "nadie duda que las impresiones vivas y las pasiones fuertes ó por mucho tiempo comprimidas que turban el sistema moral de la madre, puedan determinar en el producto de la concepcion algunas alteraciones ó cambios mas ó menos profundos" (no one doubts that intense shocks and strong passions [controlled or not] that upset the mother's moral system, can cause degrees of profound alterations and changes in the conceived child).[83] Many women, therefore, likely felt obliged not only to control their actions and words, but also their thoughts.

Breastfeeding in particular became linked to theories of degeneration. Just as Spain's first *pícaro*, Lazarillo de Tormes, in an apparent slip of the tongue, claims to have acquired his skill at begging through his mother's milk ("Mas como yo este oficio le hobiese mamado en la leche" [But as I acquired this vocation through my mother's milk]),[84] nineteenth-century medical experts also believed that children inherited various physical and emotional traits through breast milk. The medical texts of the time condemn the use of wet nurses when the biological mother is herself physically capable of nursing, because many doctors believed that the employment of a lower-class woman to nurse one's child meant that the child would inherit the less desirable characteristics of the lower social classes. Furthermore, doctors argued that the quality of a mother's milk was not only determined by physical factors, such as heredity and diet, but also by the mother's emotional state and behavior during breastfeeding. According to Monlau, "la lactancia es uno de los canales de trasmision así de la parte física, como de la parte moral, así de lo bueno como de lo malo" (lactation is one of the channels of transmission of physical and moral attributes, both good and bad).[85] Monlau therefore advises nursing mothers to "evitar las excitaciones morales, las lecturas prolongadas, los bailes, los espectáculos, y cualquier ejercicio violento de las facultades intelectuales" (to avoid moral excitations, long periods of reading, dances, spectacles, and any intense exertion of the intellectual faculties).[86] He also advises against sexual intercourse during lactation since it could turn the breast milk into "un fluido seroso, insipido y amarillento" (a serous fluid, insipid and yellow).[87]

Pulido Fernández dedicates an entire chapter to the topic of lactation in which he condemns women who choose not to breastfeed. Since he also associates breastfeeding with hereditary transmission, he goes so far as to blame the use of wet nurses for the decline of great societies: "siempre que los pueblos han caido en la degeneracion y el envilecimiento, la lactancia mercenaria ha sido una de sus practicas mas extendidas" (whenever a nation has fallen into degeneration and debasement, mercenary lactation has been one of its most extended practices).[88] These hygienists portray women who choose not to breastfeed as selfish and frivolous. For example, according to the Marquis del Busto, women who employ a wet nurse do so in order to have the free time for "la inútil y murmuradora visita ó para la arruinadora competencia de los trajes y los adornos en los paseos, y las noches, para brillar en los salones y en los teatros ricas galas y joyas" (the useless and gossip-filled visit or for the ruinous competition of dresses and accessories during the afternoon stroll, and in the evening, in order to show off one's attire and jewels in drawing rooms and in lavish theaters).[89] In this way the new medical demand that the biological mother breastfeed her baby not only served as a form of monitoring a woman's thoughts and actions, which were believed to affect the genetic information of the breast milk, but it also further restricted a woman's freedom by insisting that women limit social and leisure activities.

The socialization of procreative behavior also redefined female sexual pleasure. Although all the hygiene manuals of the time insist that women need sexual intercourse, it becomes less and less attached to sexual pleasure. The discovery of spontaneous ovulation in the nineteenth century led to an attempt to move the site of female pleasure and satisfaction over to the organs directly involved in reproduction.[90] As Jagoe has shown, this change is seen from Viguera to Monlau.[91] Since Viguera still believed that female orgasm was necessary for ovulation and, therefore, for conception, the clitoris's role in producing female pleasure was still emphasized.[92] However, Monlau, more informed than his predecessor, understands that women can be impregnated even if they are totally indifferent to, or even repulsed by, sex.[93] He adds that women can become impregnated even while they are unconscious or sleeping.[94]

Because, according to nineteenth-century hygienists, only sexual activities that led directly to reproduction were legitimate, heterosexual coitus became the only "normal" form of sexual expression. Although nineteenth-century doctors still recognized the clitoris's role in female excitation, many sought to pathologize it by linking overdevelopment of this organ with so-called diseases and perversions such as hysteria, masturbation, nymphomania, ambiguous sexuality, and same-sex desire, as we will see in our discussion of the psychiatrization of perverse pleasure. Since female orgasm was now pathological, male orgasm became the new female orgasm. In other words, doctors now asserted that what women really needed was to have their reproductive organs sprayed with the male semen. This was believed to calm down the uterus and bring an end to the contractions and spasms that the female body underwent during coitus. According to Peratoner: *"El baño local de sémes es indispensable á la mujer para apagar la incitación que acompaña el coito y para hacer recobrar la calma á sus órganos sexuales y á toda la economia"* (italics in the original; A bathing of the area in semen is essential for the women, to calm down the incitement that accompanies coitus and to allow her sexual organs and entire body to recover its equilibrium).[95] And Giné y Partagas states that

> los cóitos incompletos, esto es, sin emision, acarrean en la mujer induraciones en el cuello uterino, que pueden pasar á verdaderos

cánceres. El útero, que en el acto de la cópula sufre una excitacion vivísima, necesita experimentar el tibio contacto del licor esper-mático para que se disipe la irritacion de que se ha hecho asiento, cesando así su eretismo: faltando aquel, el orgasmo se convierte en una irritacion de carácter crónico.[96]

incomplete intercourse, that is, without ejaculation, gives rise in women to the hardening of the cervix, which can actually turn into cancer. The uterus, which in the act of copulation experiences an extremely strong arousal, needs to feel the warm contact of the spermatic fluid in order for the irritation to dissipate, in this way ending its erethism: without this, orgasm becomes a chronic irritation.

By claiming that the female reproductive organs needed the male ejaculate in order to recover from sexual arousal, these doctors made male orgasm synonymous with female orgasm. Both the male and female body now climaxed in unison when the male ejaculated.

However, since conception was the ultimate goal of sexual inter-course, many doctors maintained that a woman's ultimate sexual satisfaction (which was believed to be essential for her overall gen-eral health) was in giving birth. Pulido Fernández, for example, begins his *Bosquejos medico-sociales para la mujer* with the chapter entitled "El arbol sin fruto" (The tree without fruit), which recounts the stories of two women who had trouble conceiving. Dr. Pulido met the first woman during a visit to an insane asylum in Lisbon. She was an upper-class woman from Lisbon who, after not being able to conceive with her husband, began kissing and attempting to abduct all the children she encountered on the street, believ-ing they were her own. Obviously insane, the woman was commit-ted to an asylum. Some time after that visit Pulido discovers that this woman has killed herself (1–3). The second story is about a woman who forces a doctor to perform a risky operation on her by threatening to kill herself if he will not do it. The operation is intended to correct her infertility (3–4). The doctor performs the operation; it is successful, and today the woman "vive dichosa en esta corte, con dos hijos de sus entrañas, que hacen las delicias de

los amantes esposos" (4; lives happily in the capital, with two biological children that are the delight of the married couple). The
lesson of this chapter: a woman's health, happiness, and sanity
depend on her having children. Or in the words of the Marquis del
Busto: "La mujer casada siente como una necesidad de su espíritu
el deseo de ser madre; son para ella estos deseos como unos nuevos
amores, y no se cree del todo feliz si no los ve satisfechos" (A married woman feels the desire to be a mother like a spiritual necessity;
these desires are for her like new loves, and she cannot be completely happy if she does not see them satisfied).[97] Since women
are said to only find true satisfaction in motherhood, childbirth
discursively replaces female orgasm.

Although the socialization of procreation did not only affect
women, it did play a large role in the control and conception of
the female subject. Marriage and childbirth were now said to be
both a social and a natural duty, making it increasingly difficult
for women to fight for equal rights in society. Moreover, theories
of degeneration served as a form of both thought and behavior
control since women were led to believe that their actions, as well
as their thoughts and emotions, could result in the degeneration
of their offspring. Yet, perhaps the most striking phenomenon is
the medical reconstruction of the female sexual response. In order
to make female sexual pleasure better conform to the new social
imperative to reproduce, female sexual arousal was transferred
to those organs and processes directly involved in reproduction.
Female orgasm became conception and childbirth. Therefore, in
many ways, Sigmund Freud did not say anything new in his essay
on female sexuality.[98] Like Freud, these doctors had already established that true femininity consisted in transferring female sexual
gratification from the clitoris to the vagina.

Psychiatrization of Perverse Pleasure

The psychiatrization of perverse pleasure involved the classification
of all sexual behaviors as either normal or perverted.[99] Through the
diagnosis of perversions, medicine was able to usurp the role of both

morality and law by converting sinful/criminal acts into illnesses or perversions of nature.[100] The establishment of sexual perversions helped to solidify the heterosexual norm established by the socialization of procreative behavior since, in order for the standard to exist, it had to be contrasted with the aberration. In other words, the sexually normal individual could exist only as long as she could be compared to the pervert; otherwise, there would be no defining limits of normative sexuality. According to Butler, the "abject beings" of marginal sexualities are seen as constituting the "outside" of the legitimate subject. They are forced to live in the "zone of uninhabitability" which "will come to constitute that site of dreaded identification against which—and by virtue of which—the domain of the subject will circumscribe its own claim to autonomy and to life."[101] Nymphomania, masturbation, pseudo-hermaphroditism, and tribadism were the most discussed female "perversions" of the nineteenth century, and all were directly linked to the clitoris.

Although nymphomania, like hysteria, was a rather elusive illness that encompassed a wide range of symptoms and causes, an overdeveloped sexual appetite was its main symptom. While nymphomania is a direct descendent of uterine fury, a "disease" described by the second-century Greek physician Galen, who argued that a lack of sexual fulfillment in women, particularly in young widows, could lead to madness,[102] the modern concept of nymphomania was invented in 1778 with the publication D. T. de Bienville's *La nymphomanie, ou, Traite de la fureur uterine* (published in English in 1775 as *Nymphomania, or, A Dissertation Concerning the Furor Uterinus*). In Bienville's conception of the disease, masturbation was linked directly to nymphomania.[103] Although solitary sex was certainly not new in the eighteenth century, it was not until then that masturbation became a medical concern.[104] There were two eighteenth-century texts fundamental to the establishment of masturbation as a disease. The first, published anonymously somewhere between 1708 and 1716, was *Onania, or, The Heinous Sin of Self Pollution, and All Its Frightful Consequences, in Both Sexes Considered*.[105] The other text, first published in 1760, was Samuel Auguste Andre David Tissot's *L'Onanisme, ou, Dissertation physique sur les maladies produites par la masturbation* (Onanism, or, Physical dissertation on the diseases produced by masturbation).[106] Tissot's text in particular sparked off a proliferation of writing on the subject.[107]

Although Foucault discusses masturbation as part of the pedagogization of children's sex,[108] everyone, that is, children and adults, both men and women, were suspected of this "vice." Moreover, many doctors argued that female onanism, which almost always involved the manipulation of the clitoris, only further aggravated the female system. Since doctors believed that women needed to have their uterus sprayed with the male ejaculate in order to calm down their systems, it was asserted that onanism, in any form, could not provide the sexual relief that women needed. Instead, it was said to only increase sexual desire and further irritate the female body. Masturbation in women, therefore, was said to create a vicious cycle in which a woman masturbated more and more, hoping to find relief, but only to cause further agitation. In this way masturbation and nymphomania were linked. According to Viguera, for example, nymphomania began precisely with a feeling of sexual desire that caused women to "rub" themselves:

Empieza, pues la escena, por una sensacion entre placentera e incómoda de ardor, prurito y cosquilleo en la vulva y vagina, que por un impulso involuntario obliga a las pacientes a restregarse, con tanta mas intension cuanto que de ello esperimentan un dulce placer y calma. Pero, estos repetidos actos, lejos de corregir sus sensaciones, las avivan cada vez mas, y despiertan en las doncellas los deseos del legítimo específico regulador.[109]

The scene begins with an equally pleasurable and uncomfortable burning, itching, and tickling sensation in the vagina and vulva, a sensation that makes patients involuntarily rub themselves with ever-increasing intensity as the act produces a sweet pleasure and calm. But, these repeated acts, far from correcting the sensations, make them more powerful each time, and awaken in maidens the desire for the real regulator.

Viguera claims that while this practice may initially lead to a feeling of pleasure and calm, like many other physicians of the time he also argues that, ultimately, it only increases desire rather than satiates it, making women yearn more ardently for sexual intercourse.

However, whether an overdeveloped clitoris caused women to masturbate, or whether women developed a large and/or swollen clitoris because they masturbated, was debated. Even in the second half of the nineteenth century, many doctors still held that masturbation, as well as other forms of sexual excess, actually deformed the external genitalia.[110] Peratoner asserted that the clitoris itself can reach an extraordinary size in a woman who masturbates: "el clitoris aumentado en volumen, puede haber adquerido dimensiones extraordinarias, cómo acontece a menudo bajo la influencia de hábitos de onanismo (the clitoris, increased in size, can acquire extraordinary dimensions, as happens often under the influence of habits of onanism)."[111] Although not all nineteenth-century doctors necessarily believed that masturbation led to deformed genitalia, nymphomania and masturbation remained tied to a large clitoris, in part, because it was believed that women with large clitorises would inadvertently stimulate themselves since the enlarged organ would easily rub up against clothing and other foreign objects. For example, Juan Cuesta y Ckerner states that "el clitoris puede encontrarse enormemente desarrollado, y semejante disposicion puede llegar a producir la ninfomania por el orgasmo constante que ocasione el roce de los vestidos" (the clitoris can be enormously overdeveloped, and such a situation can produce nymphomania due to the constant orgasm produced by the contact with clothes).[112]

Large clitorises were also viewed as an indication of pseudo-hermaphroditism and tribadism.[113] According to Cleminson and Vázquez García, "the 'science of hermaphroditism,' emerging from the mid-nineteenth-century onwards, was an attempt by medical and legal authorities to manage a cluster of 'deviant' representations and acts around the body, sex and gender."[114] Starting in the 1840s, doctors argued against the existence of true hermaphroditism in humans and began to employ the term "pseudo-hermaphroditism" in its place.[115] Masculine traits, a large clitoris, and attraction to one's own sex were all associated with female pseudo-hermaphroditism. According to Monlau, for example, female "hermaphrodites" have overdeveloped clitorises, very small breasts, manly features, and facial hair; they enjoy engaging in manly activities; and are sexually inclined toward members of their own sex. Monlau argues, however, that these women are not "true" hermaphrodites because they would have to have the internal reproductive organs of both sexes. Rather, Monlau prefers to refer to these individuals as monsters or "marimachos ó mujeres hombrunas (*viragines*), de costumbres masculinas, voz ronca, barba poblada, clitoris muy abultado, etc." (butch women or mannish women (viragines), of masculine habits, deep voice, hairy chin, swollen clitoris, etc.).[116] Later on in his work, Monlau will assert that such women are also often sterile.[117]

The term *lesbiana* (lesbian) was not used in most hygiene manuals of the time, although V. Suárez Casañ does use the term *lesbia* (lesbian) as early as 1892.[118] Rather, terms such as *tribadas* (tribades), *marimachos* (butch women), or *viragines* or *viragos* (mannish women) are most often employed. Peratoner uses to the term *tribadas* to refer to women with large clitorises who are sexually attracted to other women, and consequently indifferent to men: "el desarrollo excesivo [del clítoris] hacia las mujeres indiferentes á las caricias de los hombres y las arrastraba a apetecer asiduamente la sociedad de las personas de su sexo. La voluptuosidad clitoridea es para esta clase de mujeres, llamadas TRIBADAS entre los antiguos, una necesidad imperiosa que acrecenta incesantemente el delirio de sus imaginaciones" (the overdevelopment of [the clitoris] made women indifferent to the caresses of men and led them to assiduously desire the company of people of their own sex. For this type of woman, called TRIBADES by the ancients, the clitoridian voluptuousness is an imperative necessity that ceaselessly increases the delirium of their imaginations).[119]

Thus, the creation of the "perversions" of nymphomania, masturbation, pseudo-hermaphroditism, and tribadism aided doctors' in their pathologization of the clitoris and nonreproductive sexual activities. The clitoris's lack of purpose in reproduction and its similarity to the penis challenged nineteenth-century views on sexuality. It not only undermined theories of the sexes that posited woman was man's polar opposite, but it also contested the medical assertion that sexual pleasure had a solely reproductive purpose. To avoid such challenges, nineteenth-century medical experts converted the clitoris into the organ responsible for unfeminine and lascivious behavior in women. Similar to Freud's assertion that clitoral masturbation was a masculine activity, and that women who refused to give up this habit suffered from a "masculinity complex,"[120] nineteenth-century doctors insisted that women who engaged in clitoral masturbation, or who had excessively large clitorises (although doctors linked the two), were manly, sterile, lascivious and/or sexually inclined toward members of their own sex.

The establishment of the "perversions" of nymphomania, masturbation, pseudo-hermaphroditism, and tribadism clearly served to uphold the polarization of the sexes. Women who defied the boundaries of femininity by seeking the right to use birth control, to pursue sexual satisfaction, to move freely outside the home, to vote, or to have equal access to education and job opportunities could now be accused of sexual deviancy. Truly feminine women were to find complete satisfaction in their domestic role of wife and mother. Doctors and hygienists would argue that only perverted women, such as manly women with large clitorises and voracious sexual appetites, would want anything more.

However, none of these theories were monolithic. This is evident in the case of nymphomania, where the "disease" was also specifically related to so-called normal heterosexual, procreative urges in women. For, as in the case of hysteria, another major cause of nymphomania was believed to be chastity, which was most often associated with young unmarried women, nuns, and widows. According to Viguera for example, nymphomania "es una inevitable consecuencia de la castidad, cuando es mantenida con heroica firmeza en medio de los mas porfiados aguijoneos" (is an unavoidable consequence of chastity, when maintained with heroic resolve in the midst of the most persistent incitements).[121] Many nineteenth-century doctors believed that women's biology was so programmed for childbirth that if the female body was not being put toward such purposes, it caused all sorts of disturbances. But what about the nun, whose religious calling required that she remain chaste? Not surprisingly, many nineteenth-century doctors felt that nuns were most susceptible to nymphomania. Viguera feels great pity for these women, who are deprived of the most effective antidote to this terrible disease:

> En [estos casos] la esperanza de un porvenir lisongero, que es el mas oportuno calmante para las que no estan ligadas con los votos monasticos, nada puede consolar a las infelices victimas de una eterna clausura [. . .], mientras que sola la idea de no poder mejorar su triste suerte, es un tremendo aguijon que exalta mas su fuego [ninfomaniaco], y las precipita en el furor melancolico.[122]

> *In [these cases] the hope of an agreeable future, which is the most appropriate antidote for those women who are not tied by monastic vows, nothing can console the unfortunate victims of an eternal cloister [. . .], while the mere idea of not being able to improve their sad situation, is a huge trigger that excites their passion even more, and sends them into [nymphomaniacal] furor. I have witnessed it with much pain, and I also have seen some of these women die overwhelmed by the distress.*

From these doctors' perspective, attempts on the part of women to pursue a chaste and spiritual life were unnatural and occasioned a variety of sexual pathologies. This line of reasoning would bring many nineteenth-century doctors to diagnose contemporary and former female mystics as hysterics or nymphomaniacs. According to Francisco Vázquez García, in the nineteenth century, "la mujer casta será siempre 'insatisfecha'; patologizada en las formas de la 'histérica' y de la 'ninfomaniaca'; el rostro inmaculado de la 'virgen' puede anunciar la mueca salvaje y espasmodica de la 'ninfómana,' conduciendo de los desenfrenos masturbatorios a los abismos de una prostitución sin límites" (the chaste woman will always be "unsatisfied"; the immaculate face of the Virgin, pathologized in the form of the "hysteric" and the "nymphomaniac," can announce the wild and spasmodic grimace of the "nymphomaniac," taking her from unrestrained masturbatory practices to a life of prostitution without limits).[123]

One of the most important, and perhaps most curious, supposed causes of nymphomania was the over-excitation of the imagination caused by reading, specifically by reading novels. Bienville argued that the imagination was one of the most important factors in the production of this female "disease."[124] Since nymphomania was linked to masturbation, and since masturbation was accompanied by fantasy and an over-excited imagination, the connection between nymphomania and the imagination was made. Thus, it was argued that in order to prevent masturbation and cure nymphomania, the imagination had to be controlled. This meant the proscription of novel reading by women. Bienville's ideas definitely made their way to Spain because the link between reading novels, masturbation, and nymphomania was explicit in the Spanish hygiene manuals of the time. Pulido Fernandez's *Bosquejos medico-sociales para la mujer* contains an entire chapter on the pernicious effects of novel reading on women. According to Pulido, the intense emotions that these novels elicit in the reader produce all sorts of nervous disorders. Pulido discusses the role of the imagination in this process: "el primer blanco que recibe siempre los disparos de la novela es la imaginacion, la cual los refleja despues a todo el resto de la economia humana" (the first target to receive the novel's arrow is the imagination, which then transmits it to the rest of the human organism).[125] Pulido goes on to describe how the situation deteriorates: "cuando los hábitos son malos, las tendencias lúbricas, y la lectura lanza en el delirio de los placeres avivando el fermento de los deseos, esta infeliz solitaria, tras una larga lucha, y hasta sin ella, concluye por dejar el libro, cerciorarse de su soledad, y . . ." (ellipsis in original; when one has bad habits and lewd tendencies, and the reading shoots off into a delirium of pleasures causing the fermentation of desires, this unfortunate solitary woman, after a long struggle, and even without one, ends up dropping the book, checking to insure she is alone, and . . .).[126]

To those who are skeptical that this truly happens, Pulido claims that he could invoke "el recuerdo de tanta infeliz *ninfomaníaca*" (italics in the original; the memory of so many unfortunate *nym-phomaniacs*) and detail "las mil impresiones que hemos sentido, cuando hemos sido llamados para prestar los auxilios de la ciencia a alguna joven que se agitaba convulsiva en su lecho entre espasmos cinicos y estros venales" (the thousands of shocks we have experienced when we have been called to lend science's help to a young women who was shaking convulsively in her bed between shameless spasms and venous estruses).[127] Thus, Bienville's connection of novel reading, masturbation, and nymphomania finds echoes in the Spanish nineteenth-century hygiene manual.

Although these doctors claimed, and probably truly believed, they had women's best interests in mind, their pathologization of novel reading was also an attempt to get women to regulate their own thoughts and behavior. By instilling a fear of disease in women, doctors could convince women to censor their own ideas and fantasies. It was also a way to control what women did when they were alone and unsupervised. Since a male authority figure, such as a doctor or husband, could not be present at all times, making women conscious and fearful of what they did when they were alone was a means of getting women to police themselves.

While Foucault talks about the psychiatrization of perverse pleasure as one of the four strategies of the deployment of sexuality, separate from the hysterization of the female body, hysteria itself can be viewed as one of the central female perversions of the time. In fact, the difference between hysteria and nymphomania is far from clear. Both diseases were supposedly caused by an out-of-control female sexual desire, both were manifested by a wide variety of symptoms, from epileptic-type seizures to defiant behavior, both were said to arise from enforced chastity and the natural biological phases of the female body such as puberty and menstruation, both could be caused by lascivious sexual behavior, and both were said to find their most effective cure in marriage and normal heterosexual coitus and conception. Even Viguera admits that it is difficult to distinguish between the two diseases since their causes and symptoms are nearly identical.[128] Thus, hysteria is nymphomania's twin sister and deserves a place in the psychiatrization of perverse pleasure.

The establishment of nymphomania as a female perversion worked to control the female subject in several ways. First of all, since it was directly linked to masturbation, same-sex desire, and an overdeveloped and/or highly sensitive clitoris, it pathologized female sexual pleasure. Clitoral stimulation became related to unfeminine behavior and an out-of-control sexuality. Nymphomaniacs were portrayed as subversive women whose challenges to the boundaries of "natural" femininity converted them into monsters of nature, into manly, sterile women, who could no longer fulfill their natural and social duty to procreate. Secondly, those theories that related the disease to chastity bolstered the belief that women were programmed biologically for procreation and helped to condemn the one legitimate female community of the time, the convent. Finally, by associating reading and imagination with masturbation and nymphomania, medical experts were able to get women to police themselves; out of a fear of disease, many women were made to censor their own thoughts and imaginations.

Conclusion

According to Foucault, as European societies became more democratic, a new, more subtle form of power began to operate that was more effective in controlling the growing populations of Europe.[129] From the exploration above, it is clear that this new type of power also took hold in nineteenth-century Spain. One manifestation of this "bio-power," as Foucault refers to it, was the rise in social importance of medicine and hygiene, particularly as they related to questions of human sexuality.[130] The new authority of medical discourses on sexuality was especially effective in keeping down the rising female emancipation movement, which had gained force since liberal theory seemed to promise that all human subjects, regardless of their gender, were equal and therefore deserving of the same rights.[131] However, the growing capitalist economies were soliciting more able bodies to fuel the labor market and strengthen the military power of the state, and female emancipation conflicted with these aims. For many, women's role in society had to continue to be that of procreator. By establishing the polarization of the sexes which claimed that woman, as man's opposite, was completely controlled by her reproductive organs and her instinctual drives, doctors were able to insist that the female body was naturally programmed to serve solely for the purposes of reproduction. Medical physicians, claiming, and probably believing, they had objectively and empirically studied the female body, argued that woman's role in society should be restricted to that of wife and mother and demands for equal rights for women were absurd.

The antifeminist agenda of medicine makes it necessary to reexamine the friction between religion and science in the nineteenth century. Although science is frequently portrayed as a progressive social force, in terms of gender and sexuality it was merely reaffirming traditional Catholic morality. This issue is of particular importance in the chapters that follow in which the battle between the two discourses to define the female body comes to the forefront. It is also key in the analyses of the works and ideology of Eduardo López Bago, Leopoldo Alas "Clarín," and Emilia Pardo Bazán. While the anticlericalism of the first two authors is sometimes seen as progressive, their literary works uphold the same misogynist beliefs that were historically upheld by the Church. On the other hand, Pardo Bazán, who is often portrayed as a conservative because of her distrust of scientific discourses on women and her adherence to the Catholic faith, was the fiercest proponent of gender equality. This, as we shall see, problematizes facile dichotomies between progress and reaction, and religion and science, in Spain in the nineteenth and early twentieth century.

2 Women, Mysticism, and Hysteria in Fin-de-Siècle Spain

IN 1880, THE well-known Cervantes scholar Ramón León Maínez Fernández (1846–1917) published his highly critical and unapologetic *Teresa de Jesús ante la crítica* (Teresa de Jesús in the face of the criticism) in which he attacks the Spanish saint's character and writing abilities and dismisses her mystical experiences as hysteria.[1] Not surprisingly, his essay proved to be highly polemical.[2] This same year, 1880, in preparation for the 1882 tercentennial celebration of Santa Teresa's death, essays were solicited for a literary and artistic contest in which one of the proposed topics was to prove Santa Teresa's capacity to distinguish between the natural and the supernatural.[3] The most noteworthy of the submissions was that of the Belgian Jesuit priest G. Hahn, who was also a disciple of Charcot. His essay titled "Les phénomènes hystériques et les révélations de sainte Thérèse" (Hysterical phenomena and the revelations of Santa Teresa) made its argument from a scientific perspective and sought to demonstrate that although Teresa de Jesús suffered physically from a form of hysteria similar to epilepsy, unlike most hysterics, she was psychologically and morally sane. He concluded, therefore, that her mystical experiences were indeed divine.[4] Hahn's essay was well received by the jury in Salamanca in 1882 and awarded a golden medal.[5] Yet, the essay met with opposition in Rome and was placed on the Index of Prohibited Books in 1886.[6]

The winner of the essay contest for topic 5 was the Spaniard Dr. Arturo Perales y Gutiérrez, a professor of medicine at the University of Granada who also held a doctorate in theology.[7] His work was titled *El supernaturalismo de Santa Teresa y la filosofía médica, ó, Sea, los éxtasis, raptos y enfermedades de la santa ante las ciencias médicas* (The supernaturalism of Santa Teresa and medical philosophy, or, The ecstasies, raptures, and illnesses of the saint in light of the medical sciences). A self-professed Catholic scientist, Perales arrived at a conclusion similar to Father Hahn's; that is, he concluded that Santa Teresa physically suffered from hystero-epilepsy, but that her mystical experiences of the divine were authentic. In order to avoid the criticism and attacks Hahn had suffered, Perales asked the Archbishop of Madrid to vouch for the work's orthodoxy. The Archbishop obliged, and his approval was included at the beginning of the 343-page publication (1894).[8] Since Perales was not a member of the clergy, he could not be punished by the Vatican. However, like Hahn, he was confronted with published refutations of his ideas.[9]

Not long after the tricentennial celebration, Leopoldo Alas Clarín published his masterpiece, *La Regenta* (1884–85), which dealt extensively with the question of female mysticism and hysteria. At about the same time, 1885–86, the radical naturalist Eduardo López Bago published his *Cura* trilogy—*El cura* (The priest), *El confesionario* (The confessional), and *La monja* (The nun), which, unlike *La Regenta*, was entirely unambiguous in its sexualization of religious ecstasy. Later, in 1893, a lesser-known naturalist writer, Eduardo Zamacois, published a medical treatise titled *El misticismo y las perturbaciones del sistema nervioso* (Mysticism and disturbances of the nervous system), in which he asserted that mystics, like criminals, had a unique physical and psychological makeup, and that hypnosis had proven that all mystical phenomena were pathological in origin.[10] In 1907 Eduardo Ovejero translated Auguste Armand Marie's *Mysticisme et folie*, in which Dr. Armand Marie argued that mystical rapture was a physiological phenomenon produced through *coitos imaginarios* (imaginary coituses) with the divine (170), into Spanish under the title *Misticismo y locura* (Mysticism and insanity).[11]

And Pardo Bazán would again weigh in on the debate surrounding women, mysticism, and hysteria, although from a different angle, in two of her last novels, *La Quimera* (1905; The Chimera) and *Dulce dueño* (1911; Sweet master). Not only did both Alas and Pardo Bazán personally express their opinions about Santa Teresa in literary and nonliterary works, but they both also revealed a life-long interest in mysticism in their writings.

Of course, all of this was part of a larger debate taking place in Europe at the time that was directly tied to new scientific understandings of female sexuality. As we saw in the previous chapter, many nineteenth-century doctors were assuming roles previously assigned to members of the Church by prescribing certain sexual practices and proscribing others. This medical "knowledge" simply reaffirmed the misogynistic prejudices already in place. It is not surprising, therefore, that just as the counter-reformation Church had often interpreted mystical rapture in women as sexual deviance and demonic possession, nineteenth-century physicians would now diagnose manifestations of female mysticism as hysteria, a disease directly related to female sexuality. This chapter explores the ways science and liberalism sought to domesticate both women and religion, as well as the ways certain doctors and intellectuals pathologized the mystical experience in order to discredit alternative models of female existence that continued to capture the public's attention and admiration.

The Rise of Science over Religion

Nineteenth-century medical and technological advances strengthened scientists' authority in society. For many liberal thinkers, science was synonymous with progress. Moreover, scientists would claim the superiority of science to other forms of knowledge, such as philosophy or religion, by insisting that it alone dealt with demonstrable facts.[12] The scientific method required that all scientific theory be the product of observation of the material world and that the conclusions drawn be repeatable and observable through scientific experimentation. Thus, it was argued that sci-

entific theories could be observed in nature whereas philosophical or metaphysical theories were a priori, internal creations, not
demonstrable in nature, and therefore not provable. For the scientist, the existence of a phenomenon was dependent on two important factors: its having a manifestation in the material world, and its
being visible or observable. The scientific gaze, therefore, became
an important measure of truth.

Auguste Comte's theory of positivism played a crucial role in
establishing the superiority of science over other forms of knowledge. Comte hierarchized the various sciences and established
three phases of intellectual development, known as the "Law of
Three States," which applied both to the development of the individual and to the development of a society as a whole. The first
stage was the theological stage, in which natural phenomena were
explained through religion that generally assumed the existence
of divine beings that willed certain events into action. The second stage was the metaphysical stage that, rather than attribut-
ing causes to divine beings, looked to abstract concepts such as
"essences" and "forces" to explain reality. The third, most evolved,
phase was the positive phase, which involved the study of observable phenomena and the formulation of natural laws that explained
these phenomena. Thus, in positivism, science was held up as the
superior and most evolved form of knowledge since its theories
were observable. Comte's theory specifically contraposed religion with science by associating religion with superstition and a
naïve, childlike way of viewing the world, and science with a factual,
adult understanding of an observable material reality.[13] Although
this emphasis on the empirical and observable phenomena of
reality did not eliminate other types of knowledge or speculation
altogether, it effectively attempted to subordinate them to science.

Scientists' assertion of the superiority of science to religion was
also part of an attempt to weaken the political power of the Church.
One of the main characteristics of nineteenth-century Spanish liberalism was its anticlerical stance. The liberal constitutions ratified
during the century greatly reduced the Church's power within Spanish society. Through the process of disentailment, the government

confiscated large portions of Church property and sold them off to the public. This naturally led to a reduction of the Church's ability to provide charity and consequently began to dissolve Spanish citizens' dependence on the institution of the Church.[14] The Church's wealth was further diminished by the abolition of the tithe and the permanent closure of many convents and monasteries that were under-populated. The nineteenth century also saw the end of the Inquisition in 1820.[15]

Even though many of the conservative governments that came to power during the nineteenth century reinstated some of the Church's lost powers, the Church did not recover the wealth and influence it had previously held. Once the Church's properties had been sold off, they were never recovered. Furthermore, regardless of the government in power, a large section of the population, particularly of the urban population, was now strongly imbued with liberal ideals, which often fomented strong sentiments of anticlericalism. In the most severe cases, the spread of anticlerical propaganda manifested itself in mob violence, such as attacks in Madrid against the Jesuit college and the monasteries of the Franciscans, Carmelites, and Dominicans.[16]

Most liberals, however, never sought to eradicate religion altogether or the institution of the Church. Rather, they sought to domesticate religion by moving it out of politics and education and relegating it to a personal, spiritual practice. Emphasizing its importance in the teaching of morality, many liberals argued that religion still should play an important role in the personal lives of citizens.[17] According to Carr, liberals had two main objectives regarding the Church: they wanted the Church to be under the jurisdiction of the laws of the state, and they wanted to decrease the Church's control over secondary education.[18] The liberal push for progress and modernity therefore did not mean a complete secularization of society, but rather an attempt to reduce the Church's influence in the political and academic arenas.

Science and liberalism not only worked together to weaken the Church's political power, but they also formed an alliance in the subjugation and domestication of women. As we saw in Chapter

1, most Spanish liberals were not promoting female emancipation. Rather, they sought to relegate women to the domestic sphere. Yet, in this new liberal mindset, liberal thinkers and hygienists had different views on whether religion itself was an appropriate space for women. According to Grace M. Jantzen, "a connection can be traced between the domestication of women and the domestication of religion such that claims to religious experience become permissible for women in direct proportion to the decline of public importance of religion."[19] This seems to be true for nineteenth-century Spain where, according to Pamela Radcliff, we witness a "general 'feminization' of religious practice."[20] While those who felt comfortable with the Church's position in society believed it was an important part of female instruction, those who felt threatened by the Church's power argued against imbuing women with strong religious beliefs. For those belonging to the former category, religion was seen as a means of controlling and regulating female behavior. For example, the feminist author Emilia Pardo Bazán claimed that religion served to uphold the patriarchal objectives of keeping women trapped in the domestic sphere; she writes, "como no es factible ponerle a la mujer un vigilante negro, de puñal en cinto, le pone un *custodio* augusto: ¡Dios!" (since it is not feasible to give a woman an African guard who carries a dagger in his sash, man gives her a majestic custodian: God!).[21]

Since, in many cases, female piety served to uphold the new patriarchal order, hygienists argued that a religious life was an acceptable alternative for women. Many liberal doctors claimed that women were more naturally suited for religious devotion than men. For example, in 1892 the Marquis del Busto made such an argument to the Real Academia de Medicina (The Royal Academy of Medicine): "La mujer, ó por devoción ó por vocación, está por su amorosa condición más dispuesta que el hombre á la piedad; y, por fortuna, el conocimiento de Dios, de sus atributos y de sus leyes y mandatos, la llevan á cumplirlos con perfección y como por providencial destino" (Women, either out of devotion or vocation, are more suited for piety than men, because of their loving nature; and, fortunately, knowledge of God, of his attributes and his laws and commandments, bring women to fulfill them with perfection and as if by providential destiny).[22] Moreover, according to Adrian Schubert, "philanthropy was the only important public activity in which respectable Spanish women could legitimately take part since it was considered merely an extension of their nature." Apparently, many liberal politicians agreed with these views since during disentailment female congregations were often spared while the closure and sale of many monasteries reduced the male clergy by over half; between 1797–1900 the number of male clergy fell from two hundred thousand to eighty-seven thousand while the number of nuns actually increased from twelve thousand in 1842 to over forty-two thousand by 1900.[23]

Yet, there were other doctors and thinkers who felt hostile toward the Church and feared extremes of female piety and therefore insisted on religion's harmful effects on women. According to Pardo Bazán, even men who were relatively comfortable with their wives' remaining devout Catholics feared the possibility that their piety would lead to "arrobos y extremos místicos" (raptures and mystical extremes).[24] Pardo Bazán writes that "Lo que desea [el hombre] para la mujer es una piedad tibia: un justo medio de piedad" (What man desires for woman is a tepid piety: a happy medium of piety).[25]

Much of the medical "evidence" of the time, however, was indicating that it was difficult for women not to be carried to extremes in religious devotion. First, women were not only less educated than men, but they were also said to be naturally less intelligent. And since secular doctors like A. Marie believed that "la ignorancia es la medida de la religión; ambas caminan del brazo. Al aumento de la ciencia corresponde la disminución de la fe" (ignorance is the measure of religion; the two go hand in hand. The decrease in faith corresponds to the increase in science),[26] they also believed women were more likely to be taken over by superstitious and religious thinking. Furthermore, as we saw in Chapter 1, according to nineteenth-century doctors, hypersensitivity was the most salient trait of the female organism, a trait that was said to be responsible for all sorts of physical and mental disorders in women. Yet, as the Spanish doctor and author Eduardo Zamacois explains, hypersensitivity was also the characteristic trait of mystics and hysterics.[27] This inevitably made women more susceptible to this form of insanity. Moreover, the highly excitable nature of the female imagination itself could easily lead to all sorts of physical and mental disorders. Citing Moreau, Viguera states that "se sabe [. . .] con qué facilidad se consigue, atacando vivamente su imaginación, diseminar el desorden en todos sus sentidos, y promover casi á voluntad furores, arrebatos, enajenaciones y convulsiones" (one knows [. . .] with what facility, by vividly attacking her imagination, disorder in all of her senses is disseminated and fury, rapture, insanity, and convulsions are produced almost at will).[28] It is therefore no coincidence that Ramón León Mainez argued that Santa Teresa's hysteria was due in part to the arousal of her imagination produced by novel reading.[29] Thus, according to the medical consensus of the time, women's ignorance, hypersensitivity, and overly active imagination made them highly susceptible to the insanity that religion often inspired.

Another point of contention was the Catholic Church's insistence on chastity. As we saw in Chapter 1, in aiding the state in its call for population increases, hygienists were insisting that sexual intercourse and procreation were necessary for the healthy functioning of the human organism. This was said to be even truer for women whose entire nature was believed to be programmed for procreation. Out of this line of thinking arose a whole new set of discourses that asserted the pathological nature of religious chastity in women. Many nineteenth-century doctors and intellectuals would claim that the celibacy of nuns was causing all sorts of disease by suppressing the female body's drive to procreate. For example, Mainez writes, "Hase sostenido, y aún sostiénese con gran razon por muchos autores, que la continencia forzada ó no, produce en los organismos delicados el histerismo, citándose ejemplos de mujeres que lo han padecido en la época de su pubertad, así como es harto frecuente en las esposas del Señor y en las viudas" (It has been maintained, and is still maintained with great reason by many authors, that chastity, enforced or not, produces hysteria in delicate organisms, citing examples of women who have suffered from it during puberty, similarly, it is very frequent in the Brides of Christ and in widows).[30] Unable to reconcile chastity in women with their construction of a highly sexualized female subject, many nineteenth-century thinkers objected to women's role in the Church on the grounds that maintaining vows of chastity would lead many of these women to disease.

Out of this pathological view of religion arose a debate on the nature of mysticism, particularly in women. The medical consensus was that mysticism was actually a symptom or manifestation of hysteria. The nineteenth-century expert on hysteria, Jean-Martin Charcot, for example, not only established the relation between hysteria and mysticism, but he also diagnosed past mystics, such as Santa Teresa, as hysterics.[31] And Charcot was not alone; he was joined by notable figures such as Max Nordau (*Degeneration*, 1892), Richard von Krafft-Ebing (*Sexual Psychopathy*, 1886), Cesare Lombroso (*Man of Genius*, 1888, and *The Female Offender*, 1893), and later Joseph Breuer and Sigmund Freud (*Studies on Hysteria*, 1895).[32] And as we have seen, Spanish doctors and intellectuals also participated in the discussion. Perhaps Zamacois summarizes the medical consensus most succinctly when he states:

el místico, como el criminal, tiene una antropología que es propia, el místico, como dice muy bien Gall, presenta ciertos caracteres anatómicos y ciertos antecedentes psicológicos, que favorecen la producción y desenvolvimiento de sus aficiones místicas; y el número infinito de apariciones religiosas, como las voces ocultas, los éxtasis, los presentimientos, el arrepentimiento en el momento de la muerte, los posesos del demonio, estigmáticos, etc., no son obra de Dios ó del diablo, sino consecuencias naturales de perturbaciones nerviosas, de preocupaciones, de histerismo, de sugestiones hipnóticas, y de otras muchísimas causas puramente patológicas.[33]

mystics, like criminals, have an anthropology that is their own, mystics, as Gall states very well, present certain anatomical characteristics and certain psychological antecedents that favor the production and develop-

ment of their mystic inclinations; and the infinite number of religious
apparitions, like occult voices, ecstasies, premonitions, conversions at
the moment of death, demonically possessed people, stigmatics, etc.,
they are not the work of God or of the devil, but natural consequences
of nervous disorders, obsessions, hysteria, hypnotic suggestion, and
many other purely pathological causes.

Thus, for thinkers like Zamacois, mysticism itself is both a physical disease and a type of nervous ailment that should be analyzed and treated by doctors.

Mysticism as Sexual Deviance: An Early Modern Precedent

Before exploring in detail the fin-de-siècle medical approach to mysticism, it is useful to examine mysticism's problematic relationship with institutions of authority in the past and how those institutions chose to deal with it. According to Foucault, the nineteenth-century deployment of sexuality had its roots in religious confession. The deployment of sexuality, like psychoanalysis, was a process in which the subject created a narrative, particularly of sexual transgressions, that was then subjected to the interpretation of an authority such as a medical expert. What was solicited from the subject was a narrative of sexual perversions. Sex and all its aberrations were believed to be the hidden "truth" behind all disorders.[34] In this way, the deployment of sexuality differed very little from religious confession. Although the religious concept of sin was not completely restricted to matters of the flesh, aberrant sexual thoughts and behaviors had always been one of the preferred topics of the confessional. Writing about the Counter-Reformation practice of confession in Spain, Adelina Sarrión Mora states that the confessors' manuals of the time show that sex was the central theme of confession.[35] Thus, Catholic confession, like the deployment of sexuality, induced the female subject to define herself in terms of her sexuality. The discourses that she was made to utter, however, belonged to the institutions of power, because, as Jeremy Tambling explains:

those addressed by a confessional discourse are [. . .] made to define
themselves in a discourse given to them [. . . while] made to think
of themselves as autonomous subjects, responsible for their acts.
Further, the confession puts an emphasis on the sexual, in both
Catholicism and Protestantism, and this connects to far more than
the desire to accentuate fleshly weakness. It is bound up, in Foucault, to the production of the subject carried out in the Renaissance and beyond, making the sexual an index to character, and
reading people as unique individuals—subjects—in light of this
confessional knowledge.[36]

Confession was the principle tool used by sixteenth- and
seventeenth-century Spanish society to control the outbreaks of
mysticism on the Iberian Peninsula. One group that operated outside of the Church and that was effectively suppressed by the Inquisition was the *alumbrados*.

It is believed that the *alumbrados* emerged during the late fifteenth and early sixteenth centuries when many laymen and
-women began to gather in private homes to pray and comment
on religious works.[37] Many of the group's members were women,
specifically *beatas*, single women belonging to the lower classes
who made religious vows but continued to live outside the convent,
in private homes, although some did live together in communities
called *beatarios*.[38] These women generally became *beatas* because
the two traditional roles open to women at the time, marriage or the
convent, were foreclosed to them because their families could not
provide them with a dowry.[39] According to Diego Pérez de Valdivia's
Aviso de gente recogida (1585; Notice to the secluded), these women
were supposed to practice a strict religious lifestyle, similar to that
upheld by nuns in the convents: they were to get up early, pray, par-
take in manual labor in or outside the home, eat sparingly, and
mortify the flesh.[40] Moreover, although not all of these women were
required to wear a habit, they were at least expected to dress hum-
bly.[41] They were also expected to remain celibate even though many
beatas were widows and therefore not virgins.[42] The reality of the
beata lifestyle, however, was quite different. Due to the fact that

many women turned to the life of a *beata* in order to attain financial independence rather than to follow spiritual pursuits, many *beatas* did not strive to emulate the religious ideals that the Church and society had set for them. What many of the *beatas* did take advantage of was the freedom and authority that this lifestyle offered. Since they were financially independent and were neither confined to the home nor the convent, they had much more mobility than other women in society.[43] They were also often able to establish a certain amount of prestige for themselves within their villages as divinely inspired spiritual leaders and healers.[44] And, what would be even more disconcerting for the institutions of power, they would be able to do this with little oversight by the Church.[45]

Although many *beatas* and *alumbradas* came to confess to non-sexual heresies, such as their practice of *dejamiento* and their disdain for Church rituals, their sexual transgressions became the grounds on which this group was ultimately discredited.[46] While the *alumbradas de Toledo* were not charged with any sexual offenses, the later groups, those of Andalusia and Extremadura, and later those in the New World, have gone down in history as sexual deviants.[47] The confessed sexual practices of the *alumbradas* went from indecent touching and sensuous kissing to masturbation, fornication, *coitus interruptus*, and even sexual activity with the devil himself, whom they said would often come to them disguised as Christ. According to the Inquisition's records, what often first appeared to them as a spiritual union with Christ was ultimately revealed to be seduction by the devil.[48] Such confessions serve as a perfect example of how these women were forced to utter the Church's discourse on female sexuality in defining themselves. Not only did many Church authorities believe that women were highly susceptible to seduction by the devil, but they were still influenced by manuals on the detection of witches, such as the infamous *Malleus Maleficarum* (1487), whose fourth chapter is titled "Here Follows the Way whereby Witches Copulate with Those Devils Known as Incubi."[49] Clearly under pressure to produce a confession that would satisfy the Inquisitor, these women simply defined themselves in terms of the Church's conception of female sexuality.

María Emma Mannarelli, in her discussion of the Inquisition trials of *beatas* in Peru, argues that this was an area of particular interest to the Inquisitor.[50] A transcription and English translation of the testimony of the *beata* Marina de San Miguel shows that Mannarelli's argument is well founded. Marina, a native of Cordoba, Spain, who in her early adulthood moved to the New World, gave several testimonies before the Inquisition in New Spain. But it is not until the sixth testimony, after what appears to be a two-month period of solitary confinement in her cell, that Marina begins to confess to a series of carnal sins, one of which is having copulated with the devil.[51] This confession—in contrast to her earlier attempts not only to exonerate herself, but also to prove her mystical powers— is believable because Marina has changed her story to produce the confession the inquisitor sought. Yet the fact that Marina held out on giving such confessions until her sixth testimony suggests that she did not initially cooperate.

The effectiveness of the confession in creating a deviant female subject can be seen in the way that posterity has continued to understand these women. The most extensive work on the topic, Álvaro Huerga's five-volume *Historia de los alumbrados* (History of the *alumbrados*), takes the Inquisition's presentation of female *alumbradas* at face value and dismisses them as sexual deviants. In volume five, which was published in 1994, Huerga dedicates an entire chapter to defaming these *beatas*. Using chastity as the touchstone for true spirituality, he concludes that these women were sexually depraved religious frauds: "Las beatas caían y recaían en lo más opuesto a su estado: profesaban castidad, practicaban lujuria; anhelaban pureza, se doblegaban a lo que Pérez de Valdivia llama "tentación deshonesta"; soñaban vivir un amor espiritual, despertaban encendidas en amor erótico" (The *beatas* fell again and again into the most opposite condition of their state: they took chastity vows, they practiced lechery, they desired purity, they gave in to what Pérez de Valdivia calls "dishonest temptation"; they dreamed of experiencing spiritual love, they awoke burning from erotic desire).[52] Moreover, Huerga completely rejects any reevaluation of the *beatas* as a marginalized group rebelling against their low standing in society. For Huerga, their motivation is to be found in their female vanity and their obvious sexual neuroses: "El recurrir a tópicos como el de la protesta o de la marginación no es suficiente para interpretar el fenómeno socio-religioso de las beatas. Hay otras constantes más profundas, como la neurosis sexual, o la simple vanidad femenina, que explican el comportamiento de las beatas" (Resorting to clichés such as their rebellion against their marginalization is insufficient to interpret the socio-religious phenomenon of the *beatas*. There are other more profound recurrences that explain the behavior of the *beatas* such as sexual neurosis or simple female vanity).[53]

What Huerga and other historians have failed to recognize is the role played by the deployment of sexuality in their understanding of these women. In other words, these women were coerced through confinement as well as through psychological and physical violence to define themselves in terms of an aberrant sexuality. Sex was the truth solicited by the Inquisitor who sought precisely to discredit them. Yet it is not a matter of whether the *alumbradas* truly engaged in such activities, since respectable members of the Church were living in open defiance of the Church's teachings on sexuality.[54] Rather, the crucial factor is that these women were forced to make a narrative of their supposed sexual transgressions, which would then be used to define their subjectivity. And this narrative would not only be diligently recorded for posterity but would also be made public during the autos-da-fé, in which the women had to repent of their sins publicly. Thus, these women's involuntary narratives discursively fixed their subjectivity from the moment they uttered them.

This brings us to the inevitable question of Santa Teresa. As in the case of the *alumbradas*, Santa Teresa's practices and beliefs became suspect. Even though Santa Teresa had been denounced to the Inquisition more than once during her lifetime, it was not until seven years after her death, in 1589, that Alonso de la Fuente sent several letters to the Inquisition requesting that it censor her writings. De la Fuente, the man principally responsible for bringing the *alumbrados*, both male and female members, to the attention of the Inquisition, was convinced of Santa Teresa's guilt.[55] Indeed, both

Santa Teresa and the *alumbrados* read the same spiritual works, stressed the importance of maintaining a personal relationship with God, practiced mental prayer, and showed a certain disregard for the ecclesiastical knowledge held by the clergy. Santa Teresa, however, was able to clear her name because she was in a more advantageous position than the *beatas* simply because she was a nun and therefore a member of the Church. Unlike the *alumbradas*, Santa Teresa could not be said to show disdain for the Church's role as an intermediary between herself and God. Her affiliation with the Church also meant that she had been given access to education, unlike many of the lower-class *beatas* who could neither read nor write. Moreover, in contrast to the *alumbradas* who were forced to confess extemporaneously before the Inquisitor, Santa Teresa gave her confession in the form of a written autobiography, which she had the opportunity to revise in consultation with her confessor, a learned and respected member of the Church. Santa Teresa therefore had the time and learning to create a confession that would actually serve as an apologia, rather than a declaration of guilt.[56]

Nevertheless, even though the Catholic Church finally canonized Teresa and other female mystics like her, their trials in Spanish and European society were not over yet. In the modern era, beginning in the nineteenth century, their cases would be exhumed by physicians eager to apply medical diagnoses of hysteria and nymphomania. Thus, while the *alumbradas* were discredited in the sixteenth and seventeenth centuries through the deployment of sexuality, the canonized mystics would be subjected to the same technique in the nineteenth century, but now power and knowledge lay with science and medicine rather than with the Church. And modern medical knowledge would not distinguish between the heretical mystic and the saintly mystic. The highly sexualized nature of the female body would "prove" that all mystical experience in women was sexual.

Mysticism as Hysteria in Fin-De-Siècle Spain

Many nineteenth-century physicians set out to show how the Church had erred in its judgment of the mystics. They argued that the clergy's superstitious, religious worldview had clouded their thinking and made them unable to perceive that such people were actually ill. In other words, trapped in the theological state of thought (according to Comte, the least advanced of the three stages), Church authorities were unable to progress to the positive phase and recognize that these aberrations were due to physical disorders and not to divine and supernatural forces. Zamacois clearly expresses this idea when he writes:

> Lo que parece imposible, es que por espacio de tantos siglos se haya venido creyendo en esas ridículas apariciones de vírgenes y de diablos, que solo sirven para asustar á los niños, y que los pobres tontos que las han tenido, hayan pasado como inspirados por Dios, y no como personas ignorantes y supersticiosas.
>
> Ahora, afortunadamente, ya no sucede lo mismo; ya se pide y se busca en la ciencia lo que antes se pedía y buscaba en el cielo, y la historia de las apariciones religiosas apenas si sirven para distraer; hasta aquí, las alucinaciones, éxtasis, calambres, llagas, etc, han sido consideradas como manifestaciones del poder divino, y ahora, como simples fenómenos patológicos del espíritu; la humanidad ha dado, por tanto, un gran paso en el camino de la verdad.[57]

> *What seems impossible is that for so many centuries people have continued to believe in these ridiculous apparitions of virgins and demons, that only serve to scare children, and that the poor fools who have had [these apparitions] have passed themselves off as inspired by God rather than as ignorant and superstitious people.*
>
> *Today, fortunately, this does not happen; nowadays one looks to science for answers where it once looked to the heavens, and the story of religious apparitions only serve as entertainment; until now hallucinations, ecstasies, shocks, wounds, etc., were considered manifestations of divine power, now they are considered simple pathological phenomena of the spirit; humanity, therefore, has taken a huge step on the path of truth.*

Many writers also argued that when the Church had a dominant presence in society, people held very conservative views on sexuality that prevented them from recognizing or acknowledging the sexual nature of such diseases and prescribing the "appropriate" treatment, which was often sexual intercourse. For example, Mainez asks his reader: "¿Se hubiera aventurado [. . .] á decir á una monja que sus éxtasis, que sus apariciones, que sus risibles teomanías, sólo se fraguaban en el arsenal de su contrariada voluntad física, y en el forzado completo reposo de las funciones sexuales?" (Would they have dared [. . .] to tell a nun that her ecstasies, that her apparitions, that her laughable obsessions with God, were only forged in the arsenal of her unmet physical needs, and in the forced complete inactivity of her sexual functions?).[58]

Yet the relation between hysteria and female sexuality goes back to the ancient Egyptians. And, as we saw, the connection was also made by the medieval and early-modern Church since, even though sexual intercourse was never prescribed as prevention or treatment, the decision of whether to condemn or exonerate a female mystic of heresy often depended on her professed sexual behavior. In other words, according to the Church, a true mystic was chaste while the heretic led a sexually lascivious life. Thus, the connection between sexuality and hysteria goes back to ancient Egypt, and the connection between sexuality and mysticism can be traced to the Middle Ages. These nineteenth-century physicians and intellectuals were merely reviving original notions of the two related phenomena.

Not only did these doctors and hygienists pat themselves on the back for their superior knowledge and their open-mindedness regarding issues of sexuality, they also insisted that they were more compassionate than their predecessors. These doctors argued that Church authorities, in their judgment of cases of mysticism as demonic possession, persecuted the ill for something that was beyond their control. Although one cannot deny the barbarism and cruelty of the Church's persecution of such people, the compassion of the nineteenth-century medical community deserves some scrutiny. Not only were doctors merely replacing one stigma with another (demonic possession with mental illness), they were also applying their diagnoses more indiscriminately. Unlike Church authorities in the past, these doctors blurred the Church's distinction between true mystics and demonically possessed women. For nineteenth-century physicians, both were truly cases of hysteria. Doctors made a point of arguing that the Church's persecution of one group and exaltation of the other was wholly unfounded. In his introduction to Dr. Marie's work on mysticism and insanity, the renowned French anthropologist Dr. Henri Thulié states Dr. Marie "prueba precisamente por estrechas analogías e identidades de síntomas, que gran parte de místicos privilegiados que en el cielo están sentados a la diestra de Dios padre, lo mismo que los poseídos destinados a arder eternamente, atizados por su horquilla, no han sido sino simples alienados" (proves precisely through close analogies and the identical nature of symptoms, that the majority of privileged mystics that are seated to the right of God in heaven, just like the possessed destined to burn eternally, stoked by his pitchfork, were nothing more than simple insane people).[59] While the Vatican had made room for certain mystics who were supposedly able to prove the authenticity of their experiences through their humility and subservience to the Church, nineteenth-century medicine sought to discredit all self-proclaimed mystics.

In fact, doctors' portrayal of female mystics/hysterics was usually far from favorable. They described them as capricious, defiant women who, because their imaginations had gotten the better of them, were chronically unsatisfied with their "real" lives. For some doctors, hysteria, at least in its less severe manifestations, was not even a "disease" at all, but rather an exaggerated form of a natural female condition. For Charles Richet, who worked with Charcot at the Salpêtrière, hysteria, in its milder forms, was simply one type of female character.[60] Hysterics were not only said to be carried away by fantasy but also unable to resist pleasure, particularly sexual desire. Henri Legrand du Saulle, another French doctor who worked with Charcot at the Salpêtrière and who dealt with religious hysteria in women, believed that hysteria led many women to abandon their families and take on a life of prostitution.[61] In addition to their lasciviousness, hysterical women, like spoiled children, were said to become irritable and to throw temper tantrums when they did not receive immediate satisfaction. For example, according to Father Hahn, a Jesuit priest who observed Charcot's patients, "Les hystériques de la Salpêtrière sont pour la plupart des jeunes filles volages, légères, qui n'ont pas trouvé en elles-mêmes assez d'énergie pour résister aux attraits du plaisir et d'une vie licencieuse. Si elles n'ont point la candeur et la simplicité des enfants, elles en ont les caprices et les lubies, s'irritant, pleurant, riant pour des riens" (The hysterics at the Salpêtrière are for the most part flighty, capricious young girls, who have not found within themselves enough strength to resist the attraction of pleasure and a licentious lifestyle, if they do not have any of the candor and innocence of children, they have their whims and tantrums, they become irritated, they cry, and they laugh for the smallest reason).[62] Hysterics were also said to be prone to all sorts of deceptive behavior such as lying and faking certain states or illnesses. Their skill at deception was cause for concern since hysterics, unlike other types of mental patients, remained completely lucid. In other words, their intelligence, which was usually very sharp in such women, was not affected by their disease.[63] For this reason, Father Hahn warns that one must take precautions so as not to be deceived by the hysteric.[64]

It was believed that the hysteric's keen intelligence and highly imaginative nature led her to feel nothing but chronic dissatisfaction with her domestic life. Such women even began to feel indifferent and hostile toward their families, toward both their children and their husbands.[65] Summarizing the case history of the "hysteric" Juana Sagrera, recorded by José María Esquerdo in 1862, Catherine Jagoe gives an example of a Spanish hysteric who exemplified these characteristics:

> La encerrada era perfectamente lúcida pero presentaba rarezas de conducta: desatendía el gobierno de su casa, se mostraba indiferente ante su familia, y deseaba separarse de su marido; era demasiado locuaz; contaba a los criados y los hombres los pormenores más íntimos de su matrimonio, se mostraba irreverente en la iglesia, faltaba al decoro, usando gestos vulgares; salía sola de casa y frecuentaba los bares de los jóvenes militares, con quienes jugaba a los naipes.[66]

The locked-up woman was completely lucid but exhibited strange behavior: she neglected the care of her home, she showed herself indifferent to her family, and she desired to separate from her husband; she was overly talkative; she told the servants and men the most intimate details of her marriage, she was irreverent at church, she lacked decorum, using vulgar gestures; she went out alone, she frequented the bars of young military men, with whom she played cards.

From this description, it is clear that the Spanish doctor José María Esquerdo viewed hysteria as a form of rebellion on the part of the woman. Any behavior that contravened the norms of femininity that nineteenth-century liberal societies were trying to uphold could be classified as "hysterical." This has led modern-day feminist scholars such as Elaine Showalter and Carroll Smith-Rosenberg to conclude that women who rebelled against nineteenth-century gender roles by, for example, not following the norms of femininity or fighting for the right to vote, were often labeled hysterics.[67] The hysterical woman's defiance of the norms of femininity threatened to destabilize the "natural" polarization of the sexes.

Thus, like the Inquisition in its portrayal of heretical female mystics, the nineteenth-century medical community portrayed female hysterics as arrogant and defiant women who disrupted the social order. While in early modern Spain, hysterical mystics such as female members of the *alumbrados* were accused of arrogance because they dared to question and defy the knowledge and authority of the Church, in nineteenth-century Spain, hysterics were accused of arrogance for defying the scientific knowledge of the time that had proven that a woman's role as wife and mother was biologically determined. Since these women, like early modern female mystics, chose a view of reality, and more importantly, of the self, that contravened the authorized discourses of the time, their reality was discredited by the institutions of knowledge. Marie, for example, accused female mystics/hysterics of arrogance because they believed that they were capable of contesting science. According to Marie, the self-proclaimed female mystic, "lo sabe todo sin haber aprendido nada, se reirá de la ciencia humana, tan defectuosa y tan lenta" (knows everything without having learned anything, she laughs at human science, so defective and so slow).[68]

Moreover, while the early modern Church had viewed humility as the touchstone of the true mystic and arrogance as the defining trait of the heretic, nineteenth-century medical doctors accused all mystics/hysterics (even canonized saints) of arrogance. For example, Mainez, in his attempt to portray Santa Teresa as a hysteric, insisted on her vanity: "Tan engreida y tan maniatica desde su delicada infancia. [. . .] Aquella adolescente, que ántes se dedicaba incesantemente á la oracion, al ayuno, al retiro, gustaba despues usar galas, parecer hermosa, ser adorada, oir frases aduladoras" (So conceited and manic since childhood. [. . .] This adolescent, who previously dedicated herself incessantly to prayer, fasting, and retreat, later enjoyed fineries, looking beautiful, being adored, receiving flattery).[69] Such arrogance, according to Marie, contributed to the mystic/hysteric's exaggerated sense of self-worth and importance: "El eroticismo sensorial primitivo [de la mujer mística] provocará la exageración, la hipertrofia del yo, como se ha dicho, y la megalomanía verdadera o su desdoblamiento consecutivo. [. . .] Desde el punto de vista psicológico, sería más justo decir *autofilia*, amor de sí mismo, que exageración del amor de Dios" (The primitive sensory eroticism [of the mystical woman] will provoke exaggeration, hypertrophy of the I, as has been said, and true megalomania or consecutive split personality. [. . .] From a psychological point of view, it would be more accurate to say narcissism, the love of one's self, than an exaggerated love of God).[70] In this way, all mystics, even saints, were portrayed as egotistical and vain. Women were not to turn to Santa Teresa as a model, any more than to female mystics from heretical sects such as the *alumbrados*. Rather than following in the steps of arrogant mystics, women were to emulate the submissive, selfless, nurturing *ángel del hogar* (angel in the house), who willingly accepted her humble position within the family and society.

The diagnosing of mysticism as hysteria was then, in many ways, an attempt to control what doctors perceived to be a threat to the family and the social order. Hystericizing women who did not accept their proper roles in society, enabled doctors to discredit them by converting their mystical experiences into symptoms of a sexual disease. Interestingly, this process involved techniques similar to those employed by the sixteenth- and seventeenth-century Spanish Inquisition. Doctors would attempt to challenge these women's claims by turning the spiritual into the sexual through confessional narratives and through the assertion of the superiority of scientific knowledge to religious perceptions of the world. While the Church's counterattack had been to force such women to re-create the Church-imposed subjectivity of themselves through a confession of their sins, usually sexual in nature, in the nineteenth century women were induced to confess indecent sexual activities to their doctor, from which a diagnosis of hysteria was made. In addition, just as the Church had asserted the superiority of orthodoxy (the official, monolithic Church doctrine), over heterodoxy (varied beliefs), science would insist on the superiority of its knowledge over Church doctrine by stressing science's use of empirical evidence. In other words, through the scientific gaze, or the observation of the female body during mystical rapture/hysterical fit, doctors would claim that their version of reality was factual because it was based on empirical evidence, whereas religious understandings of the same phenomenon were not.

Medical practice took over the confessional in the nineteenth century in two ways. The first way was by inciting women to discuss their sexual behavior with a doctor. Some of the sexual hygiene manuals of the time mention the doctor's role as confessor. For example, in his discussion of masturbation in women, V. Suárez Casañ claims that the only way to make an accurate diagnosis is to elicit a confession from the patient: "lo más acertado es provocar una confesión del paciente, que un médico instruido sabrá arrancarle con facilidad" (the best way is to provoke a confession in the patient, which a trained doctor will know how to do with ease).[71] In addition, in a talk to La Academia de Medicina de Madrid in 1867 about the reason why diseases of the womb had become so much more prevalent, Francisco de Cortejarena y Aldebó argued that women had become more willing to consult their doctors for all sorts of matters, even for the slightest symptom or most personal problem. Cortejarena y Aldebó maintained that women, convinced of the necessity of frequently consulting and confiding in their doctor, were now more willing to confess to things that women would have been loath to discuss with their doctors in previous eras. Because of this, doctors had become "poseedores de los más íntimos secretos de las familias" (the possessors of families' most intimate secrets).[72] Not surprisingly, the case histories related in such works often read as confessional narratives in which the female patient confesses to her doctor.

As the doctor assumed his new role as confessor, the role of the priest in the practice of religious confession was put into question, particularly in regard to women. Seemingly aware of the position of power held by the Church confessor, many anticlerical liberals objected to the great influence priests had on women in this role. Leopoldo Alas serves as a case in point. In *Solos de Clarín* (Solos by Clarín), the Asturian author sarcastically expressed the threat that the religious confessor posed: "no digo que la confesión sea un arma terrible en manos del clero; lo que digo es que, si no lo es, parece mentira" (I'm not saying that confession is a terrible weapon in the hands of the clergy; what I'm saying is that, if it is not, it seems like a lie).[73] And in *Preludios* (Preludes), pretending to exonerate women for their susceptibility to religious fanaticism, Alas places the blame once again on the clergy: "¿Quién tendría la culpa de que tantas mujeres (porque son muchas) se conviertan en otros tantos Quijotes con devocionarios? ¡Sus directores espirituales!" (Who could be guilty of the fact that so many women (because there are many) turn into equally as many Don Quixotes with prayer books? Their confessors!).[74] Pardo Bazán added to the debate by calling attention to men's fears of extreme religious devotion in women and to the role of the confessor in bringing about such fears:

[El hombre liberal] le prohíbe [a la mujer] ser librepensadora, mas no le consiente arrobos y extremos místicos. Detrás de la devota exaltada ve el padre, hermano o marido alzarse la negra sombra del director espiritual, un rival en autoridad [. . .]. Así es que de todas las prácticas religiosas de la mujer, la que el hombre mira con más recelo es la confesión frecuente.[75]

[The liberal man] prohibits [his wife] from being a freethinker, but he does not allow raptures and mystical extremes. Arising from behind every female religious fanatic, the woman's father, brother, or husband sees the black shadow of the woman's spiritual guide, a rival in authority. [. . .] This is why of all of women's religious practices, the one which men view with most suspicion is frequent confession.

Thus, many nineteenth-century thinkers recognized, as did Foucault much later, that confession was a form of surveillance and control exercised by the confessor who was able to elicit the desired narrative from the confessant. For this reason, many anticlerical liberals sought to transfer this power out of the hands of the religious confessor and into those of the liberal physician. Yet for the woman the result was the same. In both cases, she was supervised and regulated by a patriarchal institution that would insist she define herself in terms of her sexuality.

Another strategy to contain female mysticism that took on the confessional form was the reinterpretation of the texts of past mystics. These writers attempted to convert mystical narratives into confessions of behaviors indicative of hysteria. This was done by creating accounts of defiant behavior, particularly of aberrant sexual behavior, that would then be used to create the female mystic's subjectivity. Teresa de Jesús was one of the preferred targets of this attack since, as Tomás Álvarez points out, Santa Teresa's extensive written account of her experiences made her a preferred subject of retrospective scientific study.[76] A perfect example of this is Ramón León Mainez's *Teresa de Jesús ante la crítica*, in which the author cites Teresa's own writings to demonstrate her histeria: "Lo que vamos á hacer es [. . .] manifestar de un modo terminante, *y con el propio irrecusable testimonio de sus palabras*, que Santa Teresa sufria cruelísimos males físicos" (emphasis mine; What we are going to do is [. . .] show once and for all, *and through the damn-*

ing testimony of her own words, that Santa Teresa suffered from terrible physical illnesses).[77] Zamacois also cites Teresa's account of her mystical experience to then imply a connection between her experiences and the experience of two lovers: "¿No es cierto que hay alguna semejanza entre las sensaciones que experimentan los místicos y esa inexplicable felicidad que inunda el corazón de un amante, al reposar su frente sobre el blanco seno de su amada?" (Is it not true that there is some similarity between the sensation that mystics experience and that unexplainable happiness that inundates the heart of a lover, when he rests his head on the white breast of his sweetheart?).[78]

The attempt to sexualize the mystics' texts was facilitated by the fact that many nineteenth-century doctors had already linked sexuality to religion. For example, Richard von Krafft-Ebing, in his highly influential *Psychopathia sexualis*, originally published in 1886, claimed that "religious insanity was often to be found in the sexual aberration." Moreover, Krafft-Ebing argued, religious ceremonies "often degenerated into orgies, or into mystic cults of a voluptuous character" while unappeased sexuality often found "a substitute in religion."[79] Spain's first gynecologist, Baltasar de Viguera, writing in 1827, well before Krafft-Ebing, made a similar connection. In his four-volume *Fisiología y patología de la mujer*, Viguera recounts the case of a young woman in love who, because her sentiments were not reciprocated, was overtaken by hysteria. This illness endured until the young lady found a substitute for human love in religion and became a nun.[80] Zamacois relates a similar case in which a young woman, who had lost her fiancé, came to experience mystical rapture during which she would embrace and pretend to kiss an imaginary being.[81] The implication is that spiritual love (*agape*) and sexual love (*eros*) satisfy the same instinct and can therefore replace one another.

Not only did many doctors assume a direct link between sexuality and religion, they had also established that mysticism/hysteria was a sexual disease of which either chastity or sexual excess was the cause. Thus those who argued that mysticism in women was merely a sign or symptom of hysteria simply needed to highlight the sexual aspects of mysticism to confirm their preconceived ideas about religion and sexuality. This was easily achieved by emphasizing the ambiguity of the mystics' language and its sexual connotations. In so doing, many writers were able to convert the spiritual into the material by showing that mystics were really having a bodily, sexual experience. Marie, for example, claims that sexual perversion and mystical deliria are often linked. He cites another expert in the field who argues that the sexual arousal experienced by the mystics is produced by fantasizing about having intercourse with God/Jesus. Although merely a figment of the imagination, the mystic's fantasy of union with the divine produces a material, bodily experience: "Más de una religiosa, dice Ball, escogía a Jesús como santo, y el papel de este divino personaje no es siempre tan inmaterial como podría creerse" (More than one nun, Ball says, chose Jesus as her saint, and the role of this divine figure is not always as immaterial as one might think). In other words, the mystics' supposed spiritual unions were really "coitos imaginarios" (imaginary intercourse) that led to physical orgasm.[82] To prove his argument that mystical rapture is really sexual arousal and orgasm produced through fantasizing about having sexual relations with God, Marie quotes a number of mystical texts, first amongst them Santa Teresa's passage of the transverberation vision in which an angel of God thrusts an arrow into her heart; the arrow reaches her intestines, producing both intense pain and delight.[83] This passage, taken from her *Libro de la vida* (Book of her life) and given visual representation in Gianlorenzo Bernini's famous statue of the Spanish saint (1645–52) in the Vatican in Rome, has often been cited for its sexually charged imagery. Thus, for Marie, it serves as evidence of the physical and sexual nature of the delights Santa Teresa experienced in her union with God.

These doctors' sexual reading of mystical union between the mystic and the divine resembles the narratives that the Inquisitor solicited from the female heretical mystic, who was often brought to confess that her spiritual unions were actually sexual transgressions. For example, in the trial of the *alumbrada* mystic Marina de San Miguel, the accused ultimately admitted that her proclaimed mystical union with Christ was actually fornication with the devil.[84] Just as this female *alumbrada* mystic was made to confess to the carnal nature of her so-called mystical experiences with Christ, many nineteenth-century thinkers would reinterpret, or rewrite, Santa Teresa's experiences of the divine as sexual fantasy and physical orgasm.

A direct relation was also made between masturbation and mystical ecstasy. In fact, for doctors it was not clear which came first: did mysticism produce masturbation, or did masturbation bring on mystical ecstasy? Thésée Pouillet, whose book on onanism in women was translated into Spanish in 1883, condemns the "abominable redacción de los libros místicos y de los cánticos en que el amor divino se halla explicado por frases demasiado sensuales" (the abominable writing style of mystical books and poems in which divine love is explained through very sensual phrases) since it led youth to the practice of autoeroticism.[85] However, later in his work, Pouillet claims that masturbation itself can produce states of ecstasy.[86] Thus, hysteria/mysticism was both the cause and the result of masturbation.

Moreover, a connection was made between masturbation and mystical rapture by emphasizing the role of the female imagination in both. As we saw in Chapter 1, in the nineteenth century many hygienists warned against over-exciting the female imagination. Claiming that the "real" world could never compete with the pleasures of the imaginary world, many doctors and writers argued that women were prone to abandon themselves to fantasy and completely lose touch with reality. Yet the pleasure procured through the use of imagination was not solely mental. Following the lead of Samuel Auguste André David Tissot's *L'Onanisme* and D. T. Bienville's *La Nymphomanie*, many nineteenth-century doctors argued that fantasy and imagination, particularly when incited by novel reading, led to sexual arousal and masturbation. This was particularly dangerous for women since in the female sex masturbation was said to be a practice that exacerbated desire rather than placating it.[87] Because texts on both onanism and mysticism stressed the fundamental role of imagination, mysticism and masturbation were linked in women.

   Those writers involved in the reinterpretation (or sexualization/
hysterization) of mystical texts often exploited the connection
between mysticism, imagination, women, and masturbation. For
example, on more than one occasion Mainez makes reference to
Santa Teresa's overly active imagination, connecting it to the Spanish nun's avowed affinity for novel reading.[88] Thus, through the
implied connection between the Spanish nun's imagination and her
engagement in solitary sex, Mainez sexualizes Teresa's narrative. Not
surprisingly, masturbation was also one of the sins female *alumbradas* confessed to before the Inquisitor, a fact that ultimately served
to discredit their mystical experiences. For example, María Palacios
Alcalde, taking the *alumbradas'* confessions before the Inquisitor at
face value, claims, "en la forma en que estas mujeres viven su sexualidad, lo que más llama la atención es la frecuencia con que se regis-
tra en su comportamiento la autosatisfacción sexual, bien medi-
ante la masturbación, bien por medio de la imaginación intensa
del encuentro sexual, somatizada hasta la experiencia del orgasmo"
(of the form in which these women live their sexuality, what is most
striking is the frequency with which solitary sexual practices are
recorded, either through masturbation or through intense fantasies
of sexual encounters somaticized to point of orgasm).[89]

   In addition to the deployment of sexuality, or the confessional
narrative, doctors were also able to sexualize the mystical experience by asserting the superiority of scientific knowledge. Since scientific theories were demonstrable through observation, the visual
aspects of the mystical rapture/hysterical fit were stressed, for they
served as scientific evidence of the sexual nature of the disease.
By employing the scientific gaze to read the female body, doctors
could empirically "prove" that their theories on the nature of this
religious disease were correct. This technique was also applied to
canonized mystics/saints. By observing artistic representations of
these mystics' spiritual ecstasies, many doctors easily could "read"
the female body in order to reveal the sexual nature of their experiences. For example, according to Cristina Mazzoni, much of the
controversy on Santa Teresa at the time focused on Bernini's statue
of her in Rome, rather than on her texts.[90]

The best example of the employment of the scientific gaze in the study of mysticism/hysteria was Charcot's famous "stage" for hysterics at the Salpêtrière hospital in France. During the *sessions de lundi* (Tuesday sessions), Charcot would hypnotize many of his female hysterics and induce a hysterical attack before an audience. These hysterical fits often resembled mystical rapture. In fact, the third phase of the hysterical fit, as developed by Charcot, was the *période des attitudes passionnelles* (period of passionate attitudes), in which the hysteric took on certain religious poses.[91] Since Charcot needed a means of circulating this empirical evidence beyond the hospital walls, there was a special photography laboratory in the hospital where hysterical poses were captured on film. These images, which were published by two of Charcot's disciples, D. M. Bourneville and P. Régnard, in the three-volume *L'Iconographie photographique de la Salpêtrière* (1876–1880; The photographic iconography of the Salpêtrière), would have an even wider audience.

But what were people seeing at the Salpêtrière and in these photographs that proved that these women were hysterics? Through the clinical gaze, a connection was made not only between the hysterical attack and mystical rapture, but also between the two and female orgasm. The link between orgasm and mystical rapture was strengthened by theories that claimed the hysterical fit itself was a type of pathological female orgasm. For example, Viguera, still believing that female orgasm was necessary for conception, viewed hysteria as a diseased type of orgasm that occurred when the womb was sexually unsatisfied. According to Viguera, through intercourse and orgasm the womb could be pacified.[92] To prove the effectiveness of producing a "normal" orgasm to treat hysteria, Viguera relates a case that he himself treated. A widow, who was living with her aunt, suffered from hysterical attacks only when her aunt was away. According to Viguera, "Esta circunstancia de que se lisongeaba, me hizo sospechar alguna maniobra indecente, y en efecto [la tía] me confesó que la onanizaba al instante que la veía acometida del paroxismo y que estaba bien persuadida que este auxilio la habia arrancado muchas veces de la agonía" (This circumstance, for which she praised herself, made me suspect some indecent maneuver, and indeed [the aunt] confessed to me that she manually stimulated her the moment that she saw her overtaken by the paroxysm and that she was very convinced that this assistance had saved her many times from agony).[93] Thus, for Viguera, normal female orgasm was the antidote to the pathological orgasms of the womb of the hysterical woman. However, the pathological orgasm and the normal orgasm were nearly indistinguishable: "estos dos fenómenos, aunque el uno sea fisiológico y el otro patológico, tienen entre sí tanta conformidad" (these two phenomena, although one is physiological and the other pathological, are very similar).[94] Doctors such as Viguera helped to support the link between the hysterical fit/mystical rapture and female orgasm.

Even though Viguera distinguished, to some degree, one type of orgasm from the other, other doctors would see both types of orgasm as pathological. Monlau, for example, warning women against the danger of sexual indulgence, stressed the similarities between female orgasm and the hysterical attack, as well as the disorders normal orgasm can produce: "los sacudimientos nerviosos que experimenta la mujer en el cóito han sido comparados á un acceso de histerismo" (the nervous spasms that the woman experiences in coitus have been compared to the hysterical fit).[95] Mystical rapture's similarity to the hysterical fit/female orgasm would convert female mysticism into a sexual aberration that needed to be addressed by the medical community.

The sexual nature of hysterical fits/mystical raptures was also underscored in accounts that emphasized the role of the female sexual and reproductive organs in these attacks. According to Charcot and his followers, the hysterical fit could be both incited and arrested by manipulating the female reproductive organs, particularly the ovaries. Richet described this phenomenon based on what he had observed at the Salpêtrière:

> Pendant tout le temps que l'ovaire est comprimé, la malade a toute sa conscience; elle peut remettre en ordre ses vêtements que les contorsions ont dérangés, causer, rire, s'amuser tranquillement avec ses voisines; mais si l'on vient à relâcher quelque peu la com-

pression de l'ovaire, aussitôt l'accès reprend avec tout autant de force qu'auparavant. En comprimant de nouveau l'ovaire, l'accès cesse encore.[96]

During the whole time that the ovary is compressed, the afflicted woman is completely conscious; she can straighten out her clothes that the contortions had messed up, chat, laugh, calmly enjoy herself with her neighbors; but if the compression on the ovary is released a little, the fit returns immediately with just as much force as before. By compressing the ovary again, the attack ceases again.

According to such descriptions the hysterical attack could simply be turned on and off merely by manipulating the female ovaries.

A general fear of female sexuality also played a role in the pathologization of female orgasm. This fear was due in part to texts that stressed the discrepancy between male and female sexual capabilities. Doctors argued that for men sexual intercourse drained and weakened the physical body since it was believed that each ejaculation deprived the male body of a vital life substance.[97] On the other hand, since female orgasm did not produce an ejaculation, women's bodies were not necessarily weakened by the sexual act. Thus, there seemed to be no natural limits on women's sexual abilities. As a result, any man who tried to placate an overly sexed woman's desires risked weakness, infirmity, and serious debilitating diseases that could bring on an early death. These lascivious women, otherwise known to the medical community as nymphomaniacs, were portrayed as ravenous beasts who had the supposed potential to devour men sexually:

La vista de una de estas dementes es un espectáculo horripilante y conmovedor al mismo tiempo. Sus ojos parecen querer saltar de sus órbitas; dilatadas las narices; la respiración jadeante; bañada la boca en viscosa saliva; contraídos los labios, por entre los cuales se ve asomar la lengua; desordenado el traje; suelto los cabellos y descubierto el seno, parecen unas furias, unas bacantes. No pudiendo apagar el fuego interno que las devora, se golpean con furor y desgarran sus carnes con las uñas, dan gritos y alaridos terribles y agotan el vocabulario de frases obscenas.[98]

The sight of one of these demented women is horrifying and moving at the same time. Their eyes appear to want to jump out of their sockets; their nostrils dilated; their breath panting; their mouths bathed in viscous saliva, their lips, through which one sees their tongue appear, are contracted, their dress in disarray; their hair down and their breasts showing, they look like the Furies or bacchantes. Unable to extinguish the internal fire that devours them, they beat themselves with fury and tear their flesh with their fingernails, they give off screams and terrible shrieks and exhaust their vocabulary of obscene phrases.

Richet gives a similar description of the hysterical attack:

Il n'est peut-être pas de spectacle plus effrayant que celui de ces accès [hystériques]. Le corps est agité de tremblemen[t]s et de secousses violentes. Tous les muscles sont contractés, tendus au point qu'on les croit toujours sur le point de se rompre. Des bonds prodigieux, des cris et des hurlemen[t]s épouvantables, des vociférations confuses, des contorsions inouïes qu'on n'aurait jamais supposé une créature humaine capable de faire, tel est le hideux tableau que présente une hystérique lorsqu'elle est en proie à une attaque."[99]

There is perhaps no spectacle more frightening than that of the [hysterical] attack. The body is shaken by violent quivers and temors. All the muscles are taut, stretched to the point that one believes they are always about to break. Extraordinary leaps, frightening cries and howls, confused rants, unbelievable contortions that one would have never believed possible for a human being to do, such is the hideous scene that a hysteric creates when she is suffering from an attack.

Thus, female sexuality and orgasm were presented as a sinister threat. The physical similarities between hysterical/nymphomaniacal fit and mystical rapture made both the former and the latter frightening spectacles. The implicit message was that a woman who gave free reign to her sexuality threatened male strength and dominance in society. The pathologization of the sexuality of mystics/hysterics/nymphomaniacs combined with discourses idealizing the passionless, bourgeois *ángel del hogar* turned mysticism into a menacing defiance. Mysticism/hysteria/nymphomania, as a type of uncontrolled female sexuality, not only wreaked havoc on the household and the institution of the family in general, but challenged patriarchal society by threatening to undermine male strength.

Although the scientific gaze did not involve eliciting a confession from the subject under study, it did involve eliciting certain behaviors from these women. The fact that Charcot labeled the various phases of hysteria and then was able to demonstrate them on command indicates some complicity on his part. Carroy-Thirard has pointed out the similarities between the religious art of the Counter-Reformation that Charcot and Richet allude to in their *Les démoniaques dans l'art* (1887; The demonically possessed in art) and the images of the hysterical patients captured by Charcot's photographers at the Salpêtrière.[100] It therefore seems likely that Charcot derived his concept of the hysterical attack from religious art and was actually inducing, although not necessarily consciously, his patients to perform his notions of the disease.[101] In fact, after observing the hysterics at the Salpêtrière, Father Hahn described the role of the physician as that of "director": "Les hystériques hypnotisées se changent en véritables statues de cire molle, auxquelles on imprime toutes les poses que l'on désire, poses toujours naturelles et par là même gracieuses. [. . .] Les attitudes les plus diverses, les jeux de physionomie les plus variés peuvent être ainsi provoqués à volonté; tout dépend de l'habilité de l'opérateur." (Hypnotized hysterics change into veritable statues of soft wax on which one impresses all the poses one desires, poses that are always natural and as a result gracious. [. . .] The most diverse attitudes, the most varied acting expressions can be in this way provoked at will; it all depends on the skill of the director).[102]

All of this seems to suggest that the hysterical fit was nothing more than a performance or a simulacrum. Even the famous English political philosopher John Stuart Mill argued that hysteria in women was more the product of cultivation than of a natural disposition.[103] Thus, just as nineteenth-century doctors were eliciting a sexual confession from their patients in the practice of the deployment of sexuality, through the scientific gaze and assertion of the superiority of scientific theories over other types of knowledge, they were also producing desired behaviors in their patients. In both instances, both the discourses and the behavioral norm were products of authorized knowledges (medicine/liberalism). The female subject was merely made to utter the words and/or act out the behaviors that the authority figure sought. This serves as a perfect example of Foucault's concept of "productive" (versus "deductive") power. Rather than exercising power through punishment, through denying the individual certain freedoms and even life ("deductive power"), "productive" power produces the discourses and behaviors it desires so that it can then regulate and control them.[104]

Of course, many mystics voluntarily used the physical body as a sign of their mystical experiences. Through bodily signs such as injuries and illnesses caused by self-mortification, stigmata, and certain poses during mystical raptures, many mystics sought to give external signs of the ineffable, internal experience of union with God/Universe, as well as validity to their claims. However, this may have been, in part, an attempt to persuade and appease those with the authority to sanction their experiences. Moreover, one of mysticism's greatest strengths was precisely that it allowed for the affirmation of a unique and ineffable human existence that could not be defined and controlled by signs (either language or the body). By insisting that true being transcended human sign systems, the subject was freed from the restrictions of culturally and linguistically constructed subjectivities. Nevertheless, in the age of science, when that which could be seen (and subsequently explained) existed and that which could not be seen or adequately expressed did not, the defense of ineffability would mostly fall on deaf ears. While in the early modern era the Church openly attacked those forms of knowledge that contested its own by labeling them heresies and by brutally persecuting their proponents, in the nineteenth century many scientists' marginalization of alternative knowledges was more subtle. By emphasizing the visual and material aspect of a phenomenon, scientists could subjugate metaphysical concepts of the female subject without employing physical violence. This is what Carroy-Thirard has called the nineteenth-century hegemony of seeing, or *l'hégémonie de voir*.[105] However, despite the lack of physical violence, the scientific gaze was a form of suppression in that it subjugated those discourses that sought to liberate women by claiming that a woman's essence could not be revealed by an empirical study of her physical body.

Conclusion

What explains nineteenth-century doctors and writers' interest in discrediting female mysticism? At the time, religious life remained an alternative path for women who sought to escape domestic life and actively engage in intellectual and social pursuits. Moreover, religious history had not only provided examples of alternative lifestyles for women but also of women who had been able to distinguish themselves and earn the reverence of the Church and society. Pardo Bazán points out, for example, that in the Middle Ages, when social issues and spirituality were intricately entwined, many women, such as the female saints and mystics, held prominent roles in society.[106] This is what led contemporary theorist Luce Irigaray to assert that mysticism "is the only place in history of the West in which woman speaks and acts so publicly."[107] It also can be tied to Kathy Bacon's more recent concept of "saintly capital." Bacon argues that in nineteenth-century Spain, sainthood was "an essentially social phenomenon, and one which requires explanation in terms of power and agency."[108] In other words, since saintliness conferred power on the individual who is believed to possess it, it was a form of currency that women could acquire at a time in which they were denied access to positions of power and authority in other areas of society. Thus, from this perspective, mysticism not only offered a means of transcending a domestic existence but also of aspiring to greatness.

Specifically, in terms of the continued fascination with Santa Teresa, DuPont asserts that Teresa was "a symbol for mysticism in its historical context, neomysticism as a rejection of positivism, disavowal of the present in general, resistance to the diagnosis of hysteria by way of an empowered, self-generated, self-analyzing discourse, and new currents in feminism."[109] Thus we see that Santa Teresa continued to serve as model for women who sought more active roles in society, such as female intellectuals and writers. In terms of writing, she was one of the few role models available to women. Her prominence in her role as a female author is attested to by Carolina Coronado who, in *Los genios gemelos*, asserts that "Teresa como poetisa no tuviera rival en el mundo si no existiera el nombre de Safo" (Teresa as a female poet would not have a rival in the world if the name of Sappho did not exist).[110] Similarly, Rosalía de Castro, in the prologue to her first novel, *La hija del mar* (1859), claims that the Spanish saint was one of the few female authors who inspired her to dare to write a novel.[111] And of course Pardo Bazán also held a great admiration for Santa Teresa. She praises the Spanish saint's work for its beautifully refined language, spontaneity, and literary value, and lauds her as an exemplary writer and national figure.[112]

The debate between science and religion regarding mysticism and hysteria found expression in the literary movements and works of the time. By the mid-nineteenth century, anticlerical themes as well as scientific theories, particularly those relating to degeneration and hysteria, began to exercise a direct influence on literature. These scientific theories played a particularly prominent role in the realist and naturalist novel. Signs of mysticism were generally interpreted as symptoms of hysteria in these novels and were given a primarily ironic and negative representation. Notable examples include Gustave Flaubert's *Madame Bovary* (1857), Leopoldo Alas's *La Regenta* (1884–85), and Eduardo López Bago's *Cura* trilogy (1885–86). In all these works the female protagonists' bouts with mysticism are portrayed as causes and signs of their hysteria.

While I analyze the mystical discourses in *La Regenta* in Chapter 4, in Chapter 3, I explore Eduardo López Bago's *Cura* trilogy in order to show how a radical naturalist used mysticism and mystical discourse to portray various female sexual "pathologies." López Bago's novels give fictional expression to all the medical theories previously discussed to create a series of novels that simultaneously seek to sexualize and domesticate women, discredit the Church, and provide sexual titillation for the reading public through the portrayal of sexual behaviors that the novels simultaneously condemn. Thus, despite López Bago's liberal political views by the standards of the time, on questions of gender and sexuality, I argue, he was no less reactionary than the church and society he virulently attacks.

3 Eduardo López Bago's Hysterics, Tribades, and Nymphomaniacal Nuns

IN THE 1880S Eduardo López Bago led a movement of writers known as the radical naturalists. Other authors in this group include José Zahonero, Eugenio Antonio Flores, Alejanndro Sawa, Enrique Sánchez Seña, and Remigio Vega Armentero.[1] These writers sought to use literature to promote a political agenda informed by the medical and scientific knowledge of the day. Taking Émile Zola's theory of naturalism to the extreme, they combined melodrama, lewd topics, and contemporary medical knowledge to create novels with characters who were subjected to a fatalistic material determinism. And while many of these novels were subject to censorship and have never been incorporated into the canon, their immense popularity with the contemporary reading public suggests their influence on, and representation of, the cultural imaginary of the time.[2]

Passionately embracing the rise of science, López Bago not only subscribed to all of Zola's postulates, but also assumed the principles of Claude Bernard's *Introduction à l'étude de la médecine expérimentale* (1865; Introduction to the study of experimental medicine), positivist philosophy, evolutionary theory, Hippolyte Taine's ideas on *race, milieu, moment* (race, environment, and time), Prosper Lucas's hereditary theories, Charles Letourneau's theses on the biological heredity of feelings and passions, and Max Nordau's theory of degeneration.[3] Comparing his writing style to a medical experiment, and even to a vivisection, López Bago claimed that his objective as a writer was to show both the wound and its cure.[4] The author's unwavering allegiance to matter over spirit leads narrators and characters alike to argue against the existence of a soul.[5] It is precisely López Bago's fervor for material determinism as an explanation for everything that leads Pura Fernández to refer to him as a "mesiánico discípulo que raya en el fanatismo" (a messianic disciple who verges on fanaticism).[6]

The drives that were of interest to López Bago were specifically those involved with human sexuality, explicitly linking his determinism to his conviction that the "natural" sexual instinct could not be controlled without causing great harm to the human organism.[7] It was on these grounds that he decried the hypocrisy of religious morality.[8] Obsessed with the pernicious effects of chastity vows, he argued that the Church did more harm than good by imposing practices that went against human nature. Indeed, like many of the hygienists of his day, he embraced legal medicine claiming that any law that contravened nature could not be enforced.[9] His belief that society could only be improved by creating laws based on human nature rather than on religious beliefs largely explains the author's seeming obsession with what he perceives to be the unnaturalness of celibacy in members of the Church.[10]

Like his contemporaries, López Bago also denounced the confessor's role in manipulating his female confessants to the detriment of the family.[11] This concern with the confessor's pernicious influence over women and the family was a commonplace in canonical and popular anticlerical literature of the time, particularly in France and Spain. Examples include Jules Michelet's *Du prêtre, de la femme et de la famille* (1845; Priests, women, and families), Émile Zola's *La conquête de Plassans* (1874; The conquest of Plassans), the Goncourt brothers' *Madame Gervaisais* (1869), George Sand's *Mademoiselle de la Quintinie* (1863, Miss Quintinie), Joséphin Péladan's *Le vice suprême* (1884; The supreme vice), Léo Taxil and Karl Milo's *Débauches d'un confesseur* (1879, A confessor's debauchery), Benito Pérez Galdós's *La familia de León Roch* (1878; The family of Leon

Roch), Leopoldo Alas Clarín's *La Regenta* (1884–85; The regent's wife), López Bago's *El confesionario* (1885; The confessional), and José Zahonero's *Mi mujer y el cura: Confidencias de un aldeano* (1900; My wife and the priest: A villager's secrets). These works not only present the confessor as a rival to the husband but also denounce the confessional practice for lending itself to the crime of solicitation.[12] All these issues are put on display in López Bago's *El confesionario* where the priest Román uses the confessional not only to seduce a married marchioness, but also to manipulate her into giving the Church large sums of money to win the Pope's favor, and to engage in behaviors that are destructive to herself and her family.

Despite López Bago's proclaimed adherence to the scientific method and display of familiarity with medical texts of the day, many critics have rightfully questioned the degree to which his works are truly scientific.[13] For example, critics such as Pura Fernández and Yvan Lissorgues argue that he was just as fanatical in his views as a religious zealot. Lissorgues asserts that López Bago confuses literature and scientific experimentation by egregiously overlooking the fact that the author of a literary work always gets the results he wants, something that is not the case for the scientist.[14] Pura Fernández argues that López Bago holds up heterosexual union and reproduction as his religion, as scientific dogma that offers up a simplistic theory of everything, which actually flies in the face of the experimental method.[15] Thus, as Maite Zubiaurre notes, despite López Bago's claims to absolute objectivity, his novels are quite tendentious.[16]

Several critics have also raised the issue of whether López Bago's works are merely pornography disguised by a political and scientific agenda. The fact that the author was taken to court on obscenity charges for his novels *La prostituta* (1884; The prostitute) and *La pálida* (1884; The pale woman) shows that many readers at the time considered his works obscene.[17] Indeed, López Bago's novels, like the hygiene manuals dealing with sexuality, are more accurately described as pseudoscientific, erotic, naturalist fiction.[18] The focus on female sexual deviance, related through a voyeuristic gaze, likely appealed to the fantasies of many readers.[19] For example, as

Zubiaurre writes, in regard to one character's hysteria in *El cura*, "lo que interesa es ver Gracia distorsionar y desnudar su cuerpo durante unos ataques histéricos que peligrosamente recuerdan al acto sexual" (what is of interest is watching Gracia undress and writhe during hysterical attacks that dangerously remind one of the sexual act).[20] Also likely erotically appealing to the readers was the female characters' initial ignorance about their own sexuality and what was causing their problems.[21]

Due to the author's embrace of legal medicine, hygiene, biological determinism, and anticlericalism, the *Cura* trilogy is a good place to examine the issues discussed in Chapters 1 and 2. In the first novel, *El cura (Caso de incesto): Novela médico social* (The priest [A case of incest]: A socio-medical novel), upon being ordained a priest, the twenty-two-year-old Román invites his fifteen-year-old sister Gracia to come to live with him. Both characters are initially naïve, but Gracia's immediate transition to womanhood and Román's simultaneous sexual awakening, combined with a lack of outlets for either's newly awakened erotic desires, lead them to become attracted to one other and to consummate their relationship at the very end of the novel. *El confesionario (Satiriasis): Novela médico social* (The confessional [Satyriasis]: A socio-medical novel) picks up where *El cura* leaves off. Out of shame about the act he has committed, Román ignores Gracia, leaving her in the care of his new maid and his neighbors, a situation that worsens Gracia's hysteria and leads to her death by the end of the novel.[22] While Gracia is left to waste away from her illness, Román becomes consumed with his new confessant, the thirty-year old marchioness of Florida, Gertrudis, whom Román desires both for her physical beauty and her wealth. Her riches, he believes, are the means of eventually becoming Pope. By the middle of the novel Román loses his moral compass entirely and becomes sadistic in his interactions with Gertrudis. He insists that she sleep with her syphilitic husband, which provokes the man's death and risks infecting Gertrudis with the same illness, manipulates Gertrudis into giving most of her money to the Church (thereby disinheriting her daughter), and forces himself on her sexually at the end the novel.[23] The third novel in the trilogy, *La monja: Novela médico-social* (The nun: A socio-medical novel), takes its focus off Román in order to study the sexual deviance that takes place in the convent. Román convinces Melita, Gertrudis's daughter, to become a nun. There she is manipulated into believing that the homoerotic activities in which she is inducted are spiritual ecstasy. When Román discovers the same-sex orgies that take place in the convent at night, he finds a way to insinuate himself into the sexual activities. Melita dies a premature death from tuberculosis caused by the unhygienic conditions and activities of the convent, and the only nun to resist the lesbian practices, Soledad, whose hysteria is cured by becoming impregnated with Román's child, is buried alive by the other nuns.

Not only do all the discourses on women and sexuality come into play in this trilogy, but the novels give special attention to mysticism as a manifestation of hysteria, nymphomania, and homoeroticism. The stated purpose of the trilogy is to show how the Church's insistence on chastity vows goes against nature and occasions a variety of sexual aberrations.[24] Although Román is the protagonist of all three novels, and his diagnosis is satyriasis, the male form of nymphomania, the novels actually emphasize more than anything, as Zubiaurre notes in the case of *El cura*, the medicalization of female sexuality.[25] Moreover, as Isaac García Guerrero points out, *El cura* provides detailed and lengthy explanations of Gracia's illness, but does not give similar medical explanations of Román's satyriasis: "This different treatment helps, in the end, to focus on the feminine body as a potential source of problems, while the masculine one is merely out of balance without causing issues beyond that."[26] While Román's satyriasis receives more attention in *El confesionario* and *La monja*, the space dedicated to his "illness" still pales in comparison to the amount of description given to Gracia and Soledad's hysteria, Melita's protracted puberty and subsequent tuberculosis (supposedly brought on by her engagement in homoerotic activities), and Gertrudis's sudden menopause. Furthermore, in contrast to medical descriptions of satyriasis that suggest men suffering from this "disease" will fall ill from seminal depletion,[27] Román comes out at the end victorious and more powerful, whereas, in contrast, Gracia, Soledad, and Melita die, and the thirty-year old Gertrudis becomes old and infirm overnight. Indeed, Gracia and Melita serve as medical case studies who pay with the loss of their health, their moral integrity, and even their lives for their attempts to find a substitute for their sexual and reproductive urges in religious faith and practice. Román's experience, on the other hand, shows that the Church can in fact serve as a means for successfully satiating the most perverse sexual impulses and political goals.

Some critics have argued that López Bago's radical naturalist agenda was progressive.[28] Juan Ignacio Ferreras, for example, views the radical naturalists as unambiguous challengers of conservative values and social injustice,[29] and Zubiaurre has argued that López Bago's *El cura* actually celebrates sexuality. She argues that the novel denounces the absence of sex, and that the protagonist, Román, is portrayed as healthy for having violated his chastity vows.[30] While it is true that López Bago insists on the naturalness of human sexuality in his oeuvre, it should be underscored that it is only heterosexual sexuality employed in the service of reproduction that he embraces, a view that varies little, if at all, from the Church's position on these matters. Consequently, I would highlight that the problems that arise in the novel are due to the absence *of the right kind of sex*, as determined by the medical discourses of the day. Moreover, female sexuality in particular appears as pathological in all its forms. In López Bago's trilogy, as in the sexual hygiene manuals discussed in Chapter 1, women are inherently ill, their essence is defined by their reproductive organs, and they are consequently deprived of true personhood.

Thus, even though López Bago decried the lack of education and economic opportunities afforded to women, and the economic exploitation that ensued,[31] his biological determinism supported the medical theories being used to deny women more equality in Spanish society. Like the hygienists, he set out to reveal the essence of woman through a scientific observation of her physical body, thereby combining voyeurism and epistemophilia.[32] Akiko Tsuchiya argues that the aim is not only to observe but also to keep watch over and control supposedly deviant expressions of sexuality.[33] This radical naturalist technique, as Fernández notes, connects to the rising national interest in the sexual practices of a nation's citizens.[34] Furthermore, I agree with Isaac García Guerrero's assertion that López Bago explicitly attempts to take sexuality out of secrecy so that it can be "regulated" and geared toward "the multiplication of healthy life." In other words, "the aim is to subjugate readers to new old structures of patriarchal domination [. . . an] ideology [. . .] informed by the very same religious principles López Bago allegedly tried to attack."[35]

Returning to the Foucauldian technologies discussed in Chapter 1, then, this chapter explores the ways López Bago's *Cura* trilogy presents us with a clear literary example of the hysterization of the female body, the socialization of procreative behavior, and the psychiatrization of perverse pleasure specifically in relation to women, and how these novels consequently advance social efforts to keep women restricted to the domestic sphere. I also add to the extant criticism on these novels by exploring the ways López Bago's trilogy partakes in the late nineteenth-century trend of diagnosing female mysticism (past and present) as hysteria, nymphomania, and pseudo-hermaphroditism/tribadism in order to discredit alternative paths of female existence.

Hysterization of the Female Body and the Socialization of Procreative Behavior

The first novel in the series, *El cura*, immediately presents us with a case of hysteria. Fifteen-year-old Gracia is sent to live with her brother, the twenty-two-year-old priest Román. Already in chapter 2, the focus is on Gracia's struggles against the changes in her own body as she goes through puberty. In accordance with nineteenth-century doctors' assertion that hysteria occurs with great frequency during a girl's transition to womanhood,[36] puberty in and of itself brings on the "disease."[37] Gracia soon comes to exhibit all the classic symptoms: she suffers from outbursts of tears, numbness in the limbs, convulsive laughter that she cannot control, a choking sensation in the throat that is later specifically referred to as the *globus hystericus* (173), and hysterical attacks–epileptic-like seizures that prove to be sexually arousing not only to her brother Román, but also to her friend and neighbor Ana (180–81).

In order to subdue Gracia during one of her attacks, Fermín throws Román on top of his sister insisting that he press his body up against hers. This simulated sex act leaves Román depleted and almost hysterical himself (183).[38] Scenes like this one underscore doctors' and society's link between hysteria and sexual frustration, and between the hysterical attack and female orgasm, reinforcing the notion of hysteria as a disease resulting from repressed sexual desires and of the "hysterical paroxysm" as an oblique form of sexual release—a "crisis" of a "disease."[39] Moreover, don Fermín's suggestion that Román subdue the attack by getting on top of his sister echoes society's belief that what hysterical women needed was sexual intercourse. Furthermore, the hysterical attack is sexually arousing to the onlookers, both male and female, and appears to be contagious, producing symptoms of the attack in the woman who observes it: "Anita, extremadamente pálida, la miraba, y se iba contagiando de aquella convulsión, de tal manera, que imitaba las contracciones de los músculos de la cara, los movimientos de los brazos y piernas" (180–81; Anita, extremely pale, watched her, and became infected by that convulsion, in such a way, that she imitated her facial muscle contractions, and the movements of her arms and legs). This suggestion of same-sex desire is also developed earlier when the narrator compares the beginnings of the young women's intimate friendship to the beginnings of an orgy: "el principio de su amistad tan alegre como el principio de una orgía" (90; the beginning of their friendship as happy as the beginning of an orgy). And shortly thereafter they seal their friendship with "Un beso sonoro en plena boca" (98; a loud kiss right on the mouth).

When a doctor is finally brought in, he explains to Román in detail the causes, symptoms, and cures of Gracia's illness, which he immediately diagnoses as hysteria. He asserts that Gracia's age and sex make her predisposed: she is fifteen and women between twelve and twenty-five are most susceptible to the disease (185–86).[40] A female neighbor's reading of novels to Gracia is another cause,

as is Román's nightly readings of Santa Teresa de Jesús's *Vida* (187)
As a cure, the doctor recommends that Gracia get married immediately (187). In this way, the doctor makes it clear that the real cause
of Gracia's hysteria is her celibacy. He argues that marriage will
resolve the situation, whereas if she is not given a legitimate outlet for her sexual urges, her hysteria will turn into nymphomania:
"¿Sabe usted cuál es una complicación que puede sobrevenir en el
histerismo? ¿Sabe usted lo que es esa complicación y el nombre
que recibe? Esa es la temible, esa se llama ninfomanía" (189; Do you
know what complication can arise after hysteria? Do you know what
it is and what it is called? It is frightful, it is called nymphomania).
The doctor proceeds to give a detailed description of nymphomania: intense burning, itching, and pressure in the breasts and genitalia that lead women first to masturbate and then to engage in
sexual activity with whomever incites their desires, even with other
women. This is accompanied by a disturbance of their intellectual
and moral faculties that causes them to lose all sense of shame
and moral responsibility to the family. This situation deteriorates
until the nymphomaniac turns to prostitution, only to find therein
an early death. Then, in a prophetic revelation, the doctor asserts
that while Gracia only suffers from hysteria at the moment, if she
does not marry, she will sleep with the first man who enters in the
house, even if that man happens to be her own brother (194), which
is indeed how the novel ends.

While the contemporary reader would probably be inclined to
agree with Román when he tells the doctor that his description of
nymphomania shows that science has its own legends, the doctor's description corresponds to the scientific discourses of the
time in their connection between nymphomania and masturbation ("buscan en el vicio de nombre bíblico, en el onanismo, un
alivio insuficiente y pasajero" [117; they look for an insufficient and
passing form of relief in the vice of a biblical name, in onanism]),
the role of the imagination in the exacerbation of the disease ("la
imaginación se exalta" [117; the imagination becomes over-excited]),
and the dangers of inadvertent stimulation of the genitalia ("se ve
obligada á andar lentamente, separando las piernas para evitar el

más pequeño roce" [117; they are obliged to walk slowly, separating their legs in order to avoid the slightest friction]). Nevertheless, in this description of nymphomania, the stress is not on these women's supposed lesbian proclivities, but rather on the nymphomaniac's overly determined feminine characteristics, strong heterosexual inclinations, and desire for procreation. Here the hysterical woman predisposed to nymphomania has pronounced hips and a wide pelvis (supposedly signaling her childbearing abilities), large, well-formed breasts (suggesting a facility for nursing), and an exaggerated desire, at least initially, for heterosexual intercourse (191). Thus, while there is some mention of masturbation and same-sex desire, and an indirect reference to the clitoris in discussions of these women's inadvertent self-stimulation, these "abnormal" characteristics are associated with the disease's more advanced stages—stages that are explored in more detail in the last novel in the trilogy, *La monja*. What is highlighted in Gracia's case is the unmet, "natural" heterosexual urges that are the initial cause of the disease. Gracia's hysteria diagnosis is repeated in the second novel, *El confesionario*, making clear that her incestuous sexual relationship with her brother does not cure her hysteria, but only makes it worse, and leads to her early death at the end of the second novel.

It is also important to note that while the doctor does not explicitly connect Gracia's hysteria to her desire for a child, the text itself does, most notably by emphasizing the maternal attentions she gives to a mahogany statue of the baby Jesus and the scene in which her cat gives birth on her bed. Gracia treats her *Niño de la Bola* (Baby Jesus with the Globe) like a doll, pampering it and changing its clothes, which she herself sews (31–33): "en realidad, era el niño de Gracia" (33; in reality, it was Gracia's child); "había en el culto de Gracia las manifestaciones todas del sentimiento maternal" (35; in Gracia's devotion were manifestations of the maternal sentiment). When Román reproaches his sister for the maternal familiarity with which she treats the baby Jesus (34), Gracia simply responds, "como si fuera hijo mío, aunque te parezca un disparate" (35; as if he were my own child, even though it may seem ridiculous to you). Later the *Niño de la Bola* is related to her hysteria when she has her first full-blown attack. The *globo histérico* (globus hystericus) was a classical symptom of the hysterical attack. Doctors believed that it resulted from an unsatisfied uterus wandering throughout the woman's body and eventually choking her.[41] In *El cura*, the *globus hystericus* is referred to as both a *globo* (globe) and a *bola* (ball), thereby making a clear connection to the *Nino de la Bola* that serves as a substitute for the child she so desires: "El ataque de Gracia empezó por la sensación de un frío interior, propagándose á los miembros y el tronco, y seguido muy pronto de la sensación de *la bola* que dijo sentir en el vientre, una contracción dolorosa; luego *la bola* se corrió el pecho hacia la faringe, produciéndole falta de respiración, casi asfixia" (181; emphasis mine; Gracia's attack began with an interior cold sensation, spreading to her members and trunk, and followed suddenly by the sensation of the *ball* that she said she felt in her abdomen, a painful contraction, then the *ball* moved through her chest up to her larynx, producing a lack of breath, almost suffocation).

The *Niño de la Bola* also reappears the night Gracia's cat gives birth, another scene that signals Gracia's unmet desire for a child. Gracia wakes up one night to find that her cat, Morroña, has given birth to kittens on her bed, which is also her parents' marriage bed and the bed in which she will commit incest with her brother. She is clearly moved by her cat's motherly attentions to her kittens and refers to it all as a "maravilla" (216; marvelous thing). The feline not only gives a meow of satisfaction but communicates with her eyes that Gracia and Román ought to follow her example: "aprendan ustedes" (217; learn from this). This unspoken conversation between the cat and Gracia continues after Román leaves: "'¡Ah! ¿Conque eso es así?' parecía preguntar la virgen, y la contestación de la recién parida resultaba '¡Así es!'" (222; "Ah! So that's how it is?" the virgin seemed to ask, and the answer from the one who had recently given birth was "Yes, this is how it is!"). As this conversation takes place the night lamp shines its light simultaneously on the newly born kittens and on the *Niño de la Bola*: "La lamparilla de noche [. . .] alumbraba débil y temblorosa esta escena. [. . .] *El Niño de la Bola* era el que recibía la claridad más directa" (222; italics in the original; the small, weak, flickering night lamp illuminated this scene. [. . .] Baby Jesus with the Globe was the one on which the light shone most directly). Shortly thereafter Gracia places the kittens between her thighs as if she were the one to have just given birth, and sleeps with them the rest of the night in this position (225). The next hysteric appears in the third novel of the trilogy, *La monja*. By following Melita, Gertrudis's daughter, into the convent, the reader discovers the rampant nymphomania and homoerotic practices there. Yet, while Melita, naïve and fully indoctrinated in the Catholic dogma, is susceptible to the nuns' manipulation, it is another novitiate, Soledad, who understands that the nuns' supposed spiritual ecstasies are physical, and that the nuns are actually engaging in sexual activity with each other.[42] As her own sexuality awakens, Soledad, like Gracia, begins to suffer from hysterical fits.[43] However, Soledad, rejecting the nuns' homoeroticism, realizes she is naturally meant for heterosexual intercourse and motherhood: "vióse tal como era, mujer, nacida, no para inutilizar su sexo en las nocivas soledades del claustro, sino para entregarlo al hombre, para compartir los goces del amor legítimo, y sentir, en la agitación de las entrañas, cumplido el fin del amor, esperando enternecida el desgarramiento doloroso que produce el primer grito de júbilo inmenso de la maternidad" (164–65; she saw herself for what she was, a woman, born, not to render her sexual organs useless in the harmful solitary confinement of the cloister, but rather to give them to a man, to share the pleasures of legitimate love, and to feel, in the agitation of her womb, the objective of love achieved, anticipating with emotion, the painful separation that produces the first cry of the immense jubilation of motherhood).

Soledad, therefore, finds an antidote to her disease by sleeping with a man, in this case the priest Román, and getting pregnant. Clearly anticipating Freud's notion of the child as a substitute phallus for women, Soledad's pregnancy not only cures her hysteria, but gives her a feeling of superiority over the other nuns, whom she now views as "seres incompletos" (166; incomplete beings). This understanding of female sexual pleasure as conception and motherhood is also tied to the socialization of procreation.

As we saw in Chapter 1, the socialization of procreative behavior, which sought to direct the individual's sexual practices toward increasing the size and health of the nation's population, had a direct effect on women as it was actively involved in the redefinition of female sexual pleasure. Through the medical legitimization of sexual activities that led to reproduction, and the pathologization of those that did not, heterosexual intercourse became the only legitimate sexual activity. The clitoris and its role in female orgasm were pathologized by being linked to masturbation, tribadism, pseudohermaphroditism, and nymphomania. In contrast, healthy female pleasure was now tied to male orgasm and its role in conception. Not only did doctors argue that women needed to have their uterus sprayed with the male semen in order to calm down the excitation of their reproductive organs, but they insisted that conception was the ultimate form of sexual pleasure for women. We see this in the characters of Gracia and Soledad. Gracia dies an early death in *El confesionario* because, after consummating her incestuous relationship with her brother, Román distances himself from her. Not only is this sexual act portrayed as an unhealthy aberration, but it does not lead to conception, leaving Gracia alone and childless. These circumstances exacerbate her hysteria and lead to her early death.

In contrast, Soledad finds complete satisfaction in having sexual intercourse with a man and becoming pregnant and is consequently cured of her hysteria. Tsuchiya perceptively notes that the narration of chapter 11 is not only focalized through Soledad, merging her views with those of the narrator, but also that in the next chapter the narrator subsequently validates Soledad's choices by contrasting her with Melita, who has fallen ill from tuberculosis. Tsuchiya argues that Soledad "reconoce que el acto sexual con Román no le ha dado ningún placer, sino que fue hecho por compulsion" (recognizes that the sexual act with Román has not given her any pleasure, but was committed out of compulsion).[44] However, the objective of the redefinition of the female sexual response, and later Freud's theory of female sexuality, was precisely to transfer female sexual pleasure away from sexual acts involving the clitoris and orgasm toward coitus, conception, and motherhood.[45] In fact, in the passage from *La monja* cited above, childbirth itself is described as "el primer grito de júbilo inmenso de la maternidad" (the first cry of the immense jubilation of motherhood)—in other words, as orgasmic. In short, it is not that Soledad does not experience pleasure, it is that she experiences the "right kind" of pleasure, according to the new sexual hygiene regimes.

In contrast to Soledad, Melita, rather than fulfilling her "natural" heterosexual urges, falls prey to the nuns' same-sex practices. However, unlike Gracia in *El cura*, rather than succumbing to hysteria, her immersion in female homoeroticism leads her to die of tuberculosis. According to doctors like V. Suárez Casañ: "Las lesbias acaban casi siempre por morir devoradas por terrible tísis" (Lesbians almost always die devoured by terrible tuberculosis).[46] It is suggested that Melita's taking of the habit during puberty slows her physical development and makes her predisposed to the illness. Our attention is drawn to both the fact that Melita's transition through puberty was arrested and that the cause of the disease "en los púberes," is "la permanencia en habitaciones oscuras y mal ventiladas, los excesos del onanismo y del coito [. . .] siempre que el gasto orgánico es mayor que el ingreso, puede decirse que está creada la condición generatriz de la tuberculosis" (221; in adolescents [is] staying in rooms that are dark and poorly ventilated, the excesses of onanism and coitus [. . .] whenever the organic expense is greater than the deposit, one can say that the condition that generates tuberculosis is created).[47] The dark and poorly ventilated rooms are clearly a reference to what is considered to be the unhygienic conditions of the convent, and the reference to onanism to the nonprocreative homoerotic activities in which the nuns engage Melita. Moreover, references to bodily savings ("ingresos") and expenses ("gastos") were commonplace in nineteenth-century discussions on sexual activity that warned against "overspending."[48]

It is also worth noting that the description of Melita's tuberculosis, the sole subject of the penultimate chapter of the novel, includes not only extensive citations from an unnamed medical text on the subject, but also lengthy descriptions of the most gruesome aspects of the disease. The sordid description of Melita's demise serves to punish the recalcitrant female body and exact poetic justice. In his book *Body Works: Objects of Desire in Modern Narrative*, Peter Brooks analyzes the way the body is manifested in modern narrative where readers, narrators, and characters alike gaze at and unveil the body, usually the female body, in order to make it signify and thereby satiate both scopophilic and epistemophilic desires: "What presides at the inscription and imprinting of bodies is, in the broadest sense, a set of desires: a desire that body not be lost to meaning—that it be brought into the realm of the semiotic and the significant—and, underneath this, a desire for the body itself, an erotic longing to have or to be the body."[49] We also see this phenomenon with Gracia and Gertrudis. Gracia's healthy, youthful, and physically attractive body is the object of erotic desire of the entire first novel, *El cura*, a desire fulfilled at novel's end by the consummation of the siblings' relationship. In the second novel, *El confesionario*, however, Gracia's now sickly body is a tool for giving meaning to the novel's events. Indeed the novel closes precisely with Gracia's death.[50] This disturbing death scene not only highlights Román's moral depravity, but it tells us how to read all that has happened in the novels so far: the infertile, incestuous relationship between the siblings is a crime against nature to be punished by death.

Similarly, Gertrudis's beautiful, and still youthful, body is the object of desire of the second novel, *El confesionario*.[51] Román tries to resist his attraction to Gertrudis, as he did with Gracia in the first novel. But in both cases his "natural" desires win out by novel's end. In the case of Gertrudis, he rapes her (after she taunts him). The rape is recounted in the last chapter, right before the description of Gracia's death. While in *El confesionario* the desire for Gertrudis's body is satiated through her rape, in *La monja*, this once desirable female body, now is punished in a sudden passage through menopause that corresponds with the character's anagnorisis in which she comes to understand the true nature of her relationship with Román and her role in her only child's imminent death.[52] Menopause is described as "aquel período que los antiguos médicos consideraban como el de mayor peligro para la mujer" (116;

that period that ancient doctors considered to be the most dangerous for a woman). We are privy to a several-paragraph description
of symptoms and the reasons why the dangers of menopause will
be exacerbated by Gertrudis's life choices, among them, only having had one child: "hembra, se vió fecundada una vez tan solo, y
luego tuvo que condenarse á las inacciones de la esterilidad" (118;
a woman, she only saw herself fertilized once, and then she had to
condemn herself to the inactivity of sterility), and to the fact that
the aging of Gertrudis's thirty-year old body happens overnight.[53]
Once again, after the scopophilic desires the female body incites
are satiated by an aberrant sexual act (with Gracia, incest, with
Gertrudis, rape), that same body is then inscribed with meaning
by being punished for challenging the dictates of the socialization
of procreative behavior (for Gracia and Melita death, for Gertrudis
age and infirmity).

Psychiatrization of Perverse Pleasure: Onanism, Tribadism, and Nymphomania

As we saw in Chapter 1 the psychiatrization of perverse pleasure
enforced the state's pro-natal agenda by labeling all sexual behaviors that did not lead to reproduction as perverted. Usurping the
role of the Church, doctors simply redefined sexual acts that the
Church had labeled "sinful" as "illnesses" and "perversions." The
primary female perversions were onanism, tribadism, and nymphomania, all three of which were related.[54] Both masturbation
and tribadism were nonprocreative and put into question women's
dependence on men. Similarly, nymphomania was seen as a threat
to male dominance. Suárez Casañ, for example, writes that since "el
hombre pierde antes las fuerzas y la potencia que la mujer, las nin-
fomaniacas buscan en su sexo, como más resistente, la continua-
ción de unos placeres que siempre quisieran estar reanundando"
(since men lose their strength and prowess before women, nymphomaniacs look for the continuation of pleasure that they always want
to resume in their own sex, as the more resistant [sex]).[55] Indeed,
perhaps the lengthiest account of the time on same-sex desire in

women is Suárez Casañ's *El amor lesbio* (Lesbian love).[56] Echoing ideas expressed in other texts of the period, Suárez Casañ asserts that the principal cause of "el amor lesbio" is "el desarrollo excesivo del clítoris, que en algunas toma todas las proporciones de un verdadero pene" (lesbian love [is] the excessive development of the clitoris, which in some women takes on the size of an actual penis).[57] Like other doctors of his day, he also notes that the size of a woman's clitoris can be determined by nature or because the woman herself engages in masturbation or homoerotic activities, thereby explicitly tying all three together.[58] Asserting that many *lesbias* (lesbians) are also nymphomaniacs, and vice versa, he claims that when these two perversions are combined, the affected woman becomes totally depraved and even commits acts of violence. He writes that nymphomaniacal lesbians are "quizás las más peligrosas por su atrevimiento y desmoralización que lo avasalla todo, y en todas partes hace víctimas. Muchas veces se la ha visto emplear la violencia, ni más ni menos que un hombre desalmado" (perhaps the most dangerous for their daring and lack of morals, which dominates everything, and everywhere takes victims. Many times, such women use violence, neither greater nor less than that of the most heartless man).[59] These are precisely the types of women we encounter in *La monja*, where "el convento toledano en que ingresa Melita es un gineceo donde se practica el lesbianismo y se castiga con la muerte a las desertoras" (the convent in Toledo that Melita enters is a gyneceum where they practice lesbianism and punish deserters with death).[60]

While Soledad represents a clear case of hysteria, a hysteria cured by the fulfillment of "natural" heterosexual urges, the novel portrays the other nuns, who did not choose the same path as Soledad, as tribades and nymphomaniacs, that is as hysterics whose disease has progressed to the next, more dangerous, stage.[61] The nuns' same-sex activities are initially revealed, unsurprisingly, through mystical double entendres. Sor María Josefa explains to Melita that the third and final stage of the mystical path, *la vía unitiva* (union), usually takes fifteen days to reach, but that she can get her there faster another way (104–5). She informs Melita that all the nuns regularly enjoy states of ecstasy,[62] and subsequently forces herself on Melita in the name of obedience:

> —*Se trata, sí, de una . . ., ¿cómo le llamaremos? . . . Como tú quieras . . . Una operación. Eso es, una operación que te hará sentir los inefables goces del éxtasis.*
>
> Y fuera de sí ya, con las mejillas más arrebatadas y los ojos llenos de fulgores:
>
> —*Ya verás.*
>
> La pluma se resiste á describir aquella repugnancia. Melita se sintió empujada dulcemente, tendida en el camastro; y la monja, sentada en el borde, inclinándose sobre ella, besábala en la boca, y sus manos se perdían entre las ropas de la inocente novicia, que, asombrada al principio, iba á dar un grito.
>
> —*¡La obediencia!*—la dijo sor María Josefa. –*La obediencia, no la olvides. Me debes la obediencia.*
>
> La infamia aquella se consumó. Adquirió el organismo de la virgen el primer vicio, vicio contra naturaleza. La credulidad propia de su absoluta ignorancia, confundió la sensación corporal con una explosión de sentimiento. El éxtasis. (108)

> —It is about, yes, a . . . how should we call it? . . . Whatever you want . . . An operation. That's it, an operation that will make you feel the ineffable pleasures of ecstasy.
>
> *And beside herself already, with her cheeks more flushed and her eyes beaming:*
>
> —You will see!
>
> *My pen refuses to describe that repugnant act. Melita felt herself softly pushed, stretched out in the rickety bed, and the nun, seated on the edge, leaning over her kissed her on the mouth and her hands got lost amongst the clothing of the innocent novitiate, who, shocked at the beginning, was about to scream.*
>
> —Obedience—María Josefa told her—obedience, don't forget it. You owe me obedience.
>
> *The above disgrace was carried out. The virgin's organism acquired its first vice, vice against nature. The credulity characteristic of her*

complete innocence confused the bodily sensation with an explosion of feeling. Ecstasy.

Not only do the nuns engage in same-sex practices, but masturbation is alluded to when the abbess suggests that María Josefa teach Melita how to reach ecstasy by herself (153). And later, when the nuns arrange a group sexual encounter with Román, we discover that they are also well versed in birth control practices (198), also considered a form of onanism in its original sense. All sexual practices that did not lead to reproduction were said to occasion hysteria and nymphomania in women. And just as hygienists cautioned that the homoerotic practices of nymphomaniacs could become so deep rooted that they would lose interest in men altogether, the mother superior expresses this very concern when she fears that the nuns may not be interested in a man when they discuss their plans for meeting Román's request for a group sexual encounter (158).

The sexual orgies between the nuns and Román also resemble the "infernales orgías" (infernal orgies) described in *El amor lesbio*. V. Suárez Casañ describes one such orgy as an "aquelarre" (witches' Sabbath) and a "misa negra" (black mass), citing a 1610 Inquisition case where twenty-nine witches and sorcerers, but mostly female witches, fornicated with the devil and each other, including men with men and women with women.[63] The orgies between Román and the nuns, which are not explicitly depicted but only alluded to, mirror this event. Román, as priest and confessor, is the leader and initiator of the group sex, and thus resembles "Satanás" (Satan) or the "macho cabrío" (he-goat/devil) who was the initiator of the Sabbath Suárez Casañ describes. The implicit comparison of Román with the devil is reinforced by the frequent references to him as a faun and a satyr (because of his satyriasis), and satyrs' connection to goats and the devil.[64] For example, Gertrudis describes her sexual encounters with Román through therianthropic tropes: "ella sentía siempre el contacto duro del *fauno*, los brazos que la estrechaban, no como caricia, sino como agresión; los dos *zarpazos de fiera* que desgarraban su traje, desataban su cabellos, la sujetaban, la inmovilizaban en poder, no de un hombre, sino de un loco furioso" (84, italics mine; she always felt the hard contact of the *faun*, the arms that held her, not as an embrace, but as aggression; two *clawings of a wild beast* that tore her dress, undid her hair, subdued her, immobilized her in power, not of a man, but of a violent lunatic).[65]

Similarly, the nuns' comparison to witches is reinforced by their sadistic behavior. The nuns' exhibition of sadism, a characteristic that psychology has historically tended to associate with men and masculinity, also signals their sexual deviance as they assume the characteristics more often attributed to the opposite sex. Since Soledad apparently obtained what all the other nuns "really" wanted, they start targeting her. They make mean, suggestive comments and force her to kiss their feet. The mother superior is also physically abusive, requiring Soledad to fast for a week and to kneel next to a wall for two hours, knowing that this posture is particularly difficult since she is pregnant (206). Soledad suspects the nuns are trying to cause her to miscarry. The nuns' envy and depravity ultimately lead them to brutally murder Soledad and the child she is carrying by burying them alive, a heinous act that closes the last novel in the trilogy and reinforces the comparison of the nuns to evil witches who participate in a black mass and conduct a human sacrifice.[66] Jules Michelet's *La sorcière* (published in English in 1863 as *La sorcière: The Witch of the Middle Ages*), originally published in 1862 and republished in several subsequent editions, outlines the rituals of the black mass in which a woman's body was both altar and host, and was offered up as sacrifice along with "the newest born child in the district."[67] The 1911 edition of the French version of the work included illustrations by Martin Van Maële that show group sex and same-sex desire (Figure 2) as well as a woman's body as an altar and a child sacrificed as host (Figures 3 and 4). In Figure 3, the devil is also present. Thus, the nuns' delight in the brutal murder of Soledad and the child she conceived with Román (the symbolic representation of the devil) parallels the rituals of witches' Sabbaths as depicted in literary and nonliterary works of the time where the sacrifice of a woman and a child was central.[68] López Bago was most certainly aware of the work of Jules Michelet. Indeed, the narrator of *El confesionario* specifically mentions Michelet's *La sorcière* (212) and the author cites Michelet again in the appendix

FIGURE 2. Illustration by Martin van Maële of a witches' Sabbath from the 1911 edition of *La Sorcière*, by Jules Michelet. Courtesy of Wikimedia Commons.

FIGURE 3. Illustration by Martin van Maële of a witches' Sabbath from the 1911 edition of *La Sorcière*, by Jules Michelet. Courtesy of Wikimedia Commons.

FIGURE 4. Illustration by Martin van Maële of a witches' Sabbath from the 1911 edition of *La Sorcière*, by Jules Michelet. Courtesy of Wikimedia Commons.

to *La monja* (274). López Bago and doctors such as Suárez Casañ, likely influenced by such texts, belie their own claims to scientific objectivity and come full circle by using the very same imagery as the Early Modern Inquisition to connect sexual "aberrations" to demonic activities.

Of course, some of these "perversions" first appear in the earlier novels. In *El cura*, Gracia's long, unsupervised, and frequent baths incite homoerotic and incestuous desires and lead to onanism. According to Peter Ward, while nineteenth-century hygienists on both sides of the Atlantic encouraged cleanliness, they simultaneously feared bathing because of "the stimulus to sexual desire offered by nudity, warm water, and privacy."[69] This was then connected to fears about masturbation and incest, the latter supposedly caused by nudity in the home.[70] The doctor in *El cura* articulates similar fears when he warns Román that Gracia's bathing is producing "una excitación demasiado considerable de los sentidos" (188; too much excitement of the senses). We witness this phenomenon firsthand when the narrator informs us that during one of her lengthy baths Gracia finds herself aroused by the observation of her own naked body "mirando su desnudez como en un éxtasis" (155; observing her nudity in a state of ecstasy). There is a clear homoerotic element to her being sexually aroused by her own naked body, a homoeroticism reinforced by earlier suggestions of sexual desire between Anita and Gracia. Moreover, in a different scene, when Gracia is unable to bathe, presumably because of her menstrual cycle, the lack of access to the sexual release bathing provides leads her to rub herself up against her bed to point of orgasm, a scene oddly focalized through her cat Morriña (116–17).[71] Portrayals of masturbation and homoeroticism, in addition to incest, occur from the very first novel in the trilogy, and are tied, at least in part, to the sensuousness of bathing.

Mysticism as Sexual Deviance

El cura, *El confesionario*, and *La monja* not only give fictional representation to ideas about women and sexual pathology found in nineteenth-century hygiene manuals, but they also show the way mystical discourse was coopted to signify the sexual rather than the spiritual. In fact, one of the crucial themes that arises from the very first novel in the trilogy is the sublimation of sexual desires and urges through religious practices and discourses. Whenever the word "mystical" is used, it is almost always a synonym for "sexual." For example, Gracia's presence produces in Román "infables gozos místicos" (*El cura*, 54; ineffable mystical pleasures) which the reader knows to be truly sexual in nature. And Santa Teresa herself is called out in a comparison with Román's confessant Gertrudis for wrongly labeling her sexual desires as religious ones: Román wants Gertrudis to give in to "un éxtasis tal, que, así como el de Teresa de Jesús era sensualismo y anhelo de una posesión sexual, más que del Hijo de Dios" (*El confesonario*, 159–60; such ecstasy, which was sensualism and longing for sexual possession more than for God's Son, like Santa Teresa's ecstasy). Moreover, when Román becomes a priest, he thinks of the Song of Songs (or Song of Solomon), while the narrator reminds us that his mysticism is a cover for his repressed sexuality (*El cura*, 10). The Song of Songs, a collection of love poems found in the Old Testament, was interpreted allegorically in Christian traditions as describing the love between Jesus and the Church and between Jesus and the human soul. However, the verses were considered so open to alternative interpretations that Fray Luis de León's translation of the Song of Songs into the vernacular was one of the main reasons he was charged and imprisoned by the Inquisition for heresy.[72] *El cura* comes full circle with this Biblical allusion when, toward the end, there is a transcription of a passage of the Song of Songs right before Román commits incest with his sister. This happens right after Román officiates a real wedding and attends the wedding reception, a clear carnivalization of the supposed spiritual meaning of the Biblical passage, an event that leads Román to a clearer understanding of the "natural" meaning of marriage.

Mystical literature in all its forms is always overtly sexualized. Two of the books Román gives Melita in order to convince her to become a nun are *La vida de Santa Teresa* (*La monja*, 8) and *Tratado del amor de Dios* (19; Treatise on the love of God). And once in the convent, the nuns use mystical texts to seduce Melita; two texts mentioned by name are *Ejercicios de Santa Gertrudis* (Exercises of Saint Gertrudis) and *Palacio del amor divino* (Palace of divine love).[73] The mother superior, Sor María Egipcíaca, whose name evokes the saint who began her life as a dissolute prostitute, puts the book between her thighs and asks Melita to read from there. As Melita reads sensual passages full of metaphors of sexual love, Sor María Egipcíaca strokes her hair and face (60). The sexual feelings this arouses in Melita are confused with spiritual love: "¡Oh, mi buena madre! ¡Mi buena madre! ¿Sería aquello la iniciación en el Amor divino?" (62; Oh, my good mother! My good mother! Could this be the initiation of Divine Love?).

The nuptial and family metaphors associated with mysticism are further exploited in the eroticization of the religious figures of Jesus and Mary. After experiencing a hysterical episode, Gracia enters her brother's study when he is not home, to gaze upon the figure of Jesus, "en aquel gran cuerpo de varón desnudo, cuyos brazos no le parecían abiertos para el martirio, sino para cogerla en ellos y levantarla hasta la cruz, estrechándola en una sobrehumana caricia. Sentíase removida en todo su ser, dolorida dulcemente: algo se quería desprender de ella, salir de su seno al encuentro de cosas desconocidas, de placeres ignorados" (*El cura*, 26; in that great body of a naked man, whose arms did not appear to be outstretched for martyrdom, but rather to embrace her in them and lift her up to the cross, to hold her in a superhuman caress. She felt moved in her entire being, sweetly in pain: something wanted to detach from her, leave her breast to encounter unknown things, unknown pleasures). Here Jesus is not God, but a strong, naked man who wants to hold Gracia in a firm embrace. This sexualization of Jesus foreshadows the eroticization of her brother as a priest and is reminiscent of Marie's claims that Santa Teresa herself had fantasies about having a physical relationship with Jesus.[74] Román is similarly aroused by images of the Virgin Mary, who represents, in many ways, his young virgin sister: "de pronto creyó ver, como á la claridad de luna gran luz, que estaba en pecado mortal, que la imagen de la Virgen le excitaba los sentidos tanto como la vista de Gracia." (220; suddenly, he believed to have seen a huge light with the clarity of the moon, that showed that he was in mortal sin, that the image of the Virgin excited his senses as much as the sight of Gracia). And later, in the last novel, *La monja*, a pregnant Soledad finds in the Virgin Mary an appropriate model of emulation, a model of heterosexual love and maternity (202–3). Moreover, as we saw above, Gracia's reproductive urges find an object of projection in representations of the baby Jesus (*El cura*, 33–34). Thus, the very religious figures who are supposed to represent purity and chastity become admirable embodiments of "healthy" heterosexual love: Jesus stands in for the husband and lover, Mary as the wife and mother, and baby Jesus as the mother's longed-for child, the supposed ultimate desire of women's sexual urges.

One of the most notable ways the novel blurs mystical and sexual discourses, feelings, and actions, however, is through the constant references to Santa Teresa de Jesús, whose incorporation in the text makes sense considering the amount of debate taking place at the time regarding the true nature of her mystical experiences.[75] Echoing medical texts of the time, the novels attempt to portray Teresa as a hysteric. For example, Gracia recognizes the similarities between her hysteria and that of Santa Teresa de Jesús:

> Gracia estudiaba aquel extraño mal que hemos acusado en su naturaleza, aquellos vértigos, aquellos bostezos; la risa convulsiva y el llanto. Recordaba haber oído que tal era el estado en que se encontró otra mujer, que sin embargo, fué fundadora de conventos y canonizada por la Iglesia. Ella lo contaba, Román lo leyó. "La vida de Santa Teresa escrita por ella misma." Pero su mal tenía como *base la excitación morbosa de los nervios motores*. El colector, que había estudiado medicina, lo dijo en estos términos, explicando lo que padecía la otra santa. Luego lo explicó más claramente. Era histerismo. (emphasis in the original; *El cura*, 171–72).

> *Gracia studied that strange illness that we have shown in her nature,*
> *those dizzy spells, those yawns; the convulsive laughter and the crying.*
> *She remembered having heard that such was the state in which another*

woman found herself, who, however, was the founder of convents and who was canonized by the Church. She would tell her story. Román read it. "The Life of Santa Teresa written by herself." But her illness had its roots in the morbid excitation of the motor nerves. The collector, who had studied medicine, had said it in these terms, explaining what the other saint suffered from. Then he explained it more clearly. It was hysteria.

Beginning with *El cura*, we find Román reading Gracia excerpts from Santa Teresa's *Vida* every evening after dinner. The first night that he does so he has trouble sleeping, and when he finally does sleep, he has a dream about the lascivious women who populate the old testament. As Denise DuPont has perceptively noted, this "marks the beginning of the overt sexualization of the relationship between Gracia and Román, because after reading Teresa's story, Román dreams that his sister and the cat are one, and that this collective female figure melds with all the female Biblical characters. He awakens the next morning to discover that his body has betrayed him [. . .] and that Gracia's cat has escaped to the roof to mate."[76] Additionally, when their neighbor, the priest Fermín, finds out that Román reads to Gracia from Santa Teresa's *Vida* he insists on the pernicious effects it will have on her, particularly in light of her forced chastity (187). In his diatribe against religious celibacy, Don Fermín is unambiguous in his condemnation of Santa Teresa and other canonized mystics as hysterics: "¡Santa Teresa de Jesús, ¡otra que tal! Una histérica. Aquella mujer de que habla San Bernardo, una eretómana que por espacio de algunos años gozaba con el diablo. ¡Locos! ¡Una cuerda de locos de atar! Lea usted con detenimiento el *Año Cristiano*. La Iglesia tiene allí canonizados á todos esos enfermos" (106–7; Santa Teresa de Jesús, another one! A hysteric. That woman Saint Bernard talks about, a sex-obsessed woman who for a period of few years enjoyed herself with the devil. Crazies! A group of lunatics who should be locked up. Read carefully the *Christian Year*. The Church has all those sick people canonized there). He not only repeats Teresa's hysteria diagnosis, but he refers to claims that she had intercourse with the devil and implies

her nymphomania when he references the "ninfomanía en los con-
ventos" (106; nymphomania in the convents).

The idea that Santa Teresa's ecstasies were merely physical
orgasms produced through sexual fantasies and practices is given
clearest expression in *La monja*. As we saw in the passages cited
earlier, talk of mystical ecstasy is merely code for sexual practices
that lead the nuns to climax. Indeed, later in the novel, when the
nuns debate the wisdom of including Román in their forbidden
encounters in order to pacify him, Sor María Egipcíaca insists on
speaking plainly: "No le llames éxtasis, no le llames amor divino.
Deja eso para engatusar á tus novias. Aquí no hay que engañar
á nadie. Al éxtasis y á la unión llámales lo que son ambas cosas.
Vicios contra la naturaleza. Aberración del instinto. Extravíos del
organismo" (158; Don't call it ecstasy, don't call it divine love. Leave
that for sweet-talking your girlfriends. Here there is no need to
deceive anyone. Call ecstasy and union what both are. Vices against
nature. Aberrations of the instinct. The erring of the organism).
And Román himself talks of Teresa's description of mystical ecstasy
both to seduce María de Soledad and to let her know that he is
aware of their nightly sexual encounters. He concludes by saying,
"¡qué mayor dicha para mi sino la de ser confesor de un convento en
que no hay una, sino tantas Santa Teresas de Jesús!" (142; no greater
fortune for me than to be the confessor of a convent in which there
is not one, but several Santa Teresas de Jesús!).

As we saw in Chapter 2, many doctors censured the Catholic
Church for both persecuting some hysterical women as witches
and for canonizing others as saints rather than viewing them all as
ill, as the contemporary medical institution had done. Such doctors consistently portrayed themselves as more compassionate
than the Church in their treatment of these mentally ill women.
However, doctors' benevolence is overstated considering their
attempts to use their medical knowledge to sexualize and pathologize all women, mystics or nonmystics. What I would propose
here, therefore, is that this criticism be extended to López Bago
himself, because he, like the doctors he so admired, used his novels
not only to condemn all forms of religious expression in women as

pathology, but to advocate for an antifeminist agenda that affirmed that a woman's anatomy determined her destiny. And while López Bago extols what he refers to as a natural, heterosexual sexuality geared toward procreation, he condemns all other forms of sexual expression. Thus, in the end, his agenda differed little from that of the Catholic Church and even makes use of diabolical imagery from the Early Modern Church to bring his point home.

Conclusion

In "Teresa de Jesús and the Creation of Gender Communities in Eduardo López Bago's *El cura* Trilogy," DuPont argues that López Bago's obsession with Santa Teresa stems, in part, from gender anxieties in late nineteenth-century Spain as well as naturalist writers' condemnation of the effeminacy of nonnaturalist fiction.[77] Teresa de Jesús, as a romantic, female writer, and as a woman who eschewed the domestic roles of wife and mother in order to found convents, continued to serve as a model of social resistance and of alternative roles for women.[78] According to DuPont, "López Bago's readers might easily look past the profanation of Teresa to realize that the female characters of this trilogy follow the Teresian model in their strategies of resistance."[79] She therefore concludes that "In *El cura* [. . .] Teresa's words remain invulnerable and continue to inspire imitators."[80] Also reading against the narrator's overt positioning of the implied reader, Akiko Tsuchiya, in "Entre la ciencia y la pornografía: Masculinidades abyectas y perversions femeninas en la serie *El cura* (1885) de Eduardo López Bago," wonders whether the male narrator of the novel has truly been able to neutralize the resistance represented by the spaces of feminine desire.[81] To be sure, despite the overdetermined message of López Bago's trilogy and the popularity of his works, Santa Teresa continued to serve as a model of resistance. Moreover, as one of only a handful of texts to represent female same-sex desire, the *Cura* trilogy was groundbreaking in bringing this alternative sexual reality to a wide reading public, who may or may not have agreed with López Bago's assessment of the practice. In fact, Suárez Casañ, in his hyperbolic medical indictment of lesbianism in *El amor lesbio*, simultaneously claims that this vice threatens to destroy society and bemoans the fact that, in contrast to male homosexuality, the general public did not see lesbianism as much of threat.[82] In the next chapters, I continue to engage the question of resistance by exploring the similarities and differences between the *Cura* trilogy and Leopoldo Alas's *La Regenta* (Chapter 4) and the way Emilia Pardo Bazán contested the ideas of both male authors (Chapter 5).

4 *La Regenta* and the *Cura* Trilogy

Novels in Dialog

NOËL VALIS, NICHOLAS WOLTERS, and Maite Zubiaurre have provided the most in-depth analysis of the dialog between the first novel in Eduardo López Bago's *Cura* trilogy (1885–86) and Leopoldo Alas's *La Regenta* (1884–85).[1] Nevertheless, a thorough comparison of *La Regenta* to the entire *Cura* trilogy has not yet been undertaken, even though the parallels continue throughout all three novels. Despite clear differences in style and literary philosophy, both *La Regenta* and the *Cura* trilogy center around a young, handsome priest with a voracious sexual appetite who seeks to climb the ecclesiastical ladder.[2] Fermín de Pas in *La Regenta* aspires to become bishop and possibly pope, and Román de Acebedo in the *Cura* trilogy to nothing less than pope, and both see their female penitents as tools to achieving these goals. In both cases the priests' sexual desires and conventionally masculine ambitions are given phallic representation in the Church tower.[3] For Fermín it is the money of wealthy parishioners like the Carraspique and Páez families that he hopes will advance his career and Ana's public displays of submission that will win his dominance over the town Don Juan and solidify his reputation as the most powerful man in Vetusta. For Román it is Gertrudis's money that serves as the means of winning him favors with the Vatican, and Gertrudis's submission the means of fulfilling his sadistic desires for domination. Both Fermín and Román sexually desire their confessants (Ana and Gertrudis respectively), seduce them through talk of mysticism and Santa Teresa, and obliquely satisfy their sexual desires through a sadomasochistic relationship where the confessant makes sacrifices on her confessor's behalf; Ana walks barefoot in the Holy Week procession in *La Regenta*; and Gertrudis fulfills her supposedly wifely and religious duty of sleeping with her syphilitic husband in *El confesionario*.[4]

For both priests, the Church-imposed chastity vows bring on destructive sexual urges that lead them to wreak havoc on the lives of others. Each finds clandestine outlets for his exaggerated sexual desires. Fermín sleeps with available women who cross his path and with his maids; each maid sleeps in the room adjacent to his own until she is married off and replaced by another.[5] Román, on the other hand, satiates his desires with his sister (who also lives with him and sleeps in the room next door), prostitutes, his confessant Gertrudis (by the end of the second novel and during the third), and later with a group of cloistered nuns. Both priests' depravity leads to the deaths of their confessants' husbands—Víctor is killed in a duel encouraged by Fermín, and the Marquis of Florida dies as a result of sleeping with his wife, which Román ordered Gertrudis to do despite his doctor's recommendation to the contrary. Furthermore, Fermín and Román both exploit the daughters of wealthy parishioners by encouraging them to become nuns: Fermín with the daughters of the Carraspique and Páez families, and Román with Melita, Gertrudis's only daughter. In each work one of the young nuns contracts tuberculosis and dies: in *La Regenta*, Rosa Carraspique, and in the *Cura* trilogy, Melita.

A vying for power between doctor and priest takes place in both *La Regenta* and the *Cura* trilogy. In *El cura* and *El confesionario*, the doctor accurately diagnoses Gracia's hysteria and makes recommendations for a cure that Román chooses to ignore. His decision results in Gracia's death. Román also defies the doctor's orders when he tells Gertrudis to sleep with her husband, an act that leads to another death. Similarly, in *La Regenta* Fermín is at odds with both of Ana's doctors. He dislikes Ana's first doctor, Robustiano

Somoza, a "volteriano" (a follower of Voltaire[6]) who implicates de Pas in Rosa Carraspique's death by insisting that the unhygienic conditions of the convent are the cause of the tuberculosis that will kill her if she does not leave.[7] Ana's second doctor, Benítez, takes over for Robustiano after the holy week procession.[8] He substitutes de Pas in his role as Ana's confessor and instructs her to read medical works that will help her better understand her hysteria, such as works by the English psychiatrist Henry Maudsley, and those by Jules B. Luys, the French physician connected to Salpêtrière hospital.[9] Moreover, Fermín hears Benítez tell Víctor that what Ana needs to cure her disease is "un estímulo fuerte" (2:404–5; a strong stimulus), words that echo again and again in de Pas's mind. Fermín rightly feels threatened by the doctor's words, as shortly thereafter Ana gives in to her desires for Don Álvaro, Fermín's rival. In both works, therefore, doctors, while not always victorious or all knowing, are shown to be both more accurate and honest in their assessment of the situation, whereas the priests' words and actions are always manipulative and destructive.[10]

Ana Ozores's character in *La Regenta* is a combination of Gracia, Soledad, and Gertrudis from the *Cura* trilogy. Ana is closer to Gracia in her early manifestations of hysteria,[11] closer to Soledad in her biologically determined surrender to her seducer, and closer to Gertrudis in her position as a strikingly beautiful, yet unsatisfied, married woman who seeks out an intimate relationship with her confessor. While Gertrudis's husband is sick from syphilis, Ana's husband is substantially older and seemingly incapable of a physical relationship with her. Both women turn to a priest and to the practice of confession to substitute for the lack of physical and emotional intimacy in their marriages. The confessions take place frequently and in private homes: Gertrudis and Román meet at Gertrudis's house, Ana and Fermín at both Doña Petronila's house and Ana's house. Both women claim to want to abandon the vanities of this world and experience mystical rapture and both try to emulate Santa Teresa. Although seemingly ignorant of the sexual nature of their religious pursuits initially, both eventually come to see the true nature of their relationship with their confessor.

Thus, Noël Valis's idea of *El cura* being a "pastiche homage" to *La Regenta* can be fruitfully applied to the entire *Cura* trilogy.[12] Not only do the similarities continue throughout the second and the third novels, as we have just seen, but both works were published over a two-year period, and the novels of the *Cura* trilogy together are closer in length to the *La Regenta*.[13] Moreover, the fact that the former was written on the heels of the latter—*La Regenta* was published between 1884 and 1885 and the *Cura* trilogy between 1885 and 1886—suggests that López Bago sought to present a cruder representation, a sexually explicit and scientifically deterministic imitation of Alas's novel. In this chapter, therefore, I explore the ways all three novels of the *Cura* trilogy dialog with *La Regenta* in their engagement with contemporary, cultural discourses on women, mysticism, and hysteria, highlighting both similarities and differences. I read all the novels specifically in relation to medical and social discourses on women, sexuality, and religion, thereby developing the suggestions of Noël Valis, Lou Charnon-Deutsch, and Maite Zubiaurre to build a more expansive dialog between *La Regenta* and the discourses of its immediate historical context.[14]

Ana, Gracia, and Soledad's Hysteria Compared and Its Connection to the Socialization of Procreative Behavior

The question of Ana Ozores's hysteria has already received substantial critical attention, with scholars focusing largely on the novel's dialog with French discourses (Saillard), Freud and/or Breuer (Aldaraca, Resina, Tomsich), or the much more contemporary psychoanalytical theories of Jacques Lacan and Luce Irigaray (Labanyi).[15] Building on Noël Valis and Maite Zubiaurre's pivotal work,[16] my focus here is on Alas's representation of hysteria and the socialization of procreative behavior in relation to contemporary Spanish discourses. Whereas the term *hysteria* or a variant is used twenty-two times in the *Cura* trilogy,[17] it appears only twice in *La Regenta* (2:98; 2:34). Rather, the narrator of *La Regenta* is able to portray Ana as a hysteric by playing off the medical clichés of the time. This avoidance of the term *hysteria* is in keeping with Alas's stated narrative technique of hiding the scientific basis of the novel, for, to call Ana a hysteric explicitly would have demystified her character.[18] While Alas prefers to leave a level of ambiguity in the narrative that gives the reader more freedom to bring meaning to the text,[19] López Bago's narrator is entirely unambiguous, leading to an overdetermination consistent with his scientific determinism. Nevertheless, in both works, the characters' hysteria strictly adheres to the predominant theories of the time that held that a woman's lack of a fulfilling heterosexual relationship and of a child were the most salient causes of the disease, clearly bolstering the idea that women must bear children or risk disease.

In Ana Ozores's case, the purported cause of her hysteria is her sexless and childless marriage. Although Don Víctor's impotence is never completely explained, the novel emphasizes his age. A significant age difference between a couple as a source of reproductive difficulties was a medical commonplace of the time. For example, as we saw in Chapter 1, the Spanish hygienist, Felipe Monlau, argued against such unions in the second edition of his *Higiene del matrimonio*, claiming that they were rarely fecund and often produced hysteria in women.[20] Suárez Casañ, in *Secretos del lecho conyugal* (189–?, Secrets of the conjugal bed), is even more emphatic, claiming these ill-suited marriages not only led women to adultery, masturbation, nymphomania, and an early death, but also plagued society either by being infecund or by producing "hijos raquíticos y enfermizos" (rickety and sickly children).[21] His outrage with the legality of such marriages leads the Catalan doctor to proclaim, "las leyes deberían prohibirlos; pero ya que así no sucede, álcese la voz de toda persona honrada para censurarlo" (laws should prohibit them; but since this does not happen, every honorable person should raise his/her voice to censure them).[22] Suárez Casañ's arguments tie women's reproductive function to their social obligation to produce healthy children, an obligation he believes should be upheld by the law.

Thus, while Gracia and Soledad's hysteria in *El cura* and *La monja* respectively is due to their single status and their celibacy— Gracia's doctor stresses the importance of her marrying immediately, and Soledad's hysteria is cured once she violates the chastity vows taken upon becoming a nun—in *La Regenta* it is Ana's marriage to a much older man. The reader is initially told that Ana and Víctor married when Ana was nineteen and Don Víctor "pasaba de los cuarenta" (1:236; was over forty). However, the narrator plays with this open-endedness referring to Víctor's age once again, ten pages later, as "cuarenta y pico, pico misterioso" (1:246; forty something, the something part being mystery). Nevertheless, many other similarities abound between these characters. First, like Gracia, Ana has her first "attack" when she reaches puberty (1:211).[23] After her father's death, Ana falls ill. However, the doctor attributes the disease to "ciertas transformaciones propias de la edad" (1:211; certain transformations typical of her age). According to the doctor, Ana's "nervous fever" is the result of her physical transformation from a girl into a young woman. Moreover, Ana's attacks subside after her marriage, as Ana's friend Visitación tells Ana's seducer, Don Álvaro, suggesting that there was some physical intimacy between her and Don Víctor when they first were married: "ya sabes que cuando se casó cesaron [los ataques], que después volvieron, pero nunca con la frecuencia de ahora" (1:333; you know that when she married [the attacks] stopped, that they later returned, but never with the current frequency). Visitación's statement not only implies that Ana's illness was temporarily alleviated when she first married Don Víctor, but also that the combination of her current state of celibacy and the continual seduction by Don Álvaro has exacerbated the illness.

In fact, just as Gracia's hysteria is aggravated by her close living quarters with her brother, Ana's attacks become particularly acute when feeling most vulnerable to Álvaro's powers of seduction. For example, at a party hosted by the Marquise de Vegallana, Ana experiences the beginning of an attack when Álvaro touches her foot with his own: "sintió un miedo parecido al del ataque nervioso más violento" (2:311; she felt a fear similar to the most violent nervous attack), and, shortly thereafter, when Ana is made to dance with Don Álvaro at Don Víctor's own request, the attack comes on in full force and Ana faints in Don Álvaro's arms. Afterward, the rumor runs through the dance hall that "A la Regenta le había dado el ataque" (2:313; the Regenta had had an attack). The subsequent scandal this incident produces and the extreme jealousy it incites in Don Fermín also attest to the perceived sexual/hysterical nature of Ana's "attack." Moreover, just as Soledad finds her hysteria cured by sleeping with Román, Ana's hysteria subsides once she gives into Don Álvaro. As Víctor notes, without knowing the cause, her nervous illness has disappeared (2:445).

The hysterical attack, often compared to a pathological form of female orgasm, had come to be the telltale sign of hysteria in women. Visitación's highly sexualized description of the convulsing Ana is striking in its similarities to the description of Gracia's paroxysm:

> ¿Te acuerdas de aquella danza de las Bacantes? Pues eso parece, sólo que mucho mejor; una bacante como serían las de verdad, si las hubo allá, en esos países que dicen. Eso parece cuando se retuerce. ¡Cómo se ríe cuando está en el ataque! Tiene los ojos llenos de lágrimas y en la boca unos pliegues tentadores, y dentro de la remonísima garganta suenan unos ruidos, unos ayes, unas quejas subterráneas; parece que allá dentro se lamenta el amor siempre callado y en prisiones ¡qué sé yo! ¡Suspira de un modo, da unos abrazos a las almohadas! ¡Y se encoge con una pereza! Cualquiera diría que en los ataques tiene pesadillas, y que rabia de celos o se muere de amor . . . Ese estúpido don Víctor con sus pájaros y sus comedias, y su Frígilis el de los gallos en injerto, no es un hombre. (1:331)

> *Do you remember the dance of the Bacchantes? Well that's what it looks like, only much better; a Bacchante similar to what the real ones would be like, if they existed there, in the countries in which they say [they existed]. That's what she looks like when she writhes. How she laughs when she is in the midst of the attack! Her eyes are full of tears and on her mouth tempting expressions, and from within her very beautiful throat one hears sounds, moans, subterranean grumblings; it seems as though the long repressed and imprisoned love is lamented from inside there. What can I say! She sighs in such a way, hugs her pillows! She cringes lazily! Anyone would say that during the attacks she has nightmares, and that she is mad with jealousy or dying for love . . . That*

stupid Don Víctor with his birds and his comedias, and his Frígiles, the
one with the grafted roosters, he is not a man.

Not only do we see the familiar tears, laughter, and strange muscle
contractions, but the sexual nature of this "danza de las Bacantes"
is emphasized, in part by Visita ending her description by reproach-
ing Don Víctor of not being able to satisfy his wife's desires. The
term *bacchante* was frequently employed in medical texts on hysteria and nymphomania in women. Saillard, for example, points
out the abundant use of the term in the description of hysterics in
L'iconographie photographique de la Salpêtrière.[24]

As in the case of both Gracia and Soledad, and in connection
with the socialization of procreative behavior, Ana's hysteria is
also linked to her lack of a child. Ana's sadness about not having a
child is made evident throughout the novel. This need for a child
is portrayed as something more than just the personal whim of
the protagonist. It is the force of nature exerting its will upon the
female body. As in the case of Soledad, Ana's lack of a child is experienced as a great "vacío" (1:203; emptiness) in her life, and she feels
"gritos formidables de la naturaleza" (2:19; formidable screams of
nature). In one instance, during one of Ana's recoveries from a bout
with her illness, she feels "palpitaciones en las entrañas que eran
agradable cosquilleo" (2:212; palpitations in her core that were a
pleasant tickling sensation) and then tries to locate the sources of
this feeling: "el sentido [. . .] se le había trasladado al pecho, más
abajo, mejor, no sabía dónde, no era en el estómago, era claro, pero
tampoco en el corazón, era en el medio" (2:212; the sensation had
moved to her chest, lower, actually, she didn't know where, it wasn't
in her stomach, for sure, but it also wasn't in her heart either, it was
in between). As Gonzalo Sobejano points out, in this passage Ana
is referring to the epigastrium which, according to neurologists, is
the region in which sensations originating from the womb are felt
(2:212n24). Thus, in accordance with the medical texts of the time
that claimed that the womb dominated female existence and that
an unsatisfied womb led to hysteria, Ana's physical and emotional
upheavals are attributed to her barren womb.

Moreover, Ana's psychological problems are partly due to her own lack of a mother. She is therefore affected twice by the violation of the socialization of procreative behavior. Lamenting her own sad life before her general confession, she notes that she has had "Ni madre, ni hijos" (1:165: neither a mother, nor children). Ana's mother died in childbirth, and her father, Carlos Ozores, left her in the care of a cold and cruel English governess who not only subjected her to harsh punishments of isolation and deprivation of food, but never hugged or caressed her. Ana is aware of this lack of affection and love and still yearns for it as an adult: "Había Ana sentido toda su vida nostalgia del regazo de su madre (1:166; Ana had felt her whole life the nostalgia for her mother's lap). Contemporary attachment theory has shown that physical affection is as important to a child as food.[25] The difference between contemporary psychological theories and the portrayal of Ana's loveless childhood is that in the latter case it is specifically the lack of a mother, a female nurturer, that is responsible for Ana's sadness. However, current research has shown that the gender of the nurturer is irrelevant, so long as the child receives the kind of affection she deserves.[26] After Ana's innocent escapade with Germán, Doña Camila subjects Ana to public shaming, one of the most painful types of emotional injury.[27] This public humiliation combined with unnecessarily harsh punishments, such as the use of isolation, and a lack of love and physical affection, shows the ways the neglect and abuse Ana was subjected to as a child are causes of her hysteria as an adult. Such psychological explanations are absent entirely from the *Cura* trilogy, where the "natural" sexual drives alone cause women's hysteria. However, the psychological explanations found in *La Regenta* merely buttress the socialization of procreative behavior by underscoring the harmful consequences of not having women assume their proper roles as mothers. By the novel's logic, nobody can replace the love of a biological mother.[28]

Another difference between Ana's hysteria and that of Gracia and Soledad is Ana's pride and intentional contravention of gender norms. As we saw in Chapters 1 and 2, for many doctors, hysteria was as much a character defect in women as it was a veritable disease. Such doctors viewed hysterics as willfully defiant women.[29] Ana is often portrayed as arrogant. In fact, one of the major causes of Ana's unhappiness is her inability to accept the mundane routine of life in Vetusta. Her desire to see herself as superior to the other inhabitants of the Asturian town leads to her chronic yearning for something better: "Ana se creía superior a los que la rodeaban, y pensaba que debía de haber en otra parte una sociedad que viviese como ella quisiera vivir y que tuviese sus mismas ideas. Pero entretanto Vetusta era su cárcel, la necia rutina, un mar de hielo que la tenía sujeta, inmóvil" (1:238; Ana believed herself superior to those around her, and she thought that there had to be a society somewhere else that lived as she wished to live and that shared her ideas. But in the meantime, Vetusta was her prison, her stupid routine, a sea of ice that held her restrained, immobile).

Ana's pride is also manifested in her mysticism. Female mystics' rejection of, or indifference to, their sexually determined roles of wife and mother, combined with their conviction of their close relationship with God, made them subject to accusations of vanity and pride. This is evident in late nineteenth- and early twentieth-century authors' treatment of mystics. For example, Ramón León Mainez Fernández, in *Teresa de Jesús ante la crítica* (1880), called the Spanish saint "engreída" (conceited), and A. Marie, in his *Misticismo y locura* (ca. 1907) accused mystics of exaggerated self-love and megalomania.[30] Ana, the mystic, is also portrayed as arrogant. In a state of mystical rapture, in which she feels one with God and the universe, Ana looks out her window and observes the insignificance of the Vetustans. She then compares the importance of the life of her fellow Vetustans to that of tiny mosquitoes whose existence consists of hovering over the shores of the river and serving as food for the fish (2:208). Later, Ana admits that "para ella la señal de la *distinción* espiritual estaba en el desprecio del vulgo, de los vetustenses" (2:424, emphasis in the original; for her, the sign of spiritual *distinction* was in her contempt for the common people, of the Vetustans). Thus, Ana uses mysticism, and her literary pretensions—the latter is discussed in more detail below—as a way of distinguishing herself from the rest of Vetusta. Or, in Kathy

Bacon's words: "Ana, the character who is most closely related to Teresa [de Jesús] in the novel, uses the saint as part of her own fantasy of distinguished identity."[31]

The condemnation of Ana's pride is a notable difference between the two works since Gracia and Soledad are, apart from their desires for sexual intercourse and motherhood, devoid of other ambitions that would contravene social norms. In fact, the sole cause of their "disease" is their celibacy, which is imposed by society or the Church, not self-imposed. In contrast, in Ana's case, it is her vanity that prevents her, initially, from giving in to her desires for Don Álvaro; she doesn't want to be like other women. Ana is aware that people view her as the only virtuous woman in Vetusta, and she wants to retain that status (1:363). It is also Ana's pride that makes her believe that she could actually make the town Don Juan fall in love with her (1:296). Pride is also the reason Ana doesn't initially have more suitors (1:247) and the reason why she rejects Don Frutos as a potential husband. While Gracia and Soledad both give into their sexual urges the first time Román initiates a sexual encounter, Ana holds out for most of the novel, fearing the way succumbing to temptation could tarnish her reputation in Vetusta. Thus Ana, unlike her hysterical counterparts in the *Cura* trilogy, is an example of the hysterical temperament, of the defiant woman who refuses to assimilate to her conventional role in society, and who doesn't want to admit she is like other women. This difference between Ana and the hysterical characters in López Bago's work is also an example of the difference in literary philosophies and worldviews of the two authors. While López Bago's female characters lack any free will because their behavior is supposedly determined by their biological make-up, Alas's female protagonist does have free choice.[32] The aporia is that even with free will, Ana's only choice is between being ill (hysterical) and moral (faithful to her husband) or being healthy (sexually active) but morally corrupt (adulterous).[33]

These differences can be connected to the authors' views on women. While López Bago has been acknowledged for bringing attention to women's sexual exploitation,[34] his advocacy of certain rights for women does not refute his assimilation of the misogynistic views of women of his day. In fact, his radical determinism meant women's entire existence was restricted to the supposed drives of their bodies, leaving no appropriate or "natural" spaces open to women outside their roles as wives and mothers. Alas also subscribed to the medical consensus that women were naturally designed as men's polar opposites, claiming that it was not an issue of inferiority or superiority but of their "diferencia complementaria" (complementary difference).[35] Moreover, the Asturian author explicitly spoke out against women seeking educational or professional parity with men. He argued that equal education for women would go against women's natures, make them physically unattractive, irritable, and overall more manly.[36] In 1890, when Emilia Pardo Bazán was pursuing a seat in the Real Academia Española (Spanish Royal Academy), which she ultimately would be refused, Clarín ridiculed her ambitions in *Madrid Cómico* (Comical Madrid),[37] and in 1892 he published a *palique* (chat) in *La correspondencia* (Correspondence) in which he mocked the idea of training women for serious professions.[38] These views may account, in part, for the novel's condemnation of Ana's literary pursuits as sign of her hysterical temperament, an element entirely absent from López Bago's work.

Moreover, according to Lissorgues, while Alas adopted the naturalist method of observation and experimentation, he rejected the naturalist philosophy of material determinism.[39] In other words, for Alas, scientific and medical theories can explain, but never justify or excuse, an individual's behavior. The importance of moral choice in Alas's literary world gives us some insight into his conception of his protagonist's adultery, as do Alas's comments on the role of determinism in the moral transgressions of women. In an 1878 review of E. Rodríguez Solís's *La mujer defendida por la historia, la ciencia y la moral* (Women defended by history, science, and morality) Alas writes, "Sería lamentable que las mujeres tomasen demasiado al pie de la letra la teoría de que son enfermas. Sea lo que quiera de la matriz, hay deslices indisculpables. [. . .] La responsabilidad moral existe a pesar del *gran simpático*, y las señoras mujeres no deben olvidarlo. [. . .] Contra la fatalidad física se defiende la sociedad" (emphasis in the original; It would be unfortunate if women took too literally the theory that they are sick. Be what it may with the womb, there are inexcusable indiscretions. [. . .] Moral responsibility exists in spite of the *great sympathetic* [*nervous system*], and women of a certain social standing must not forget it. [. . .] Society defends against physical destiny).[40] So while Alas accepted and made use of theories on hysteria that claimed women were dominated by their wombs and their reproductive functions, he also felt that morality had a role in keeping such physical drives in check. In this line of thinking, Ana's sexless marriage and barren womb provide the scientific explanation for her hysteria and her inclinations toward Don Álvaro, but do not exonerate her of the moral transgression of adultery. This is not the case in López Bago's biologically determined literary universe, where women do not exercise free will and are consequently morally exonerated, but physically punished, for the deviations from their biological destiny.

Psychiatrization of Perverse Pleasure

As in the case of the *Cura* trilogy, the primary female perversions in *La Regenta* are onanism, nymphomania, and same-sex desire. The issue of masturbation, female and male, receives notable, although oblique, treatment in the novel. While Saturnino Bermúdez is the primary male character cited for this vice, there are abundant insinuations that Ana is similarly guilty. According to Laqueur, many nineteenth-century hygienists pointed to luxurious living as a sexually corrupting influence.[41] Just as Gracia's frequent bathing is subject to the narrator's scrutiny and censure in *El cura*, Ana's bedroom is described and analyzed in detail as an unsupervised space that encourages leisure and the excitation of both the body and mind. Thesée Pouillet, in *Del onanismo en la mujer (Placeres ilícitos)* (Regarding onanism in women [Illicit pleasures]), states that "la riqueza, que autoriza una vida sedentaria é inactiva, que permite el reposo prolongado en calientes lechos de pluma, en medio de la templada atmósfera de una perfumada habitación [. . .], conduce frecuentemente á prácticas culpables, dejando a las mujeres entregadas por completo á los extravíos de su imaginación" (the richness that authorizes a sedentary and inactive life, which allows for prolonged rest in warm feather beds, in the midst of the temperate atmosphere of a perfumed bedroom [. . .], frequently leads to guilty practices, leaving women completely absorbed by the deviancy of their imaginations).[42]

Thus, the description of Ana's bedroom, with its garnet satin hangings, golden marriage bed, and authentic tiger skin rug (1:163), not only signals her repressed sexuality but also the decadent environment that is inciting her desires. Ana's bed in particular is described in detail by Obdulia: "¡Ah! Debía confesar que el juego de cama era digno de una princesa. ¡Qué sábanas! ¡Qué almohadones! Ella había pasado la mano por todo aquello, ¡qué suavidad! El satín de aquel cuerpecito de regalo no sentiría asperezas en el roce de aquellas sábanas" (1:164; Ah! She had to confess that her bedding was fitting of a princess. What sheets! What pillows! She had run her hand across all of them, what softness! The satin of that pleasing little body would not feel roughness in its contact with those sheets). The attention paid to Ana's bed is important since a soft bed and luxurious bedding were said to make one more inclined to lingering therein, which, according to Pouillet, caused "congestión pelviana y una irritación genital favorable á la génesis de la masturbación" (pelvic congestion and a genital irritation conducive to the beginnings of masturbation).[43] That is why Suárez Casañ insisted that a "cama dura" (hard bed) aided in protecting against such moral vices.[44] It therefore comes as no surprise that Ana's extended stays, alone, in the highly sumptuous environment of her bedroom lead to suspect behavior:

Después de abandonar todas las prendas que no habían de acompañarla en el lecho, quedó sobre la piel de tigre, hundiendo los pies desnudos, pequeños y rollizos en la espesura de las manchas pardas. Un brazo desnudo se apoyaba en la cabeza algo inclinada, y el otro pendía a lo largo del cuerpo, siguiendo la curva graciosa de la robusta cadera. Parecía una impúdica modelo olvidada de sí misma en una postura académica impuesta por el artista. Jamás el Arcipreste, ni confesor alguno, había prohibido a la Regenta esta voluptuosidad de distender a sus solas los entumecidos miembros y sentir el contacto del aire fresco por todo el cuerpo a la hora de acostarse. Nunca había creído ella que tal abandono fuese materia de confesión. (1:165)

After having abandoned all her clothes that were not to accompany her to bed, she stood on the tiger skin, sinking her naked feet, small and plump in the thickness of the dark spots, her naked arm rested on her slightly inclined head, the other one along her body, following the gracious curve of her robust hip. She looked like a shameless model who had forgotten herself in the academic posture imposed by the artist. Never had the Archpriest nor any confessor prohibited the Regenta this voluptuousness of extending her stiff limbs all alone and feeling the contact of the cool air on her entire body upon going to bed. She had never thought that such abandon might be material for confession.

If the reader did not already suspect Ana's behavior in this scene, the narrator underscores its sexual nature by implying that it is material for confession.

However, the most suggestive scene is the self-flagellation episode, which is striking in its similarities to the passage in *El cura* in which Gracia inadvertently brings herself to orgasm:[45]

Ana se vio como un hermoso fantasma flotante en el fondo obscuro de alcoba. [. . .] Sonrió a su imagen con una amargura que le pareció diabólica . . . tuvo miedo de sí misma . . . se refugió en la alcoba, y sobre la piel de tigre dejó caer toda la ropa de que se despojaba para dormir. [. . .] y pensando ella misma en que estaba borracha . . . no sabía de qué, Ana, desnuda, viendo a trechos su propia carne de raso entre la holanda, saltó al rincón, empuñó los zorros de ribetes de lana negra . . . y sin piedad azotó su hermosura inútil una, dos, diez veces . . . Y como aquello también era ridículo, arrojó lejos de sí las prosaicas disciplinas, entró de un brinco de bacante en su lecho; y más exaltada en su cólera por la frialdad voluptuosa de las sábanas, algo húmedas, mordió con furor la almohada. A fuerza de no querer pensar, por huir de sí misma, media hora después se quedó dormida. (2:286)

Ana saw herself as a beautiful floating ghost in the dark depths of the room. [. . .] She smiled at her own image with a bitterness that seemed to her diabolical . . . she was afraid of herself . . . she took refuge in the bedroom, and she let all the clothes that she took off to go to sleep fall on the tiger skin. [. . .] and thinking to herself that she was drunk . . . she didn't know from what, Ana, naked, seeing here and there her own satin flesh amongst the Dutch linen, she jumped in the corner, she grabbed the feather dusters with black wool trim . . . and flogged her useless beauty without mercy, once, twice, ten times . . . And as that was also ridiculous, she threw the banal whips far away from her, entered her bed with a bacchante leap, and more worked up in her ire by the cold voluptuousness of the sheets, somewhat humid, she bit her pillow furiously. As a result of her trying not to think, just so she could flee from herself, half an hour later she fell asleep.

The scene with Ana is less explicit than the scene with Gracia, yet at the same time the similarities are striking. Both Ana and Gracia throw themselves onto their beds and convulse, Gracia after thinking about her brother's good looks, and Ana after contemplating her own beauty and being sexually aroused by it, to the point of feeling the need to flagellate herself. Both get so excited they bite their pillows, and both experience a calm afterward; Ana even falls asleep.

What is compelling about the scene with Ana is not only the autoeroticism and masochistic behavior, but also the suggestion of the sexual arousal produced by contemplating her own beauty in the mirror, a theme we see in *La monja* as well when Román tells Melita to remove the mirror from her room (27). Even the spiritual guidebook Román gives Melita explicitly warns its intended female readers not to look at their own reflections in the mirror and to be quick when getting ready for bed. Melita does not understand these admonitions: "¡Qué quitara el espejo de su cuarto! ¡Qué no se mirase! Y, ¿por qué?" (27; That she remove the mirror from her room! That she not look at herself! And why?). Also,

no llegó a comprender nunca por qué el *Directorio de las cosas espirituales* recomendaba tanto que las religiosas fuesen muy ligeras en desnudarse á la hora de dormir, procurando, al meterse en la cama, no descubrir jamás ni mirar desnuda parte alguna de su cuerpo; ni por qué, por último aconsejaba quedarse dormidas con algún buen pensamiento, "porque, añadía el *Directorio*, hay un demonio que vela sobre nuestro sueño para inficionarle con feas imaginaciones." (27)

she never was able to understand why the Directory of Spiritual Matters *recommended so often that nuns be swift when getting undressed at bedtime, making sure, upon getting into bed, to never reveal or look at any part of their naked body; nor why, finally, it advised to fall asleep with good thoughts, "because, the Directory added, there is a devil who watches over our sleep in order to infect it with ugly fantasies."*

Thus, the bedtime scene in *La Regenta*, read in the light of these recommendations in *La monja*, highlights the fears about women being sexually aroused by their own physical beauty, and the consequent potential for masturbation and homoeroticism, and underscores the abundance of discourses (medical and religious) warning against the suspect bedtime behaviors in which Ana engages.

Additionally, Ana's literary interests and ambitions also are interpreted as a form of gender deviance. As we saw in Chapter 1, reading and the over-excitation of the female imagination were cited as principal causes of onanism and nymphomania in women. At a time when only approximately 20 percent of women could read,[46] and when restrictions on what women should be allowed to read were plentiful, Ana's unrestricted reading of the books in her father's library is portrayed as sexually corrupting,[47] inappropriately "masculine,"[48] and is linked to her "manly" ambition of becoming a writer. Indeed, Ana's aunts regard their niece's experiments with writing as "una cosa hombruna" (1:232; a mannish thing) and as "el mayor y más ridículo defecto que en Vetusta podía tener una señorita" (1:231; the greatest and most ridiculous defect that a young woman could have in Vetusta). Even though the Marquis de Vegallana acknowledges that Ana's poetic verses "no son malos" (1:232; are not bad), he warns that it is better that Ana abandon her writing as he has never known a "literata que fuese mujer de bien" (1:232; a bluestocking who was a respectable woman). Vetustan women mockingly refer to Ana as Jorge Sandio (1:233; George Sand) and opining on the matter, the effeminate "baroncito" (baron's son) states he wouldn't want his wife to wear the pants in this way (1:234). Because of this public censure and ridicule Ana "se juró a sí misma no ser la 'literata,' aquel ente híbrido y abominable de que se hablaba en Vetusta como de los monstruos asquerosos y horribles" (1:233; swore to herself to not be a "bluestocking," that abominable hybrid entity of which Vetustans spoke as if they were horrible and disgusting monsters). Later in the novel the narrator tells us, "lo que pensaba todo Vetusta de las literatas, lo pensaba Pedro de las cocineras. Las llamaba marimachos" (1:323; what all Vetusta thought of bluestockings, Pedro thought of female cooks. He called them butches).

On more than one occasion, Alas himself expressed similar sentiments. In a piece published in *La unión* (The union) in 1879 entitled "Las literatas" (Bluestockings), Clarín writes: "Yo, humildísimo discípulo, me atrevo a aumentar las especies de los anafroditas colocando en el género . . . a las literatas. Sí, Tomás, no lo digo a tontas y a locas; la literata como el ángel, y mejor, como la vieja, carece de sexo" (I, humble disciple, dare to increase the species of anaphrodites by placing in this group . . . bluestockings. Yes, Thomas, I don't say this willy-nilly; bluestockings like angels, and more so, like old women, lack sex).[49] To this he adds, a couple of paragraphs later, "La mayor parte de las literatas son feas" (The majority of bluestockings are ugly).[50] Not surprisingly, nineteenth-century hygienists also stressed the negative effects of women's pursuing highly intellectual tasks. Many doctors argued that it was dangerous for young girls to become too interested in learning because their sexual and reproductive organs might not develop correctly, causing them to be sterile as adults.[51] Other doctors, such as Suárez Casañ in his *Enciclopedia médica popular* (1894; Popular medical encyclopedia), warned that literary work often led women to suffer frequent nervous diseases.[52] Thus, Ana's literary ambitions not only signal her pride and defiance of the conventions of femininity, both signs of the hysterical temperament, but also open her up to accusations of sexual deviance. This then is another striking difference with the *Cura* trilogy. None of the lesbian nuns in *La monja* appear to have any ambitions other than their nightly orgies. Thus, despite their more explicit lesbianism, it is only Ana in *La Regenta* who is referred to as a hybrid creature, an anaphrodite, and a butch for daring to take up the pen.

Perhaps most revealing of Ana's repressed, voracious sexual appetite, however, are the descriptions of her hysterical attacks discussed above. Despite its sexual overtones, the hysterical attack, as Aldaraca points out, was often more repulsive than arousing.[53] As we saw in the previous chapters, fears about male seminal depletion aroused anxieties about a superior female sexual stamina that could lead their male sexual partners to an early grave. This inversion of gender roles led to general fears about an emasculated society controlled by overbearing women. The pernicious effects of such a situation is seen in many Spanish novels of the time and *La Regenta* is no exception.[54] Weak men and domineering women characterize Vetustan society. While the narrator frequently refers to Don Víctor's impotence in order to highlight it as the cause of Ana's hysteria, even the Vetustan Don Juan, the supposed epitome of hegemonic masculinity, struggles with impotence when trying to satisfy the Regenta's "hambre atrasada" (2:449–50; built-up hunger). Don Álvaro's situation is exacerbated when pressured with the burden of satisfying the desires of both Ana and her sexually promiscuous maidservant, Petra.

Despite the insinuations of Ana's potential for same-sex desire and nymphomania, the implications are still more subtle compared to the manifestation of these same "perversions" in the characters of Visita and Obdulia. Indeed, Visita and Obdulia are actually more reminiscent of the nuns in *La monja* in that their ambitions are tied only to their sexual appetites, and to seeing that those who don't succumb as they do meet a tragic end.[55] Visita's sexual perversions are tied to her adultery, general lack of concern for her family, and constant consumption of sweets.[56] We are told that Visita "Siempre hablaba con alguna golosina en la boca" (1:326; always spoke with a candy in her mouth). And in the kitchen scene with Pedro, we find her licking her syrup-covered fingers.[57] Visita's sweet tooth is portrayed as a sublimation of her sexual desires, seen most clearly when she eats sweets as she watches over Ana in her bed.[58] Indeed, Visita's attraction for Ana becomes evident when, trying to excite Álvaro, she describes in detail what Ana looks like in the midst of a hysterical fit (1:331).[59] As James Mandrell notes, "El torrente de palabras y los signos de exclamación nos dicen todo: la descripción de los ataques de la Regenta no sirve solo para informar a Álvaro, también estimula y hasta excita Visitación, como indican los puntos suspensivos" (The outpouring of words and exclamation marks says it all; the description of the Regenta's attacks not only serve to inform Álvaro, but also to stimulate and even sexually excite Visitación, as the ellipsis suggests).[60] In this instance, the relationship between Visita and Ana resembles that between Gracia and Ana in *El cura*, where the hysterical attack proves to be sexually arousing to the female friend and onlooker. Finally, Visita's intense envy of Ana—she envies her beauty, her reputation, her social standing—can also be interpreted as a desire for Ana herself. As Mathews argues, "Visita seems to use her connection with [Don Álvaro] primarily as a means of approaching the real object of her desire: Ana."[61]

Obdulia's nymphomaniacal tendencies are even more pronounced. Beginning in chapter 1, her exaggerated sexual appetite is portrayed through her flirtatious actions and her scandalous attire: she wears a crimson hood, a scarlet silk bodice, or "coraza" (breastplate), from which her bosom appears about to burst, a short and extra-tight skirt, and imperial bronze boots (1:131). She uses the confessional to casually discuss her sexual adventures, and hopes to seduce Fermín de Pas in the same way she seduced the bishop of Nauplia (1:131–32). Obdulia's possible nymphomania is also revealed through her multiple affairs, her status as a beautiful young widow, and her reputation as a loose woman.[62] Obdulia's predatory sexuality objectifies both men and women of all social classes, from the bishop of Nauplia to Pedro the cook to the Regenta herself.[63] As Lawrence Rich highlights in Obdulia's seduction of Pedro, Obdulia puts a spoon in Pedro's mouth "which she has just caressed with her lips to excite him sexually," forming a parallel with the scene in which Fermín puts a biscuit in his maid's mouth. Rich argues that "Obdulia's behavior inverts bourgeois class and gender expectations: whereas Fermín gives and Teresa receives (the biscuit), Obdulia is shown as sexually active rather than passive, as she gives (the spoon) to a lower-class male who docilely receives it from her."[64] Fermín, on the other hand, resists Obdulia's objectification of him as he does not want to play the passive role of being the object of her gaze (1:178).

Obdulia's lesbian proclivities are seen in her sexual attraction to Ana. In her assessment of Ana's bedroom, she refers to Ana as "un *bijou* tan precioso" (such a precious jewel), imagines the "satín de aquel cuerpecito de regalo" (the satin of that pleasing little body) in contact with the bed sheets, and admires "sinceramente las formas y el cutis de Ana" (1:164; truly Ana's skin and curves). Most revealing, however, is the scene in which Ana is about to appear barefoot in the Holy Week procession: "'¿Cuándo llegará?' preguntaba la viuda, lamiéndose los labios, invadida de una envidia admiradora, y sintiendo extraños dejos de una especie de lujuria bestial, disparatada, inexplicable por lo absurdo. Sentía Obdulia en aquel momento así . . . un deseo vago . . . de . . . de . . . ser hombre" (2:361; "When is she coming?" asked the widow, licking her lips, possessed by admiring envy, and conscious of the strange promptings of a kind of crazy, brutal lust, so absurd as to be inexplicable. Obdulia felt a . . . vague desire . . . to . . . to . . . to be a man[65]).

Other female characters who defy their gender roles are the working-class characters. Petra, for example, is also highly promiscuous. Petra actively seduces Víctor, Fermín, Álvaro, and her cousin the miller, whom she plans to marry if nothing better comes her way. In the case of Don Fermín, Don Álvaro, and her cousin, she revels in the sexual pleasure they provide her while always being cognizant of the ways they promise to improve her lot. Her clear enjoyment of sex leads the narrator to refer to her on several occasions as the "rubia lúbrica" (the salacious blonde).[66] Víctor refers to her as a "ramerilla" (little whore) because he suspects she intends to use his provoked sexual advances toward her to blackmail him (2:445–46). Yet, as Christine Mathews notes, "Petra, with all her zest for men, nonetheless also channels an interest in Ana through the three men she is most bent on seducing: Víctor, Mesía, and De Pas."[67] Her homoerotic desire for Ana is seen in her insinuations into these erotic love triangles, her constant spying on her mistress, and in her participation in the machinations that bring about Víctor's discovery of Ana's affair with Don Álvaro. In other words, like Visita, Petra satiates her sexual desire for the most beautiful and virtuous woman in Vetusta by playing a pivotal role in her complete demise.

The most masculine woman in the novel, however, is Paula Raíces, Fermín's mother. Even though Doña Paula retains her sexual virtue, she seduces and blackmails the first priest she works for, and she takes vicarious pleasures in her son's sexual exploits.[68] She is also more masculine in appearance and behavior than most men in Vetusta. Almost as tall as her son, and wider in the shoulders (1:412), she proved herself to be physically stronger than the men who frequented her bar in her younger years. There she regularly broke up fights among miners and single-handedly fought off these same drunken men's sexual advances (1:555). Lacking conventional feminine beauty, she wears dark, discrete clothing that hides her physique, and she smokes cigarettes, an activity reserved for men at the time (1:412–14). Like Petra, she is devoid of empathy and romantic ideals and seeks instead power through the control of the men in her life and the practice of unscrupulous business tactics. Her deviance from the supposed natural nurturing role of a mother is portrayed as a cause of Fermín's own sadism and narcissism.

The secondary characters of Doña Camila and Teresina reinforce the idea of a "naturally" perverted working-class female sexuality. Doña Camila, who despite the "Doña" is of lower-middle-class standing at best, is a "hipocritona" (a big hypocrite), who physically resembles an "estatua anafrodita" (asexual statue) and "un ser sin sexo" (an asexual being) whose "pasión principal era la lujuria, satisfecha a la inglesa; una lujuria que pudiera llamarse metodista" (1:188; principal passion was lust, satisfied English style;

a lust that could be called Methodist). This negative characteriza-
tion is reinforced by her morally suspect boyfriend who lusts after
Ana as a young girl. Doña Camila's unsuccessful attempt to improve
her standing by seducing Ana's father and her consequent ill treatment of Ana as child merely reinforce her deviance from the supposedly natural maternal role of women. And Teresina, like Petra
after her, willingly and eagerly assumes her role as priest's concu-
bine without moral scruple.[69] Thus the sexuality of the working-
class female characters is shown to be naturally deviant. The bourgeois discourses of virtue and of the Angel in the House play no
role on women forced to find employment outside the home. Most
clearly enjoy sex and none of them have any qualms about using
their sexuality as a currency to improve their social standing.

Many of these sexual perversions are put on display when Ana
walks barefoot as a *Nazarena* (penitent) in the Holy Week procession. In the same way religious practices metaphorically degenerate into sexual orgies with satanic undertones in *La monja*, the
Holy Week procession in *La Regenta* is a sacrilegious event closer
in resemblance to a black mass than to a time of contrition; just
as a pregnant Soledad is lynched and sacrificed in *La monja*, in *La
Regenta* Ana's body is offered up for the sexual delectation of all of
Vetusta. In fact, Obdulia notes the accuracy of the Marquise's terminology in describing Ana's actions: "¡Ana iba a darse en espectáculo! Cierto, ésa era la frase. ¿Qué más hubiera querido ella, la de
Fandiño, que darse en espectúculo, que hacerse mirar y contemplar
por toda Vetusta" (2:355; Ana was going to offer herself up in a spectacle! That was the right phrase. What more could she, Fandiño's
widow, have asked for, than to offer herself up in a spectacle, than to
be looked at and studied by all of Vetusta). And while Ana is not literally naked, she feels like a naked prostitute: "Aquellos pies desnudos eran para ella la desnudez de todo el cuerpo y de toda el alma.
'¡Ella era una loca que había caído en una especie de prostitución
singular!'" (2:366; For her, showing her bare feet was like having
her entire body and soul naked. "She was a madwoman who had
fallen into a unique type of prostitution!"). Indeed, all of Vestusta,
from the lower classes to the aristocracy, men and women, lust after

Ana, consuming her beauty and taking voyeuristic and fetishistic pleasures in Ana's bare feet (2:361), converting the reenactment of the burial of Jesus into a sexual orgy: "ni un solo vetutense allí presente pensaba en Dios" (2:363; not a single Vetustan present was thinking about God). Female onlookers are equated with witches through Obdulia's lesbian desires and "lujura bestial" (2:361; bestial lust), and in the comparison of the event to a witches' Sabbath: "en los cristales de las tiendas cerradas y de algunos balcones se reflejaban las llamas movibles; subían y bajaban en contorsiones fantásticas como sombras lucientes, en confusion de *aquelarre*" (2:365; emphasis mine; in the windows of the closed shops and of some balconies the moving flames were reflected, rising and falling in fantastic contortions, like shadows of light, in all the confusion of a *witches' Sabbath*[70]).

The representation of the Holy Week procession as a witches' Sabbath is reinforced by the portrayal of de Pas as a diabolical figure, and of Ana's actions as a submission to him rather than to God. Devoid of any religious thoughts, Fermín, just a "cáscara de un sacerdote" (2:368; shell of a priest), shows Ana off like "un triunfador romano a una esclava . . . detrás del carro de su gloria . . ." (2:364; a Roman victor leads a slave . . . behind his chariot of glory). Indeed, he revels in the way Ana's public debasement solidifies his power over the town of Vetusta:

> Caminaba cerca de Ana, casi a su lado [. . .] empuñaba el cirio apagado como un cetro. Él era el amo de todo aquello. Él, a pesar de las calumnias de sus enemigos [. . .] llevaba allí, a su lado, prisonera con cadenas invisibles a la señora más admirada por su hermosura y grandeza de alma en toda Vetusta. [. . .] ¿Los jesuitas obligaban a las vírgenes vetustense a ceñir el cilicio? Pues él descalzaba los más floridos pies del pueblo y los arrastraba por el lodo . . . allí estaban, asomando a veces debajo de aquel terciopelo morado, entre el fango. ¿Quién podía más? (2:367)

> *He walked next to Ana, almost right next to her [. . .] he clenched his large, religious candle, now extinguished, like a scepter. He was the mas-*

ter of all this. He, in spite of his enemies' slander, brought along, next to him, as his prisoner with invisible chains, the lady most admired for her beauty and generous soul in all Vetusta. [. . .] Did the Jesuits oblige the virgins of Vetusta to wear a cilice? Well he stripped naked the most desired feet of the town and dragged them through the mud . . . there they were, appearing now and again from amongst the purple velvet and the filth. Was there anyone more powerful than him?

The *cirio/cetro* (candle/scepter) phallically represents Fermín's power and sense of triumph in this scene. Resembling the devil, he sexually and sadistically revels in Ana's invisible chains, the way he drags her coveted naked feet through the mud, and the way all this is a reflection on himself and his sense of omnipotence. This scene foreshadows the ending of the novel in which a betrayed Fermín arranges for the public display of Ana's adultery and spiritual murder (complete social ostracism), reminiscent in many ways of the nuns' lynching and physical murder of Soledad in *La monja*. Indeed, de Pas's murderous desires are clearly seen at the very end of the novel when he moves forward with "un paso de asesino" (2:536; a step of a murderer) to strike Ana.

Nevertheless, despite the use of sexual and diabolical imagery to portray the hypocrisy of religious practices in *La Regenta*, female sexual perversions themselves are not tied to the Church in the way they are in the *Cura* trilogy, where enforced chastity vows and the seclusion of women in an all-female community are singled out as causes. In Alas's novel, no religious reasons are provided to explain Vetustan women's onanism, adultery, promiscuity, same-sex desire, or manliness. If any explanation is to be derived from the details of the novel, it is that Ana, Visita, and Obdulia are emotionally and sexually unfulfilled: Ana and Visita because of their marriages to emasculated men, and Obdulia because of her status as a widow. There is also a class determinism, suggestive of fears of degeneration, in the representation of Petra, Doña Paula, Doña Camila, and Teresina's deviation from their "proper" gender role, an element entirely missing from the *Cura* trilogy. So, while *La Regenta* engages the same discourses on onanism, nymphomania, and same-sex desire that the *Cura* trilogy does, the question of the Church's chastity vows is only of issue for men, who, in both works, still fare better than their female counterparts since they are able to find clandestine outlets for their desires. Indeed, the priests prove to be sexually potent, in Fermín de Pas's case, more so than the rest of the men in his town. In both works, however, middle-class women, and these women's cuckolded husbands, pay the price for the priests' depravity.

Mysticism as Hysteria

As we saw in Chapter 2, many late nineteenth- and early twentieth-century writers, such as León Mainez, reinterpreted hagiographical texts in order to show that these saints' mysticism was really hysteria. Alas himself was no stranger to this debate. His review of Alphonse Daudet's *L'évangéliste* (1883), published in 1883, a year before the first volume of *La Regenta* made its appearance, reveals Alas's familiarity with Charcot, the experiments carried out at the Salpêtrière hospital, and the medical connections Charcot made between religion and hysteria. The article also gives some insight into the degree to which Alas accepted Charcot's conclusion that extreme religiosity in women was a form of hysteria. Alas begins the article by noting that Daudet's novel is dedicated to Charcot, and that the hospital where the latter does his work, La Salpêtrière, "está en moda" (is in fashion). He also makes reference to *L'iconographie photographique de La Salpêtrière* (1878–1880). He then refers to a piece by the Jesuit priest Benoît, published in the *Revista del Mundo Católico* (The Catholic world review), that criticizes Charcot for not distinguishing between mystical ecstasy and hysteria, to which Alas responds, "dice que no hay que confundir los fenómenos naturales que se observan en la Salpêtrière con los arrebatos místicos del éxtasis. La imparcialidad exige declarar que los argumentos del sabio jesuita no son muy satisfactorios" (He says that we should not confuse the natural phenomena we observe at the Salpêtrière with the mystical raptures of ecstasy. Impartiality requires [us] to declare that the wise Jesuit's arguments are not very satisfactory).

He adds sarcastically that in order for Father Benoît to demonstrate that the two phenomena were indeed different, he would have to prove that Saint Thomas really levitated.[71] Moreover, while Alas criticizes Ramón León Mainez Fernández's work *Teresa de Jesús ante la crítica* (1880), in which Mainez diagnoses Santa Teresa as a hysteric,[72] as distasteful and painful, he agrees intellectually with his thesis.[73] Furthermore, a year before his critique of Mainez, in 1879, Alas claims that despite Santa Teresa's genius, she, and women like her, still "son mucho menos grandes que las grandes mujeres, que sólo como mujeres han sido inmortalizadas por la historia o imaginadas por la fábula. ¿Qué son Aspasia, Hipatia, la monja dramaturga, Madame Roland, Madame Staël, Santa Teresa, etc., etc., ante Eva, Ifigenia, Antífona, Electra, María, que sólo fueron mujeres?" (are much less great than great women, who just as women have been immortalized by history or imagined by fables. What are Aspasia, Hipatia, the playwright nun, Madame Roland, Madame Staël, Santa Teresa, etc., compared to Eve, Ifigenia, Antífona, Electra, María, who were just women?).[74] Alas also expressed cynicism about many of Santa Teresa's claims, asking his readers: "¿Creen que Jesús se le aparecía en efecto a la santa? ¿Creen todo lo que ella [dice]? No, de fijo no. [. . .] Pues, ¿entonces?" (Do you think Jesus truly appeared to the Saint? Do you believe all that she [says]? No, certainly not. [. . .] So, then?).[75]

Thus, it appears that even in the case of the canonized Spanish saint, whom Alas admired for her virtue, discipline, and artistic production, he was skeptical about the authenticity of her claims, her sanity, and even her decision to give up the traditional female role. In the case of Santa Teresa, I would therefore agree with Valis's conclusion that Alas did not completely reject the argument of Teresa as a hysteric, but that he respected the saint too much to get involved in her defamation.[76] While DuPont, in *Writing Teresa: The Saint from Ávila at the Fin-de-siglo*, makes a convincing case for the evolution of Alas's views on Santa Teresa after the publication of *La Regenta*,[77] his views at the time of penning *La Regenta* give us the best clues as to how he intended us to read the novel when he wrote it.[78]

It therefore comes as little surprise that in *La Regenta* the narrator juxtaposes Ana's mystical narrative to a more compelling hysterical narrative. To begin with, we are told that Ana has her first mystical visions as an adolescent living with her aunts in Loreto.[79] Ana's mystical visions occurred during the same period that Ana had her first hysterical attack, which, as the reader is told on several occasions, corresponds to the time she reached the "edad crítica" (critical period), or puberty.[80] Later, Ana's first confessor, Don Cayetano, trying to dissuade Ana from entering the convent, tells her that "todo aquello de haber llorado de amor leyendo a San Agustín y a San Juan de la Cruz no valía nada; había sido cosa de la *edad crítica* que atravesaba entonces" (1:241; emphasis mine; all that business about having cried of love reading Saint Augustine and San Juan de la Cruz wasn't anything; it has been related to the *onset of menstruation* that she was going through at the time). And later, Don Cayetano repeats this interpretation of Ana's early mystical experiences telling Don Fermín that "ella ha visto visiones . . . pseudo-místicas . . . allá en Loreto . . . al llegar la edad . . . cosa de la sangre . . . al ser mujercita, cuando tuvo aquella fiebre" (1:398; she had visions . . . pseudo-mystical [visions] . . . there in Loreto . . . with the onset of mens . . . the blood thing . . . upon becoming a woman, when she had that fever). This overlapping of the onset of Ana's menstruation/hysteria and Ana's first mystical visions was most certainly intentional.

As mentioned above, in 1883, a year before the publication of *La Regenta*, Alas reviewed Alphonse Daudet's novel *L'évangéliste* in the newspaper *El progreso* (Progress). Alas is generous in his praise of Daudet's novel about "la manía pseudo-religiosa [. . .] en pobres mujeres" (pseudo-religious mania [. . .] in poor women).[81] Discussing Daudet's ability to reveal all the causes of the protagonist's disease, Alas states that "el autor describe con gran maestría todas las circunstancias que contribuyeron a este resultado; hasta señala el momento, difícil para la joven, en que al hacerse mujer, sufrió gran sacudida en todo su ser, y para siempre ya fue débil y nerviosa" (the author describes with great mastery all the circumstances that contributed to this result; even pointing out the moment, difficult for the young woman, in which upon becoming a woman, she suffered a great shock in her entire being, and thereafter was always nervous and weak).[82] Alas was clearly familiar with medical theories that associated puberty with hysteria in women, and apparently felt it was appropriate material for a novel on the same subject. Thus, by connecting Ana's mystical experiences with the onset of her menstruation and her first hysterical attacks, the narrator not only presents the reader with an alternative interpretation of Ana's self-proclaimed religious vocation, but also with medical explanations for Ana's hysteria (not mysticism). In comparison with *El cura*, while Gracia's passage through puberty also brings about hysteria, it is not related specifically to religious fanaticism. However, in Melita's case in *La monja*, the beginnings of puberty correspond with her becoming a "santurrona" (religious zealot) like her mother.[83]

Ana's mystical experiences themselves are also of an ambiguous nature. The descriptions of her mystical raptures are sexualized by emphasizing the similar sensations Ana has during both religious and sexual situations. For example, in one instance of mystical rapture, the narrator tells us that Ana felt as if "sus entrañas entrasen en una fundición" (2:208; her core melted). Not only is this the part of the body associated with the womb, the organ said to cause hysteria, but the sensation is similar to the sexual arousal Ana feels right before giving in to Don Álvaro's seduction: "Ana sentía un placer *puramente material*, pensaba ella, en aquel sitio de sus entrañas que no era el vientre ni el corazón, sino en el medio" (2:426; emphasis in the original; Ana felt a *purely material* pleasure, she thought, in that place of her core that wasn't her stomach or her heart, but rather in between). This is also the very same region of the body where Ana feels sensations when recovering from her illness: "se le había trasladado al pecho, más abajo, mejor, no sabía dónde, no era en el estómago, era claro, pero tampoco en el corazón, era en el medio" (2:212; it had moved to her chest, lower, actually, she didn't know where, it wasn't her stomach, that was for sure, but it also wasn't her heart, it was in between).[84] Thus, the sensations Ana feels in a state of mystical rapture originate in the womb, the organ associated with her feelings of sexual arousal and her hysteria, blurring the lines between divine revelation, sexual arousal, and disease.

The reader further doubts Ana's ability to distinguish between the sexual and the spiritual since Ana constantly confuses the two while other characters are able to make the distinction. For example, during the theatrical representation of *Don Juan Tenorio* Ana claims to have experienced "una piedad consoladora, lágrimas de amor de Dios, esperanza infinita, caridad sin límites" (2:69; a consoling piety, tears of love of God, infinite hope, charity without limits). De Pas, recognizing the highly sexual nature of the play, responds by castigating Ana for her conflation of divine love and erotic, sacrilegious love.[85] Don Fermín's understanding of the sexual nature of Ana's "religious" experience is reinforced by the medical texts of the time that targeted the theater for exciting the female imagination and leading women into bouts of hysteria and/or nymphomania. For example, Pouillet explains how such spectacles arouse the female imagination and lead to certain vices that can cause hysteria and nymphomania.[86] Thus, Ana's inability to recognize the sexual nature of her professed religious experience is underscored by both the medical "knowledge" of the time about the pernicious nature of theater on the female imagination, and Don Fermín's recognition of the nonspiritual nature of Zorrilla's famous play. Because of Ana's tendency to confuse the sexual with the spiritual, the reader is made to doubt the authenticity of Ana's religious experiences and is more inclined to view Ana as a sexually repressed hysteric, rather than a mystic.

In the *Cura* trilogy, it is Gertrudis and Melita who confuse mystical love with sexual love. Gertrudis actively seeks to replace her former lover with religion: "había acudido á la religión y al sacerdote huyendo del amor, y al pie del altar, en el mismo confesionario, encontróse con el amor de nuevo" (*El confesionario*, 174; she had turned to religion and the priest fleeing love, and at the foot of the altar, in the confessional itself, she found love again). The sexual attraction between confessor and confessant is immediate and immediately sublimated through religious practices by which Román, although attracted to Gertrudis sexually, attempts to obliquely satiate his desires through Gertrudis's displays of devotion, penitence, and mysticism (128). Gertrudis willingly plays along in this game until she finally comes to see, in *La monja*, the true nature of their relationship. Similarly, Melita's first love is Jesus himself, a love that is expressed entirely in nuptial and sexual metaphors as Melita prepares to become Christ's bride (*La monja*, 1–13). However, it is precisely her sexual naïveté that allows her to be convinced, at the young age of sixteen, that she wants to be a nun for the rest of her life (13). And this same sexual naïveté is what allows Melita to be easily manipulated into participating in the nuns' homoerotic activities. However, unlike Gertrudis or Ana, Melita dies before she realizes the way she has incorrectly confused sexual love for spiritual love.

The effects mystical texts produce in Ana can easily be seen as a sign of her hysteria as well. The imagination and its over-excitation through reading were directly linked to hysteria and nymphomania in women in the nineteenth century. While doctors often pointed to novel reading as a source of this problem, mystical literature was also directly targeted. We see this in the *Cura* trilogy with Gracia, Gertrudis, and Melita, all of whom read Santa Teresa and other mystical texts. The French medical doctor Thésée Pouillet expresses a similar condemnation of mystical literature as a tool for inciting the behavior against which it is supposed to be fighting:

> No quiero tampoco hablar de la abominable redacción de los libros místicos y de los cánticos en que el amor divino se halla explicado por frases demasiado sensuales en nuestro entender. Algunas reformas en estas cuestiones que no hemos querido profundizar, serían muy bien recibidas por la gente imparcial, que no podría entonces repetir con el autor de *Maudit*: "Así como la dirección, las lecturas místicas y los libros de piedad escritos para los jóvenes en los que queriéndolos enseñar á ser castos, se les enseña el modo de no serlo, consuman una verdadera violación moral."[87]

> *I also do not want to speak of the abominable rhetoric of mystical books and canticles in which divine love is explained with overly sensual passages, in our opinion. Some reforms on these questions that we have not wanted to go into depth on would be very well received by sensible*

people, who would then not have to repeat along with the author of Mau-
dit:[88] *"Just like [spiritual] direction, mystical readings and pious works*
written for young people in which, in order to teach them to be chaste,
actually teach them the way not to be, they are immoral."

It is therefore not surprising that after reading San Juan de la
Cruz's *Cantar de los cantares* (Song of songs), Ana feels "nerviosa"
and "excitada" (1:208; nervous [and] excited), or that after reading
Santa Teresa's *Vida*, she falls into a state of religious exaltation and
writes a letter to Don Fermín in which she proclaims that she is in
love (*enamorada*) with God, and willing to prove her devotion to De
Pas through masochistic behaviors.[89] The ability of mystical literature to incite sexual feelings is further reinforced by the fact that
the narrator tells us that Ana's father, a secular and liberal-minded
man, kept San Juan's *Cantar de los cantares* "entre los libros prohi-
bidos para Ana" (1:208; among the books Ana was prohibited [from
reading]) since he was skeptical about the religious nature of this
text.[90] In spite of her father's prohibition, Ana reads the book any-
way and shortly thereafter has a "mystical" experience (1:210).

Many nineteenth- and early twentieth-century doctors concluded that mystical ecstasy was a pathological variation of sexual
orgasm. For example, Marie argued that mystical rapture was a
physiological phenomenon produced through *coitos imaginarios*
(fantasies of intercourse) with the divine,[91] and Henry Maudsley,
that it was a form of "vicarious sexual orgasm."[92] In his text *Misticismo y locura*, Marie suggests that the figure of Jesus is materialized and sexualized in the consciousness of the female mystic.[93]
As we saw in Chapter 2, a similar claim was made during coerced
Inquisition testimonies in which self-proclaimed female mystics
were made to confess that their professed mystical unions with
God had really been carnal acts performed with the devil disguised
as the figure of Christ. The belief that Jesus somehow materialized
as the female mystic's carnal lover is seen in the *Cura* trilogy and
in Alas's novel as well. In *El cura*, Gracia eroticizes the figure of
Christ and is sexually aroused by it (26), in *El confesionario*, Gertrudis tries to follow Román's instructions to replace human love with

divine love and to form an intimate union with Jesus (95–97), and in *La monja*, Melita falls mystically in love with Jesus while going through puberty (1–13). In *La Regenta*, on one occasion, Ana recognizes Don Álvaro, her suitor, as Jesus's rival, since a simple visit by the Vetustan Don Juan is able to upset her professed devotion to Jesus. Disturbed by this, Ana cries out: "Jesús, Jesús, tú no puedes tener un rival. Sería infame, sería asqueroso" (2:219; Jesus, Jesus, you cannot have a rival. It would be despicable, it would be disgusting). The equation of Don Álvaro with Christ is also made evident in the scene in which Ana finally gives in to Álvaro's seduction and, from the balcony, responds to her suitor's call with "¡Jesús!" (2:442). Although Sobejano appears to dismiss the mixing of the sexual and religious in this particular passage, the fact is that the confusion of the two in this phrase is in keeping with the narrator's attempt to underscore the sexual nature of Ana's religious experiences throughout the text.[94] Moreover, as the line that closes one of the most momentous chapters in the novel, it calls even more attention to Ana's confusion of carnal and spiritual love. Of course, Don Álvaro's own last name, "Mesía" (Messiah), as Sobejano points out, equates Ana's lover with the physical person of the Messiah.[95]

Another way the text sexualizes the mystical experience in the novel is through the intertextual references to Santa Teresa. As we saw in previous chapters, there was much debate in the late nineteenth century regarding whether Santa Teresa was truly a hysteric. Saillard, in fact, has studied in detail the symptoms of Ana's disease, such as migraines, nightmares, feeling of suffocation, inability to swallow, fainting, dizziness, palpitations, and fever, in order to show how they are similar to the symptoms of Santa Teresa's supposed illness as well as to nineteenth-century medical descriptions of hysteria.[96] And throughout the *Cura* trilogy, Santa Teresa's discourse is clearly code for sexual feelings and actions. Thus, the fact that Ana turns to Santa Teresa as a spiritual model already puts the authenticity of Ana's spiritual pursuits into question. Ana reads Santa Teresa's autobiography and consciously attempts to imitate the saint's life.[97] However, as Sobejano points out in his introduction to the novel, Santa Teresa is not only Ana's model, but Alas's model as well.[98] In other words, many of the events in Ana's life closely parallel those that occur in Santa Teresa's *Vida*: both Ana and Teresa grow up without a mother and attempt to compensate for this lack of motherly affection through their adoration of the Virgin; both read literature as young girls and fancy running off and participating in the crusade against the Moors; both suffer from a chronic yet imprecise illness; both recount a disturbing encounter with a toad; both share a similar vision of hell (Ana's vision comes to her in a dream); and both experience mystical rapture.[99] These intertextual references further undermine Ana's spiritual claims: first because Ana chooses an already disputed model, and second because Ana falls short of emulating the Spanish saint. Not only do Ana's feelings of piety often wane, but she also dismisses the rigors that Santa Teresa says are necessary for the spiritual life: "algunas opiniones de la Santa prefería pasarlas por alto, estaban en pugna con las ideas propias; 'al fin no en balde habían pasado tres siglos'" (2:213; she preferred to disregard some of the Saint's opinions, they were in conflict with her own ideas; "after all, it wasn't in vain that three centuries had passed"). Ana takes from Santa Teresa what she likes and dismisses the rest, making her less consistent and virtuous than the Spanish saint. When she finally gives in to Don Álvaro, Ana herself comes to recognize the difference between sexual and spiritual delights: the former is effortless, tangible, and natural while the latter is arduous, abstract, and unnatural.[100] What makes Santa Teresa more worthy of respect than Ana then is her virtue, discipline, and ability to focus on the nonmaterial abstraction of God. In contrast, Ana's pursuit of sexual pleasure is merely a passive surrender to the natural instincts of the body.[101]

It is important to point out here, however, that the distinction the text makes between Ana and Santa Teresa does not necessarily signal an acceptance of the divine nature of Santa Teresa's experiences, but rather an admiration of the Spanish saint's character and moral strength, qualities that Ana does not share. In his review of Marcelino Menéndez y Pelayo's *Historia de la literatura* in "Lecturas," Alas makes clear that for those, like himself, who are not orthodox

Catholics like Menéndez y Pelayo, what is admirable about Santa Teresa can be appreciated on a human level. He criticizes Menéndez y Pelayo because "no podrá hacernos ver lo más sublime en la Santa, que es, para muchos, para los que no participan de la ortodoxia del autor, el valor pura y exclusivamente humano del esfuerzo místico" (he cannot make us see the most sublime thing about the Saint, which is, for many, for those who don't share the orthodoxy of the author, the purely and exclusively human value of the mystical effort).[102] Therefore, although the novel makes a distinction between Ana and Santa Teresa, it does not necessarily signal Alas's rejection of Santa Teresa's hysteria diagnosis. So even though Santa Teresa's own autobiography was being re-interpreted by the medical community, and her divine favors being put into question, she is portrayed as morally superior to Ana on a purely human level, converting Ana's story into a sexual parody of the disputed saint's life.

Conclusion

Judging by the scientific determinism of López Bago's writings, there is little to indicate that he adhered to traditional Catholic doctrine in any way. However, according to one obituary, in the last year of his life he sought redemption and retracted his writings. [103] In contrast Alas's views on religion are more open to interpretation. According to Lissorgues, there have been two major trends in the interpretation of Alas's religious and philosophical positions. The first views his religious beliefs as going through a series of phases.[104] Very influential in this line of thinking was Pedro Sainz Rodríguez's *La obra de Clarín* (1921; The works of Clarín), in which he divided Alas's religious development into three distinct periods: a romantic and highly religious youth, a period of skepticism influenced by his exposure to Kraussism in which he hid his religiosity, and a final period characterized by profound spiritual reflection.[105] More recently and falling within this trend, Denise DuPont has argued that Alas's views of Santa Teresa de Jesús evolved with the years.[106] The other biographical trend sees Alas's position on religion as essentially unwavering throughout his life.[107] However, even within this second trend, there are different opinions as to what exactly Alas's beliefs were. Lissorgues himself, for example, argues that, excluding his childhood, Clarín always sought an authentic faith and an ethical existence independent from orthodox Catholic thinking. For this reason, Lissorgues sees no contradiction between Alas's spirituality and his harsh criticisms of the institution of the Church and of religious hypocrisy.[108] However, other critics view Alas's faith as more traditional. Francisco Pérez Gutiérrez, for example, emphasizes Alas's traditional religious upbringing and argues that the beliefs he acquired in his youth carried with him throughout his life.[109]

Alas's views on mysticism have also been of interest to scholars. According to Adolfo Posada, the Asturian writer confessed to having had mystical experiences as a young man.[110] Moreover, Ramón Pérez de Ayala wrote in his "Ensayo-prólogo" (Essay-prologue) to J. Díez Canejas's book, *Paisajes de reconquista* (Landscapes of reconquest), that he personally saw Clarín "llorar en la cátedra, de amor y entusiasmo, glosando al propio San Francisco o a Santa Teresa de Jesús" (cry at his professor's podium, of love and enthusiasm, commenting on the very same Saint Francis or Santa Teresa de Jesús).[111] Alas's professed proclivity for mysticism, as well as other biographical details, such as his being "un joven un tanto enfermizo, hipersensible [y] tímido" (a somewhat sickly, hypersensitive [and] timid young man) have led Pérez Gutiérrez to suggest that Alas based his protagonist Ana Ozores on himself.[112] However, such readings, as Saillard points out, not only overlook the ironic detachment with which the narrator treats his protagonist, but the unlikelihood that Alas would have portrayed his personal religious development through the character of an adulterous, female hysteric.[113] Here, Saillard touches on an important point in relation to Alas's views on religion and mysticism: the question of gender.

Alas made a point of criticizing the pernicious effect that religion had on women. As we have seen, many doctors and liberal thinkers of the time believed that religion was dangerous for women. Due to their supposed lack of intelligence, excitable imaginations, and overall sensitivity, women were said to be easily carried away by religious insanity. Alas seems to have agreed with this medical consensus, speaking out in 1875 against the abundance of female "Quijotes con devocionarios" (Quixotes with devotionaries) in Restoration Spain who had been incited to extremes by their confessors.[114] In an 1876 article Clarín wrote that one of the two main negative trends in contemporary religion was "la tendencia mística, sensual [. . .] para las damas nerviosas, de corazón sensible, entusiástico y propensas a las cavilosidades y encrucijadas de los sentimientos alambicados" (the sensual, mystical tendency [. . .] in nervous ladies, of a sensitive heart, enthusiastic and inclined to brooding and the crossing of intricate feelings).[115] And in an 1877 review of Benito Pérez Galdós's novel *Gloria*, he argued that "cuando una mujer es vulgar, como las más, y también quiere echar su cuarto a espadas en misticismo y humildad cristiana, etc., etc., el carácter se hace falso y degenera en mil abominaciones" (when a woman is coarse, as most are, and also wants to give her two cents on mysticism and Christian humility, etc., etc., her character becomes false and degenerates into a thousand abominations).[116] It would seem that just such a woman was to become the protagonist of his greatest literary work.[117]

Yet, at the same time, Clarín had no fondness for the virulent anticlerical novels dealing with similar themes being published at the same time.[118] Moreover, similar to the way he criticized Mainez for his crude manner of criticizing Santa Teresa, Alas attacked the radical naturalists for their lack of talent and art.[119] In addition to these aesthetic differences between Alas's work and that of López Bago, I have tried to show in this chapter how the *Cura* trilogy also differs from Alas's work precisely in its lack of psychological development and metaphysics, at least in its treatment of its female protagonists, and in the question of moral choice. While it is society's fault that Ana is in an ill-suited marriage, and nature's fault that she has hysteria, her adultery is the result of a poor judgment. Similarly, while Ana's dabbling with writing and mysticism is attributed to her improper upbringing and later the corrupting influence of the Church, it is also due to her pride, which is portrayed as a moral and spiritual defect. There is also a clear distinction between Santa Teresa's moral high ground and Ana's religious hypocrisy, a distinction not made in López Bago's novels where the narrator dismisses mysticism and Catholic tradition altogether since, for him, there is no virtue outside obedience to natural laws. Nevertheless, neither work holds out any real options for the typical middle-class woman who does not fit in neatly with the Angel in the House ideology. Thus, the female characters and their mystical experiences are completely sexualized in both works according to the prevalent medical discourses of the day. Despite the psychological explanations and the free will offered up in Alas's literary universe, any and all paths to self-realization outside of marriage and motherhood are still foreclosed to women. This is not the case in the writings of Emilia Pardo Bazán where it is neither nature, science, nor morality that entrap women, but an oppressive patriarchal society. Furthermore, as I argue in the next chapter, the Galician writer seeks precisely to vindicate female mystics, past and present, and to argue that mystical theology provides the philosophical basis for female emancipation.

5   Bucking the Trend

Emilia Pardo Bazán on Hysteria and Mysticism in Women

THE WRITINGS AND ideas of Emilia Pardo Bazán have often baffled critics. Although obviously progressive in her views on female emancipation, her criticism of liberalism and science, her apparent disdain for bourgeois culture, her sympathies for the Catholic Church, and her purported puritanical views on sexuality have made her a controversial and enigmatic figure. In his 1971 book on Pardo Bazán, Walter T. Pattison writes that "despite her feminism and modern views, she set great store on aristocratic rank, she was sympathetic to Carlism and the 'old' Spain, she had no faith in the democratic process, and she is not tolerant of non-Catholic religions."[1] In regard to the question of sexuality Pattison adds that for Pardo Bazán, "nature included a repugnant factor, and this element had to do with sex. [. . .] Nature, in its dependence on sexual reproduction, was bad."[2] Although Pattison is writing in 1971, more recent studies have continued to view Pardo Bazán as sexually, religiously, and politically conservative. For example, in an article dealing with Pardo Bazán's last novel, *Dulce dueño*, Marina Mayoral (1989) argues that the protagonist's repulsion toward sexuality represents the author's own feelings, and in a 1998 study on the same work, Raquel Medina points to Pardo Bazán's conservatism by arguing that the novel demonstrates the Galician author's opposition to the rise of the bourgeoisie and her support of a feudal society.[3]

Biographer Pilar Faus Sevilla (2003) argues that Pardo Bazán, in her later years, left behind her concerns about social justice and became increasingly conservative.[4] And in her 2019 biography of the author, Isabel Burdiel writes that, as part of the regenerationist movement, Pardo Bazán rejected liberalism and promoted patriotism, specifically putting the nation before all else, as the only way to move the nation forward.[5] However, examining Pardo Bazán's views on liberalism, science, sexuality, and religion in relation to her feminist agenda and to the cultural obstacles she was encountering in seemingly progressive institutions complicates such views of the Galician writer. Indeed, here I agree with Denise DuPont's assertion that "the labels of liberal and progressive are not particularly helpful when we try to describe her position on social issues."[6]

It is true that Pardo Bazán was skeptical about the promises of liberalism.[7] From her perspective, liberalism had not changed Spanish political life much at all. She claimed that liberals had not reduced the national deficit or the national debt, that they had no clearly established foreign policy, and that *caciquismo* (system of political bosses) was still the law of the land.[8] For Pardo Bazán, liberalism was nothing more than a name that still seemed to carry a promise of true political reform, while in reality it differed very little from opposing parties and political systems.[9] However, probably most important to Pardo Bazán was liberals' lack of interest in improving the situation of women. Contrasting Spanish society before and after the War of Independence (1808–1814), she argued that liberalism had actually worsened Spanish women's position because the discrepancy between the two sexes had not been legally reinforced when no one had political freedom. In the nineteenth century, however, as men claimed their constitutional rights, women became second-class citizens: "Más iguales [antes de la guerra de la independencia] el varón y la hembra en sus funciones de ciudadanía, puesto que aquél no ejercía aún los derechos políticos que hoy le otorga el sistema parlamentario negándolos por completo a la mujer, la sociedad no se dividía como ahora, en dos porciones políticas y nacionalmente heterogéneas" (Men and women [were] more equal in their exercise of citizenship [before the

War of Independence], since men still did not exercise the political rights that the parliamentary system gives them today [while at the same time] denying [these same rights] to women entirely; society was not divided as it is now, into two political groups that are nationally heterogeneous).[10] Thus, to a large degree, Pardo Bazán's lack of enthusiasm for liberalism stemmed from her anger with liberals' refusal to improve the status of women within Spanish society as well as her belief that, as men obtained greater freedoms, women's position within society became progressively worse. This view concurs with recent scholarship that has shown the way nineteenth-century Spanish liberalism specifically sought to keep women and other subaltern groups marginalized.[11]

Pardo Bazán's opposition to certain scientific theories of her time also needs to be understood within the appropriate context. She criticized the scientific movement for its reductiveness in its understanding of the human subject. For example, in *La cuestión palpitante* (1883; The burning question) she argued against naturalism's scientific determinism. In her opinion, scientific theories that held that heredity and environment completely determined the behavior of an individual denied the psychological aspect of human existence as well as any concept of individual free will. In "Reflexiones científicas contra el darwinismo" (1877; Scientific reflections against Darwinism), she objected to the way science claimed to be able to understand a human being in her entirety through the study of her body.[12] Although Pardo Bazán believed that such theories were reductive for both sexes, she stressed that they were even more so in regard to women since, in defining "woman," science looked only to the female reproductive organs and denied women any spiritual or psychological dimension beyond that which could be related to the functioning of these organs. In response to the Marquis del Busto's speech on the proper role of woman in society, Pardo Bazán criticized the Marquis precisely for this type of reductiveness:

da en el grosero materialismo de considerar que el fin de la existencia de un ser racional puede estar condicionado, en primer término, no por la racionalidad que le otorgó el Criador para distinguirle de la bestia, sino por las consecuencias de la función de aparatos y órganos destinados á la reproducción y conservación de la especie, que nos son comunes con los irracionales. [. . .] No otra cosa significa la sobada afirmación, que adopta el Sr. Marqués, de que "la mujer ha nacido para el amor como esposa y madre."[13]

[He] advances the vulgar materialism of considering that the purpose of existence of a rational being can be determined, in the first place, not by the reason the Creator gave him in order to distinguish him from other animals, but rather by the results of the functions of the organs and apparatuses involved in reproduction and the preservation of the species, which we share with irrational beings. [. . .] That is exactly what the Marquis is saying with his hackneyed statement that "women are born for love as wives and mothers.

In contrast to her skepticism about certain scientific theories and practices, Pardo Bazán often asserted her strong Catholic faith. These declarations have often automatically placed her in the conservative camp as well. However, there are many indications that her faith was not as conventional as is often stated, and some of her contemporaries even doubted that she was religious at all.[14] The aspects of Christianity that attracted Pardo Bazán, such as its advocacy of gender equality and its canonization of female mystics, were not the most orthodox. In "La educación del hombre y de la mujer" (1892, The education of men and women), for example, she praises Christianity's message of equality between the sexes, thereby directly linking her faith to her support of feminism.[15] And in her "Apuntes autobiográficos" (1886; Autobiographical notes), she defines her own intellectual outlook on life as a combination of mystical philosophy and critical thinking.[16] Her concept of mysticism, which has always held a marginal position within society and the Catholic Church, was closely related to the importance of artistic creation in her life. For her, the experience of art was a mystical one: "El arte no es otra cosa sino la comunión del alma individual con el alma colectiva" (Art is nothing other than the communion of the individual soul with the collective soul).[17] According to DuPont, "art as she practiced it was not a rival, but rather a vehicle, for religion."[18]

Pardo Bazán's affinity for mystical theology can also be related to her belief that answers to metaphysical questions cannot be obtained through science.[19] The idea that sense perception could not disclose truth/reality probably appealed to Pardo Bazán because it effectively contested scientific theories on the nature of women. In keeping with the mystical distrust in the ability of traditional forms of knowledge to reveal truth, Pardo Bazán stated that the only truly scientific assertion to be made regarding reality was that we are ignorant about it: "el modesto *Ignorabimus* de Du Bois Reymond [es] el rasgo de sinceridad más noble y más auténticamente científico de nuestro siglo" (the modest *We will never know* of Du Bois Reymond [is] the most noble and most authentically scientific gesture of our century).[20] By revealing the weaknesses of all systems of knowledge, mystical theology turned the human subject into an ineffable and transcendental signified. This obfuscation of the subject served Pardo Bazán as a powerful tool for deconstructing undesirable concepts of "woman" and, consequently, of herself. Like the mystics, Pardo Bazán could claim that the nature of her existence as a woman was beyond the realm of science.

The portrayal of Pardo Bazán as a sexual prude is generally drawn from two texts, her "Apuntes autobiográficos" where she describes her reaction upon viewing pornographic material for the first time, and her last novel, *Dulce dueño* (1911; Sweet master), where the protagonist, out of disgust, renounces sex forever. While the novel is analyzed in detail below, a few words about her "Apuntes" seem in order. In this prologue to the first edition of *Los pazos de Ulloa* (1886; The house of Ulloa), Pardo Bazán tells how, as a young girl of eleven or twelve exploring her father's library in La Coruña, she decided to look inside some books that seemed to have been intentionally placed out of reach. She describes her reaction as one of "tedio, despecho y rabia" (aversion, indignation, anger) which caused her to impulsively throw the books back on the shelf. However, Pardo Bazán adds that as a somewhat sheltered young girl, her reaction was completely instinctual. Moreover, she admits that since that time she has read many such books, although she claims that she cannot appreciate erotic material unless it is artistically presented.[21] The passage from her "Apuntes," therefore, does not necessarily indicate the prudish nature of the adult Pardo Bazán.

Furthermore, Pardo Bazán led a very unconventional lifestyle for a middle-class woman of her time. Although married, she was separated from her husband and had romantic relationships with other men. Moreover, she argued against those who censured realist and naturalist novels for containing sexually explicit material that was not appropriate for female readers. She argued that women were better off knowing what the world was about rather than remaining in a naïve, childlike state of innocence.[22] In addition, her novel *Insolación* (1889; Sunstroke), in which an unmarried woman (a young widow) chooses to sleep with a man with whom she is not married without suffering any immediate consequences, was condemned by many of her contemporaries, including Alas, the author of *La Regenta*, as immoral. Thus, in many ways the Galician author seems to have been quite modern in her thinking about sexuality.

Pardo Bazán's main objection to sexuality seems to have had more to do with the scientific trend of viewing the sex drive as the principal motivation of all human behavior, as demonstrated in the novels of López Bago. Although she acknowledged that the sex drive was very powerful in human beings, she argued that it was not the only motivation for human behavior, and that it should not be a factor that limited or restricted other aspects of human existence. According to Pardo Bazán, sexual desires are

> un móvil poderosísimo de las acciones humanas—humanas, entiéndase bien, de varones y hembras, que forman la humanidad; —mas ni son el móvil único ni el único fin de la criatura racional, ni han de ofrecerse en ningún caso como negación ó limitación forzosa de otros móviles y fines altísimos, como el social, el artístico, el político, el científico, el religioso, ni siquiera al ejercicio de la libertad individual indiscutible, que implica el derecho absoluto al celibato y á la esterilidad.[23]

a very powerful motive of human behavior—human meaning, to be
clear, men and women, both of whom form humanity; —but they are
not the only motive nor the only purpose of a rational being, nor should
they be used under any circumstances as a reason to deny or forcefully
restrict other motives and noble objectives, like social, artistic, politi-
cal, scientific, religious objectives, and much less [to limit] the exercise
of inalienable individual freedoms, which include the absolute right to
remain celibate or to choose not to have children.

Thus, Pardo Bazán's negative reactions to certain questions related to sex and sexuality derive from her aversion to the scientific theories that claimed that a woman's sexuality limited her capabilities, particularly since such arguments were ultimately used to deny women the same rights as men. Rather, Pardo Bazán desired to understand the female subject as something more than the product of the sexual instincts of her material body, a position that clearly informed her views on hysteria.

Reinterpreting Hysteria under Patriarchy in "La novia fiel" and "Error de diagnóstico"

In her literary works, Emilia Pardo Bazán both reproduced and subverted medical theories on hysteria and women.[24] She rejected the notion of the female body as inherently pathological and pointed to social and political causes for the frequent manifestation of this "disease" in women, as well as to the blatant misogyny in the practice of medicine at the time. Gabriela Pozzi has explored the ways Pardo Bazán engaged and challenged medical theories on female hysteria in her fantastical fiction, while Robin Ragan has argued that Pardo Bazán intentionally left out the symptoms of hysteria connected to female sexuality in *Los pazos de Ulloa* in order to highlight the social causes of the disease.[25] Most recently, Colleen McAlister shows how the novel *Doña Milagros* (1894) demonstrates that hysteria affects both men and women who are unable to conform to limiting and artificially constructed gender roles.[26] In keeping with these critics' arguments, I seek to elucidate the way Pardo Bazán's story "La novia fiel" (1894; The faithful fiancée) specifically engages the question of female sexual frustration and hysteria in order to dismantle prevailing notions of the disease. Then I look at the way "Error de diagnóstico" (1907; An incorrect diagnosis) takes medical doctors to task for using the hysteria diagnosis to mask their own ignorance and prejudice in regard to women and their bodies.

"LA NOVIA FIEL"

Most criticism on "La novia fiel" has explored the story as a critique of the sexual double standard and women's entrapment in, and resistance to, passivity.[27] The story, however, clearly alludes to dominant notions of hysteria as a disease that manifested itself in women who were not sexually satisfied.[28] The protagonist of the story, Amelia, is a young, unmarried woman who begins to exhibit signs of hysteria, after having waited nine years for her fiancé to marry her.[29] However, it is not until she acknowledges the cause of her "illness"—"deseo, ansia, necesidad de casarse" (1:306; desire, yearning, a need to get married)—and more importantly, the reason for her fiancé Germán's tranquility—his freedom and ability to satisfy these same desires elsewhere—that Amelia suffers a full-blown hysterical attack: "Al explicarse ahora la verdadera causa de esa paciencia y esa resignación incomparables [. . .], una carcajada sardónica dilató sus labios, mientras en su garganta creía sentir un nudo corredizo que se apretaba poco a poco y la estrangulaba. La convulsión fue horrible, larga, tenaz" (1:306–7; Learning now the true cause of [Germán's] incomparable patience and resignation [. . .], a sardonic guffaw expanded her lips, while in her throat she felt a slipknot that was being tightened little by little and was strangling her. The convulsion was horrible, long, and tenacious).[30]

The description of Amelia's hysterical attack is very similar to those described by doctors of the time and is reminiscent of Ana Ozores's attack in *La Regenta*, and Gracia Acebedo's hysterical fit in *El cura*.[31] In all three case the resemblance between the hysterical fit and female orgasm is obvious.[32] While many twentieth- and twenty-first-century feminists have sought to dismiss and/or deconstruct the medical connections that were being made in the nineteenth century between hysteria and female sexuality by pointing to the many other social factors that were making women ill, others have chosen to explore this connection further in order to better understand the strong sexual connotations of the disease.[33] In keeping with the latter approach, Rachel Maines reveals that indeed, due to the repression of female sexuality and misunderstandings about the female sexual response, many women in the nineteenth and early twentieth centuries suffered from frigidity and/or sexual frustration, which were then diagnosed as symptoms of "hysteria," a "disease" that needed to be treated by a doctor. The treatment often involved manual genital massage in order to produce an orgasm, which was referred to as a "hysterical paroxysm."[34] According to Maines, because most women could not reach orgasm through "normal" heterosexual intercourse alone, women's sexual arousal was seen as an "illness" and female orgasm, disguised as a "hysterical paroxysm," was perceived as the necessary crisis of that illness that needed to be produced in the doctor's office.[35] The practice of genital massage to relieve hysteria was not foreign to Spain. Viguera tells of various patients and doctors who effectively used various forms of genital stimulation to produce a "parosisimo" (paroxysm) and relieve hysterical symptoms.[36] Although Viguera affirms that this practice is effective as a treatment for hysteria, he condemns it as indecent.[37]

Like Viguera, Pulido Fernández, in his synopsis of the formal session on hysteria held by *Sociedad Ginecológica Española* in 1876, claims that one of the doctors mentions the practice of genital massage in the treatment of hysteria only to reject it as immoral.[38] Yet, regardless of whether these doctors were publicly willing to recommend the treatment, they acknowledged its existence and practice in Spain. While Pardo Bazán's story does not engage with the specifics of female sexual frustration and its medical treatment at the time, "La novia fiel," like the *Cura* trilogy and *La Regenta*, does reproduce the notion of hysteria as a disease resulting from repressed sexual desires, and of the "hysterical paroxysm" as an oblique form of sexual release—a "crisis" of a "disease" suffered by women in a society that gave them few acceptable ways of expressing their sexuality. The story shows that female sexual needs, when not allowed any legitimate means of satisfaction, found indirect and "pathological" channels of expression.

The difference between Pardo Bazán's representation of hysteria and its portrayal in many medical texts of the time, and in the works of López Bago and Alas, is that in her story the female body, or female sexuality, are not the problem, nor is it Church imposed chastity vows, but rather society's prohibition on female sexual expression. This is where the question of hysteria overlaps in Pardo Bazán's commentary on the sexual double standard, since it is evident to the reader that had Amelia been offered even some of the sexual outlets enjoyed by Germán, she would have fared much better. The priest in particular gives a clear indication of society's views on such matters when he tells Amelia that she has made a mistake by breaking off her engagement with Germán, a man he lauds for being "formal, laborioso, dispuesto a casarse" (reliable, hardworking, willing to get married), and whose sexual adventures he excuses: "Los hombres por desgracia. . . . Mientras está soltero habrá tenido esos entretenimientos. . . . Pero usted . . ." (1:307; Men unfortunately. . . . While single he probably has had some fun. . . . But you . . .).[39]

The problem of course is not only the message society gives to Amelia, but also the fact that Amelia herself has internalized this message. The narrator tells us that once Amelia becomes aware of her sexual desires, she must take recourse to "todo el freno de las nociones de honor y honestidad que le inculcaron desde la niñez" (1:306; the whole restraining effect of the notions of honor and modesty that they instilled in her as a girl) in order to prevent herself from expressing or acting on these desires. She later decides to break off entirely with Germán out of shame and the fear that she will no longer have the strength to restrain herself.[40] Thus, rather than openly defy the double standard, something that would indeed have been difficult to do at the time without risking social ostracism, Amelia prefers to deny her sexual needs and live alone with her "hysteria." We as readers, however, do not necessarily share the view of the priest or feel satisfied with Amelia's decision. The story makes clear that the virgin/whore binary leaves unmarried women like Amelia with two undesirable options: tarnishing their reputations and their chances of marriage or living with hysteria. In other words, unlike Ana Ozores and Gracia Acebedo, she keeps her "virtue," yet she fares no better.

Nevertheless, "La novia fiel" does not restrict its critique of the double standard to sexual matters. Unlike Germán, Amelia is also denied equal access to education, the right to practice a profession, and full participation in society. We see the negative effects these prohibitions have on Amelia. She is first abandoned by Germán when he goes off to school to complete a law degree. During these six years, while Germán is receiving an education at the university in Santiago de Compostela, Amelia remains at home, filling her hours reading, rereading, and responding to Germán's letters and longing for vacation to arrive so that she can see her fiancé again. While the narrator tries to convince the reader that Amelia was so entertained by these activities that "el tiempo se deslizaba insensible para [ella]" (1:305; time passed unnoticed by her), there are other indications in the text that this is not really the case. For instance, Amelia longs for vacation to arrive so that she can see Germán again. The visits themselves serve as a "grato paréntesis" (1:305; pleasant break) from his absences. When Germán decides to continue his education and pursue a doctorate in law and his letters become shorter and less frequent, due in part to Germán's distractions with other women, Amelia is left with even less to fill her time.

Then, when Germán, after completing his doctorate, decides to postpone the wedding again until he is able to get a stronger foothold in his career, Amelia begins to notice the stark contrast in their emotional and physical states. While Germán "engruesa[ba]" (became more robust) physically and spiritually, Amelia "se consumía" (wasted away), and while Germán appeared "chancero" (jocular), Amelia "empapaba la almohada en lágrimas" (1:306; soaked her pillow in tears). Amelia finally "veía la luz" (saw the light) realizing that the reason Germán is able to tolerate the lengthy engagement so much better is because he is allowed other "distractions," both sexual and otherwise (1:306). So while he grows in self-esteem, education, and experience, she is forced to repress her desires and ambitions and to remain physically, emotionally, intellectually, and socially deprived. Pardo Bazán expresses well the plight of women like Amelia in *El lirismo en la poesía francesa* (1916/1923; Lyricism in French poetry) when she states that "si el varón puede buscar salida y aire, la mujer acaba por enfermar de languidez y de fastidio" (if men can go out for air and look for outlets, women end up becoming ill from languor and boredom).[41] Thus, the story also points to women's lack of opportunity to grow intellectually and spiritually as a cause of their malaise.

It is not only the external restrictions placed on Amelia, however, but also her internalization of a restricting concept of femininity—one that requires passivity, sexual naïveté, and a complete erasure of the self—that lead to her "illness." From the very beginning of the story, Amelia appears as the object of Germán's gaze and desire. Not surprisingly, Germán is attracted precisely by Amelia's youth and innocence: she is young, blonde, and virginal (1:305). When he asks her to dance, "recogió un sí espontáneo, medio involuntario, doblemente delicioso" (1:305; he received a spontaneous yes, half involuntary, and doubly delicious). Her acceptance of his offer is "doubly delicious" because it is partially involuntary and is something that "he" collects ("recogió") from her, rather than something "she" offers.[42] Her suppressed desire and lack of initiative are what make her "truly feminine" and the type of woman Germán is interested in marrying. However, as she matures, and the awareness of her own desires and needs increases, she realizes she is losing the very qualities that attracted Germán to her in the first place. Immediately following her hysterical attack, portrayed as a type of sexual awakening, she decides to break off her relationship with Germán; she realizes that her body will speak its desires despite her best efforts to "disimular a toda costa" (1:306; dissemble at all costs). She fears that if he were to see that she too has needs, specifically sexual needs, he would cease to love her and/or want to marry her as she would no longer incarnate for him the ideal of virginal femininity, the ideal that she "faithfully" insists on embodying in order to remain an object worthy of Germán's love. Thus, as Joyce Tolliver explains, "she must remain passive in order not to transgress societal and religious injunctions, and yet she no longer can be passive in the same way as before." She "acts, then, in order to continue to be sexually inactive."[43]

Tolliver's analysis of Amelia's passivity in the story on a linguistic level is particularly suggestive since women's silencing of their needs has been seen as a major cause of hysteria. Faced with such restricting concepts of femininity, a woman's need to speak out, to have a voice, often found indirect expression in the form of the hysterical fit. According to Dianne Hunter, hysteria is precisely "a self-repudiating form of feminine discourse in which the body signifies what social conditions make it impossible to state linguistically."[44] Thus, Amelia's body, through the hysterical paroxysm, says what she, as well as the ellipses in the text, dare not say. Hélène Cixous also develops this idea by referring to the classical symptoms of hysteria of aphonia and of the *globus hystericus*, which Amelia exhibits, to show how the silencing of women manifests itself physically on the hysteric's body: "Silence: silence is the mark of hysteria. The great hysterics have lost speech, they are aphonic, and at times have lost more than speech: they are pushed to the point of choking, nothing gets through. They are decapitated, their tongues are cut off and what talks isn't heard because it's the body that talks."[45]

Thus, in "La novia fiel," Emilia Pardo Bazán shows hysteria to be a "disease" that society inflicts on women by not allowing them to express their needs and desires, or, in Juliet Mitchell's words, hysteria is "simultaneously what a woman can do both to be feminine and to refuse femininity, within patriarchal discourse."[46] As an unconscious form of rebellion against femininity and a phenomenon largely created and sanctioned by society itself, hysteria ultimately worked to contain more threatening types of female protest. The hysteria diagnosis, by pointing to the female body as inherently flawed and pathological, simply covers up the social and political injustices that were truly making women ill. Since hysteria often merely maintained the status quo, it was clearly limited in its reach as a form of social defiance. This has led Cixous to assert that, "in the end, the woman pushed to hysteria is the woman who disturbs and is nothing but disturbance."[47] Thus, while it is true that Amelia begins to show some agency at the end of the story by "defying the wishes of Germán, her parents, the Church and society" and by choosing "her own resolution" to the problem,[48] no new spaces are truly opened up for her and other women. Like Gracia (in the *Cura* trilogy) and Ana (in *La Regenta*), Amelia simply chooses one of the options that society allows for, and ultimately remains restricted and repressed in almost all aspects of her life. Yet, in contrast to the works of López Bago and Alas, the story itself turns the hysteria diagnosis on its head by highlighting society's unhealthy and stifling restrictions on women's lives as the real cause of the disease.

"ERROR DE DIAGNÓSTICO"

Whereas "La novia fiel" deals with the causes and manifestations of hysteria in women, "Error de diagnóstico," (1907) written some thirteen years later, deals with doctors' lack of true scientific objectivity in their diagnosis of the "disease." This story, then, markedly contrasts with the *Cura* trilogy and *La Regenta* where the doctors' diagnoses of hysteria are affirmed, rather than subverted by the narrator. Pardo Bazán's story is about Dr. Cano's incorrect interpretation of the symptoms of the illness from which the Countess's daughter is suffering. The overly confident Dr. Cano's refusal to truly question his assumption that any sixteen-year-old female suffering from "ahogos" (suffocation) must be afflicted with hysteria, leads to a misdiagnosis and to the girl's death. Although the word *hysteria* is never used in the story, the symptoms of the illness and the nonchalance with which the doctor reacts to them indicate that he has arrived at this diagnosis. First of all, the patient is exhibiting the classic *globus hystericus*, which is described as "un ataque repentino de sofocación" (a sudden attack of suffocation), "el ataque" (the attack), and as "ahogos" (suffocation).[49] Moreover, the girl's age, sixteen, is mentioned twice. In fact, Dr. Cano reaches his hysteria diagnosis even before seeing the girl, but after hearing about the symptoms and discovering that his patient is the Countess's sixteen-year old daughter, not the Countess herself (4:75). The second time the girl's age is mentioned, Dr. Cano repeats the medical cliché of the time about how the female body, in its transition to womanhood, frequently develops such symptoms: "¿Dieciséis? La lucha por el desarrollo. A cada momento vienen a mi consulta señoritas quejándose de algo muy parecido" (4:75; Sixteen? The struggle of puberty. Young girls complaining of something very similar come to my office all the time).

Dr. Cano's tendency to reach a diagnosis before observing the patient is actually seen earlier when he first receives the Countess's message and immediately assumes that the Countess herself is the patient and that she is simply suffering from her usual "cólico nefrítico" (4:75; kidney stones). Thus, despite his supposed adherence to objectivity and empirical observation, his conclusions are based more on preconceived notions and biases than on the practice of the scientific method. The doctor's demeanor, even when he attempts to appear compassionate and attentive, remains arrogant and condescending throughout his visit with his young patient. Even after the mother expresses her concern that her daughter might be dying and begs the doctor to examine her carefully, Dr. Cano merely goes through the motions in order to please the mother, apparently unable to truly heed the Countess's concerns.[50] This depiction of nineteenth-century doctors' treatment of their supposedly hysterical patients not only anticipates twentieth-century feminist critiques of "the condescending authoritarianism of male doctors towards their female patients,"[51] but it is also in keeping with Pardo Bazán's criticisms of the medical and scientific movements of her day.

As we saw above, a constant theme in Pardo Bazán's writings was her skepticism about doctors and scientists' claims about being able to answer questions that, in all actuality, went beyond the realm of science. According to Laura Otis's excellent article on the early scientific writings of Emilia Pardo Bazán, "the point of departure for [Pardo Bazán's] scientific studies was Kant's reevaluation of knowledge, his awareness of the limits of human perception, and his rigorous analysis of the categories of knowledge possible."[52] In other words, Pardo Bazán would insist that truly objective knowledge must begin "with an admission of one's own [intellectual] limitations."[53] This idea is repeated in "La nueva cuestión palpitante" (1892) when Pardo Bazán argues that science will never be able to answer metaphysical questions regarding the essence of existence.[54] This leads Pardo Bazán to portray scientific assertions that step outside of the bounds of what can be known through empirical study as on a par with superstition or, at best, with blind faith. An example of this is found in "Error de diagnóstico" through the narrator's ironic presentation of Dr. Cano's conversion of "science" into an idol of worship that he hopes will replace religion:

> El ídolo de nuestra edad le contaba entre sus devotos. Soñaba mucho, y no daba forma poética, sino científica, a sus sueños. Descreído y hasta unas miajas enemigo personal del que nos mandó amar a nuestros enemigos, se forjaba en su fantasía planes de sustituir la Providencia por el conocimiento. Era estrictamente leal, estrictamente honrado, y su culto a la verdad rayaba en fanatismo. (4:74)

> *The idol of our age counted him as one of its devotees. He dreamed a lot, and he did not give poetic form, but rather scientific form, to his dreams. A nonbeliever and even somewhat of a personal enemy to He who ordered us to love our enemies, he invented in his fantasies plans to substitute Providence with knowledge. He was strictly loyal, strictly honorable, and his worship of truth verged on fanatical.*

The doctor is so "fanatical" in his "faith" in his own scientific hypotheses that he even risks his life two or three times injecting himself with untested serums and microbe cultures in order to prove their safety and effectiveness (4:74). His dedication and zeal win Dr. Cano the respect of his scientific peers, who do not bother to evaluate his work objectively—that is, based on its veracity and/or usefulness to the field—but rather simply on the doctor's own devotion and enthusiasm.

Dr. Cano's hypocrisy in regard to his rejection of religious faith, while blindly adhering to his own "faith" in "science," is most conspicuously revealed when he orders the Countess to snuff out the votive candles that she has lit in the hopes that God will heed her prayers and save her daughter's life: "Apague usted las velas, condesa. [. . .] Si la niña mejora, el bienaventurado va llevarse la gloria de la mejoría, y si la niña empeorase, culparía a usted al tonto del doctor" (4:76; Blow out the candles, Countess. [. . .] If the girl improves, the blessed will take the glory of her recovery, and if the girl gets worse, you can blame the silly doctor). This passage proves to be highly ironic considering that the girl not only gets worse but dies that night, and that she would have been at least equally well served by the candles and/or the priest whom the Countess had thought of calling first. The discovery that the girl was really suffering from a vomica, an abscess in the lungs, which should have been treated surgically, makes it clear that had the doctor correctly diagnosed the problem, there was at least a possibility that he could have saved her life.[55] Moreover, he most likely would have treated both the Countess and her daughter more compassionately, especially considering the "faith" the young girl had placed in him.[56] This event forces Dr. Cano to acknowledge his own blindness and arrogance as well as the limitations of human knowledge in general—"He comprendido que la puerta de la ciencia es la humildad [. . .] y que no sabemos nada o casi nada" (4:77; I've learned that the door to science is humility [. . .] and that we know nothing or almost nothing)—a point on which Pardo Bazán had often insisted.

This portrayal of the doctor's blind zeal for "science" is reminiscent of Pura Fernández and Ivan Lissorgues's portrayal of López Bago himself as fanatical and dogmatic.[57] It also finds some echoes in the work of Leopoldo Alas himself, who was less dogmatic than the radical naturalists in his embrace of scientific determinism. In *La Regenta*, for example, Frígiles's scientific experiments, such as his grafting of roosters, are presented as absurd. And his biggest "experiment," his arrangement of the "perfect marriage" between Víctor and Ana, is the primary source of the novel's conflict. Similarly, the town atheist is undermined when, as soon as he is faced with his own death, he repents and takes the last sacrament, suggesting that no one is truly exempt from the need for faith. However, in Pardo Bazán's story, Dr. Cano errs precisely in his diagnosis of hysteria, whereas doctors' diagnoses of hysteria prove to be founded in the *Cura* trilogy and *La Regenta*.

From the very beginning of "Error de diagnóstico," the authority of Dr. Cano is conspicuously subverted by an ironic narrator and the use of dramatic irony. The narrator undermines the doctor's authority not only by using religious terminology to describe his scientific work, but also by contradicting his assumptions and baseless judgments, ironically enough, with facts and empirical evidence to the contrary. For example, when Dr. Cano is making his way to the Countess's estate, he calmly yet incorrectly assumes that the patient is the Countess herself and that she must be suffering from her usual complaint. The narrator immediately corrects him: "Se engañaba en sus presunciones el médico. Tratábase de un ataque repentino de sofocación, y la paciente no era la condesa, sino su hija, muchacha de dieciséis años" (4:75; The doctor was mistaken in his assumptions. It was a sudden attack of suffocation, and the patient was not the countess, but rather her daughter, a girl of sixteen). The narrator uses an antithetical juxtaposition again by contrasting the doctor's lack of concern about the grave physical condition of the patient and her mother's severe emotional distress (4:75). The doctor's "alivio" (relief) and "sonrisa bien informada, algo irónica" (well-informed, and somewhat ironic smile) contrast markedly with the "boca muy abierta" (wide open mouth) and "pecho jadeante" (panting chest) of the patient, and with her mother's emotional state: "oprimida todavía por el terror" and "loca" (4:75; still overcome with terror [and] crazy). Perhaps most effective in undermining the doctor and his diagnosis is the use of dramatic irony. It is apparent from the very beginning of the story that Dr. Cano will misdiagnose his patient's illness. Not only does the title of the story, "Error de diagnóstico," suggest as much, but also we are told in the first paragraph that "los más refinados [científicos] sufren en especial al comprobar los límites de la ciencia, lo nulo del saber, lo fatal de las leyes naturales" (4:74; the most acclaimed scientists suffer the most upon discovering the limits of science, the uselessness of knowledge, the inevitability of natural

law) and then in the second that "El doctor Cano era de estos últi-
mos" (4:74; Doctor Cano was one of the latter). These statements
foreshadow the doctor's disgrace, and lead the reader to view the
doctor's certainty and arrogance ironically from the start.

Thus, by revealing the weaknesses in the practice of medicine at
the time, the story advances the idea that hysteria is more superstition than science. The fact that its symptomatology in nineteenth-
and early twentieth-century Spain resembled that found in ancient
Greece is more suggestive of the survival of prejudices, fears, and
misunderstandings about women and their bodies than of any real
advancement in medical knowledge. Dr. Cano's patronizing treatment of the Countess and her daughter similarly conveys a lack of
respect for women in general and reveals the gender prejudices that
necessarily inform his own diagnoses of his female patients. Hysteria, then, is portrayed as a catch-all diagnosis that hides doctors'
ignorance and prejudices regarding women and doctors' dismissal
of the real afflictions from which so many women were suffering at
the time, be they physical, psychological, or both. In this way "Error
de diagnóstico" not only deconstructs the concept of hysteria as a
real disease but also serves as a vindication of women's voices, particularly in regard to their own feelings and bodies.

It is important to note that Pardo Bazán did not hesitate to relate
her critiques of science directly to the way it was being used to
argue against giving women the same rights and privileges as men.
Specifically, she opposed medical assertions about the dominant
role the reproductive organs played in determining, and limiting,
a woman's destiny in life. In other words, she objected to "el error
de afirmar que el papel que á la mujer corresponde en las funciones reproductivas de la especie, determina y limita las restan-
tes funciones de su actividad humana, quitando á su destino toda
significación individual, y no dejándole sino la que puede tener
relativamente al destino del varón" (the error in asserting that the
role that corresponds to women in their reproductive capacities as
a species determines and limits the remaining functions of their
human activity, taking from her destiny all individual meaning, and
not leaving her anything other than that which is related to man's

destiny).[58] Ultimately, Pardo Bazán's insistence on the limitations of knowledge and what could truly be revealed through empirical observation of material reality would become a crucial argument against attempts by doctors to reduce women's essence and reason for existence to their reproductive function and thereby render them "naturally incapacitated" for other pursuits. In other words, by arguing that the essence of woman could not be revealed by an empirical study of her body and reproductive organs, Pardo Bazán was able to underscore the limitations of what science could truly say about a woman's nature and destiny.

Both "La novia fiel" and "Error de diagnóstico," therefore, reveal Pardo Bazán's cynicism about hysteria as a real disease, and specifically as a diagnosis applied to women. Her works suggest that women who had difficulty conforming to a restricting concept of femininity that offered them few means for expressing intellectual, creative, and/or sexual drives understandably became "hysterical." "La novia fiel" in particular makes clear that it was not women's natures but rather artificial constructs of femininity that were making women ill, and making doctors view normal reactions to this oppression as pathology. "Error de diagnóstico," on the other hand, can be seen as an indictment of the medical establishment for its retrograde views on women that were more akin to superstition than to any truly empirical or scientific understanding of women's natures, desires, and capabilities. In this way, both stories show that the hysterical woman was, as Carroll Smith-Rosenberg has argued, at once a "product and indictment of her culture."[59]

Women, Mysticism, and Alternative Technologies of the Self

According to Elaine Pagels, the main difference between orthodox Christianity and gnosticism has to do with the understanding of Jesus's divinity.[60] For orthodox Christians, Jesus is divine in a way that humans could never be.[61] In contrast, the gnostics believed that Jesus was simply a spiritual teacher and that "once the disciple attain[ed] enlightenment, Jesus no longer serve[d] as his spiritual master: the two [became] equal—even identical."[62] This different understanding of Jesus's divinity led to a major divergence between the two traditions' teachings on Jesus's role in human salvation. According to orthodox Christians, Jesus came to earth and sacrificed himself in order to cleanse us of our sins and lead us to salvation. Since Jesus was divine in a way we could never be, He did for us what we never could have done for ourselves; as mere mortals we are not in a position to achieve equal standing with Christ. In the gnostic tradition, however, the ultimate objective was nothing less than to become equal to Christ.

Although the Catholic Church effectively suppressed gnosticism, similar mystical teachings have reappeared throughout history at different times and on different soils. In the case of Spain, for example, there are many similarities between the teachings of Santa Teresa de Jesús and the *alumbrados* and those of the gnostics. Like the gnostics, both Santa Teresa and the *alumbrados* claimed to be able to reach a state of perfection and experience union with God. However, while both heretical mystics such as the *alumbrados* and those who would later be canonized, like Santa Teresa de Jesús, shared certain beliefs and practices with the gnostics, the similarities are greater between the gnostics and heretical groups, because mystics within the Church adhered to Church doctrine.[63] Nevertheless, both forms of mysticism were often viewed as in defiance of orthodox Christianity and Church authority, which can account for why the Inquisition also investigated mystics within the Church such as Santa Teresa and San Juan de la Cruz.

Michel Foucault, in his documentation of technologies of the self from the pagan to the Christian era,[64] reveals similar differences in the understanding of the relation of the individual to authority as can be seen between the gnostic and orthodox Christian traditions (the first two centuries AD—when gnostic teachings had not yet been declared heresies).[65] According to Foucault, during the pagan and early Christian periods, technologies of the self were more concerned with caring for the self rather than in knowing the self. In other words, one was to study one's conscience and personal conduct in order to improve upon them. Although one often made use of a teacher or mentor in this process, the ultimate objective was to reach a state of autonomy in which one no longer needed to submit to an authority. A student studied under a master until the student had internalized the teachings and made them part of his/ her behavior. At this point, the student became autonomous and no longer needed a master.[66] However, Foucault argues that in later orthodox Christian technologies of the self, one sought to know the self by acknowledging one's essentially sinful nature. Confession was the principal practice of revealing this true self. Unlike in the pagan and early Christian traditions, the objective of confession was to recognize one's need for guidance and submission to authority. For this reason, under this tradition, a state of autonomy was never reached. An orthodox Christian had to continually show humility and subservience toward Church authority; one did not seek to obtain autonomy through self-perfection.[67] Thus, while in many of the early Christian traditions self-cultivation was a process that, if successful, resulted in the individual's independence from the master, even if that master was Jesus himself, in the orthodox Christian tradition, the individual always remained subjected to institutional authority.[68]

While the idea that the perfection of the self leads to a state of autonomy did not take hold in the Catholic Church, it did appeal to Emilia Pardo Bazán who, in her discussion of lyricism in *El lirismo en la poesía francesa* (1916/1923; Lyricism in French poetry),[69] argues that freedom from institutional authority is a privilege earned through education and self-cultivation. This concept, fundamental to mystical theology, accounts for Pardo Bazán's view of mysticism as a viable path for female emancipation. It explains why, in her fight for women's rights, the Galician writer emphasized the issue of equal education for women. It also provides insight into Pardo Bazán's interest in hagiography as well as her decision to write about female mysticism in her last published novel, *Dulce dueño* (1911).[70] Here I explore Pardo Bazán's belief that education provided the tools and mystical theology the philosophical basis and model for personal emancipation for women. First, I examine *El lirismo* in order to show the relationship between Pardo Bazán's philosophy of self-autonomy and early Christian technologies of the self, as outlined by Pagels and Foucault. I then turn my attention to "La educación del hombre y la mujer" (1892), a speech Pardo Bazán gave in defense of women's right to equal education, delivered twenty-four years before she taught her course on lyricism, in order to explain Pardo Bazán's philosophy of education, her belief in its fundamental role in personal emancipation, and its relation to Christian teachings. Finally, I analyze *Dulce dueño* in order to demonstrate the way these ideas play themselves out in the novel.

EL LIRISMO EN LA POESÍA FRANCESA

Pardo Bazán defines lyricism as individualistic and sentimental expression. She stresses the anarchistic aspect of lyricism and writes that "el lirismo es la afirmación del individuo, no diré que siempre contra la sociedad, pero siempre sin tomarla en cuenta, y muchas veces protestando contra ella tácita o explícitamente" (*El lirismo*, 14; lyricism is the affirmation of the individual, I won't say always against society, but always without taking it into account, and many times protesting it either tacitly or explicitly). She does not reject the subversive element of lyrical expression, but rather embraces it as both a source of artistic beauty and as a means of edifying society. She claims that a desire to break free from cultural restrictions has inspired many great artistic and literary works (25–26). She also argues that certain individuals, through their social criticism, have been able to improve their respective societies (246). However, Pardo Bazán asserts that the right to criticize and defy society should be a privilege of the highly cultivated individual and not necessarily of anyone. She elaborates on this argument in her discussion of what she perceives to be the dangerous nature of the lyricism of Jean-Jacques Rousseau.

According to Pardo Bazán, although Rousseau did not invent lyricism, he was its modern initiator and was therefore extremely influential in the formation of the romantic movement. As is typical in lyrical traditions, Rousseau exalts the individual over the group. Pardo Bazán objects, however, to Rousseau's belief that the right to rebel against society should be granted to anyone faithful to his instincts. In other words, she signals as problematic the idea that in following one's nature the individual is superior to society, which is inherently evil and oppressive (79). She argues that with Rousseau, the individual is not granted the authority to contravene society because he has demonstrated a certain degree of discipline and competence but rather because he is naturally good while society is unnatural and corrupt. For Pardo Bazán, this celebration of "natural man" is an exaltation of the characteristics that make human beings similar to animals rather than of those that distinguish man from the rest of the animal kingdom. She fears that this sanctioning of man's baser instincts will inevitably result in the decline rather than in the edification of society.

From her criticism of Rousseau, it is clear that Pardo Bazán felt that the right to challenge social norms should be a privilege earned by those who had learned to dominate their baser instincts (248–49). Only the subversive message of the educated and disciplined intellectual was worthy of being received and considered. She believed that giving everyone who acted intuitively the freedom to do as he or she pleased would be to condone even the most vile and criminal behavior (240–41). For Pardo Bazán, even exceptional individuals should hold themselves subject to morality in order to avoid a sort of over-exalted individualism that could ensue if people came to believe that they had earned the right to give free reign to any of their passions (237–49). In her opinion, the lack of moral restraint and humility before a higher ideal accounted for the perversions of the elite decadent artists who had come to "proponer, en tiempos más recientes, como ideal la perversidad, y como criterio de belleza la misma corrupción de las almas, refinada artísticamente" (247; propose, in most recent times, the ideal of perversity, and as a criterion for beauty, the very corruption of souls, artistically refined).

Pardo Bazán ties the beginning of the decline of lyricism in the 1840s with the turning away from the literary movement of romanticism (25). Nevertheless, she points out that after approximately forty years of obsolescence, romantic lyricism arose again in the literary movement of *décadence*: "nadie ignora que si el romanticismo

como escuela literaria había muerto hacia 1850, como escuela literaria reapareció hacia 1889 bajo otros nombres variados, entre los
cuales prevaleció el de decadentismo" (25; we are all aware that if
romanticism as a literary school had died around 1850, as a literary
school it reappeared around 1889 with other varied names, among
which prevailed [the label] decadentism). Out of a desire to create
an art that depicted life in its spiritual as well as physical aspects,
decadent artists tended to underscore the limitations of reason
and science. Pardo Bazán was attracted to this movement precisely
because it defied the materialism of the age and emphasized the
mystical and spiritual elements of existence.

In "El porvenir de la literatura después de la guerra" (The future
of literature after the war), a lecture given at the Residencia de
Estudiantes (Student Residence) in 1916, the same year she taught
her course on lyricism, she claimed that the decadent movement
had been able to "reaccionar plenamente contra las limitaciones
del naturalismo y añadir cuerdas a la lira de las emociones místicas,
amorosas y sentimentales, revelando aspectos nuevos de la belleza,
del alma y del infinito" (react completely against the limitations of
naturalism and add chords to the lyre of mystical, loving, and sentimental emotions, revealing new aspects of beauty, of the soul, and
of the infinite).[71] Particularly appealing to Pardo Bazán was that the
lyricism of *décadence*, in contrast to that of the romantic movement,
was expressed by a superior, cultivated individual who contravened
nature and bourgeois, modern society rather than by "natural man"
who, by following his instincts and passions, instinctively broke
rules necessary to uphold a civilized society. While Pardo Bazán
had rejected the barbarism of romanticism and the reductive materiality of naturalism, *décadence* appeared as a movement more in
keeping with her own ideas, despite her objections to some of its
perversions, as will be discussed in more detail later.

Pardo Bazán saw Christianity, particularly early Christianity,
as a perfect example of lyricism. She pointed to the years leading
up to the formation of the Catholic Church in the fourth century
as a time in which lyricism flourished because this was a period
when Christianity was a persecuted religion with a revolutionary

spirit. It was a time when Christians represented a marginalized segment of society. In their struggle to maintain their faith, the early Christians had to assert their individualism against the official religious beliefs of Roman society (*El lirismo*, 34). Up until the time of the conversion of Constantine, Christianity was a heresy, and heresy by its very nature was lyrical because it was the voice of divergent thought. However, the formation of a universal, or "catholic," church with a monolithic doctrine was contrary to the lyrical origins of Christianity: "Lo que propiamente se ha llamado la Iglesia, la ortodoxia y la jerarquía eclesiástica, si no son abiertamente opuestas al lirismo, representan lo que puede contenerle y reprimirle o encauzarle" (36; What has formally been called the Church, orthodoxy and the ecclesiastical hierarchy, if they are not openly opposed to lyricism, represent what can restrain it and repress or channel it).[72] Yet, Pardo Bazán recognized that even after the formation of an official Catholic Church, lyrical voices reemerged in the various heretical and reform movements that arose afterward (36–37). Interestingly, the Church came to embrace many of these mystics and reformers through the establishment of a hagiographic tradition that recounted their defiance and lyrical expression. Thus, even though orthodox Christianity in general opposed individualism, paradoxically, it celebrated its own "heretical" history formed by early Church martyrs who fought against Roman society, and later mystics and reformers who rebelled against the Church itself:

> Los gérmenes líricos se revelan en la herejías, tan numerosas, ya desde los primeros siglos de la Iglesia. El soplo emancipador de la conciencia individual había sido tan fuerte, tan huracanado, que las individualidades sublevadas contra la organización religiosa se contaron por centenares de millares. He aquí cómo podemos ver en cada heresiarca un lírico, y no sólo en los heresiarcas, sino también en los renovadores dentro de la ortodoxia. (36–37)

> *The lyrical seeds are revealed in the heresies, so numerous, already from the first centuries of the Church. The emancipatory wind of individual consciousness had been so strong, like a hurricane, that the individual-*

ities rebelling against the religious organization added up to hundreds of thousands. This is how we can see in every heretic a lyrical individual, and not only amongst the heretics, but also among the innovators within orthodoxy.

Furthermore, although the Church had historically excluded women from positions of authority within the ecclesiastical hierarchy, women's prominence in early Church history, as well as in their roles as mystics and saints, revealed a space within the Church where women had, and could, assume leadership roles.

Thus, Pardo Bazán clearly embraced the hagiographic tradition because she saw examples of women who were able to realize themselves in that environment. Mysticism also appealed to her because it allowed for a unique kind of self-assertion, like the lyricism that she endorsed. Through discipline, virtue, education, and submission to God, female mystics had earned the authority to contravene the rules of society and to forge new paths. It was a venue for the exceptional woman to perfect and display her talents. Nevertheless, there is a seeming contradiction between the mystic's humility and complete subordination to God and her self-assertion and defiance of society. How could mysticism allow for the bolstering of the ego and the affirmation of one's superiority while at the same time insist on complete subservience to God? This is precisely where the paradoxical nature of mysticism lends itself to the affirmation of the privileges of exceptional individuals as well as the requirement that they must govern their baser instincts. As Pardo Bazán argues in *El lirismo*, adherence to morality and ideals outside oneself was a prerequisite for personal emancipation. Consequently, for Pardo Bazán, it is precisely the state of perfection of the female mystic and her humility before God that both gave her the authority to contravene societal norms, and the means of keeping in check the potential perversions of exaggerated egoism. Pardo Bazán's belief in the need to submit to some sort of external authority serves as a check on the fall into immorality of some of the decadent artists and as the lesson the protagonist of *Dulce dueño* must learn in order to assert her individuality.

"LA EDUCACIÓN DEL HOMBRE Y DE LA MUJER"

Pardo Bazán's views on education are fundamental to her understanding of women's potential for self-realization, Christianity, and
the individual's relation to society. In "La educación del hombre y
de la mujer" (1892), she elaborates on her conception of the role of
education in improving the individual and society. She argues that
learning is the very essence of life (16), and that education aims at
the perfection of the self (18).[73] She objects, however, to the fact that
while education for men is based on the positive belief in the perfectibility of human nature since it allows men to develop all their
intellectual skills to the best of their ability, education for women
is based on a pessimistic view of women's nature and prefers to fos-
ter obedience to authority, rather than true intellectual growth and
independence (20, 51). Foucault notes similar differences in early
Christian and orthodox Christian technologies of the self where
the former stressed a state of enlightenment, self-mastery, and
autonomy, and the latter, the importance of submission to Church
authority. Pardo Bazán saw this distinction between the education
of men and women. While men were given the opportunity to edu-
cate themselves to the best of their abilities in the hopes of reaching
a state of self-perfection,[74] the lack of belief in women's ability to
rise above their supposedly inferior natures, led to women simply
being trained in "la obediencia, la pasividad y la sumisión" (obedience, passivity, and submission):

> Es la educación de la mujer preventiva y represiva hasta la igno-
> minia; parte del supuesto del mal, nace de la sospecha, nútrese en
> los celos, inspírase en la desconfianza, y tiende á impedir ó á creer
> buena y candidamente que impide las transgresiones de la moral
> sexual por el mismo procedimiento mecánico de los grillos pues-
> tos al delincuente para que no pueda dañar. La educación positiva,
> de instrucción y dirección, verdadera guía de la vida humana, está
> vedada á la mujer. (51–52)

*Women's education is preventative and repressive to the point of dis-
grace; it is based on a supposed evil, it is born of suspicion, and is fed
on jealousy, inspired by distrust, and tends to impede or to truly and
candidly believe that it prevents transgressions of sexual morality by the
same mechanical procedure of [placing] shackles on a criminal so that
he won't hurt [anybody]. Positive education, of instruction and direction,
the true guide of a human life, is prohibited to women.*

Hence, throughout her speech, Pardo Bazán argues that women,
as individuals and members of humanity, have just as much right
as men to a "positive" education in which they would be given the
opportunity for self-realization and autonomy. Pardo Bazán recognizes, however, that only a minority of people, of either sex, will
ever self-actualize. Arguing that most people are of mediocre intelligence and/or character, all other factors being equal, only exceptional individuals would rise to the top.[75] Consequently, for Pardo
Bazán, a just society was one in which superior talent was recognized and all individuals were given the tools, primarily education
and the opportunity for social participation, to improve oneself.
However, by closing off such opportunities to women, society was
inhibiting personal female development by forcing many great
female minds to languish in the stagnant environment of domestic life. Unlike a man, a woman who yearned for more was restricted
by a lack of opportunity (*El lirismo*, 270).

In "La educación," Pardo Bazán argues that Christianity itself
had not only asserted the equality of men's and women's souls,
but had also freed women's conscience and given them the right
to affirm their individuality and exercise moral choice.[76] She also
points out that Church history had provided examples of women
exercising such freedoms to the benefit of themselves and society
as a whole. As in *El lirismo*, she cites early Church martyrs and mystics as examples of consummate women who assumed leadership
roles within the Church and society:

El Cristianismo, en su pureza, en su íntima esencia, tan afirmativa
de la dignidad humana, contiene el principio armónico que puede

conciliar á las dos mitades de la humanidad. Dentro de la Iglesia, las mártires han sellado con su sangre la independencia espiritual; las predicadoras como Santa Rosa de Viterbo y las heroínas como la pastora de Orleans, han confirmado su acción social y política; las doctoras como Santa Teresa, su plenitud intelectual, y hasta—á pesar de las palabras de San Pablo,—su función docente. (38)

Christianity, in its pure form, in its deep essence, so affirming of human dignity, contains the harmonious principle that can reconcile the two halves of humanity. Within the Church, female martyrs have stamped their spiritual independence in blood; female preachers like Saint Rose of Viterbo and heroines like Joan of Arc, established their social and political activism; doctors like Santa Teresa, their superior intellect, and even—despite the words of Saint Paul—their capacity to teach.

Therefore, for Pardo Bazán, Christianity not only asserted the equality of the sexes and the right of every individual, regardless of sex, to make important choices regarding the direction of one's own life, but it also provided many examples of highly intelligent women who were able to make those choices successfully and rise to positions of power.

DULCE DUEÑO

Much of the commentary surrounding Emilia Pardo Bazán's last published novel, *Dulce dueño* (1911), is critical of the mystical conversion of the narrator/protagonist. Phoebe Porter Medina asserts that Pardo Bazán creates a female *décadente* whose cult of the self, related through Lina Mascareñas's first-person narration, is ultimately undermined by the implied author who, through Lina's fall into madness (not mysticism), conveys the message that "the individual cannot succeed in transcending the problems of origin and heredity."[77] Marina Mayoral, in her introduction to the novel, complains of what she sees as a lack of verisimilitude in the final spiritual conversion of Lina Mascareñas.[78] David Henn criticizes Lina's conversion for being a "rather traditional remedy."[79] Lou

Charnon-Deutsch reads the ending as a punishment of the superior woman who refuses "to be satisfied with what conventional society expects will make women happy." She goes on to add that Lina's mystical conversion is "an exaggerated representation of women's total submission to the masculine will" that "marks the death of the self."[80] Similarly, Raquel Medina believes that the ending converts the novel into a plea for morality in which there is no liberation for a female subject who ultimately becomes a slave to a patriarchal God and a hysteric locked inside a mental institution.[81]

Susan Kirkpatrick, although more sympathetic and receptive to the novel's attempt to redefine the female subject, argues that the ending of the novel, with the depiction of the female's submission to God as supreme patriarch, keeps intact the male/female gender binary that earlier parts of the novel seem to deconstruct.[82] Maryellen Bieder was the first critic to read the ending itself as somewhat subversive. In "Intertextualizing Genre: Ambiguity as Narrative Strategy in Emilia Pardo Bazán," Bieder argues that hagiography is merely one of the various competing genres in the text that serve to destabilize gender constructs.[83] In a later essay, she claims that the novel emphasizes the incompatibility of marriage with the emancipation of women, and that Lina's ultimate withdrawal from society allows her to assume a space of her own in which she can write.[84] In her most recent article on the novel, Bieder argues that the mystical discourse is "un discurso de apoderamiento que libera a la mujer de los hombres y de las instituciones dominantes a la vez que la subordina" (a discourse of empowerment that liberates women from men and the dominant institutions at the same time that it subordinates [women]).[85] Continuing in this vein, Pau Pitarch Fernández, Carmen Pereira-Muro, Kathy Bacon, Cristina Sánchez-Conejero, and Elizabeth Smith Rousselle and Joseph Drexler-Dreis have all explored in more detail the subversive aspects of the mystical references. Pitarch Fernández argues that Lina's mystical narrative creates an individualized space in which she can attempt to artistically recreate herself.[86] Pereira-Muro, building on the ideas of Luce Irigaray, affirms that the mystical discourse can be seen as a type of *écriture féminine* that rejects phallologocentrism and asserts a fluid, feminine subjectivity.[87] In her book *Negotiating Sainthood*, Bacon argues that Lina makes use of the misogynist narrative of saintly martyrdom by rewriting it and appropriating it "for her own ends."[88] Cristina Sánchez-Conejero shows how the mystical discourse in the novel contributes to an interdiscursive postmodern hybridity that renders the novel impossible to classify.[89] Rousselle and Drexler-Dreis argue that "Lina's mysticism subverts male hegemony" and "forms a response to modernity's ambivalence about the emergence of the New Woman."[90] Most recently, Eilene Powell argues that Lina's religious masochism is a subversive strategy to reveal the grotesque comedy of women's lives in the patriarchal society of the time.[91] In accordance with Bacon, Bieder, Pereira-Muro, Pitarch Fernández, Rousselle and Drexler-Dreis, and Powell, I argue that the protagonist and narrator of *Dulce dueño*, Lina Mascareñas, is a female *décadente* who turns to mysticism in an attempt to distinguish herself as a superior individual. While she initially attempts to cultivate her existence through luxury, artistic refinement, and the pursuit of ideal love, her efforts are thwarted by a society convinced that a woman's biology determines her social destiny and by her own egotism and moral depravity. However, through her mystical conversion, the narrator/protagonist is finally able to realize herself by dominating her baser instincts and eluding oppressive cultural discourses on gender.

As we have seen, in late nineteenth- and early twentieth-century Spain, the female body, which was being read or studied through the scientific knowledge of the time, served as a referential sign for the essence of woman. Greatly due to the influence of positivism, science sought to understand the female in terms of her material being. According to Peter Brooks, "the rise of materialism as a philosophical position made the body, in the absence of any transcendent principle beyond nature, the substance to which any metaphysical speculation must ultimately return as the precondition of mind."[92] Thus, women's mental and spiritual existence, that which could be considered the nonmaterial aspect of their being, was now understood in terms of women's material existence. This type of biological determinism was applied more to women than to men because the female's role in reproduction was used as a means of restricting her raison d'être exclusively to marriage and motherhood. Out of this understanding of women, an abundance of discourses arose on the illness of hysteria.

These purportedly scientific readings of the female body worked together with social and legal texts to further solidify woman's "natural" role in society as that of wife, mother, and homemaker. A woman's biological function was directly linked to her social destiny. In an attempt to codify the natural role of women, the domestic woman was idealized as the *ángel del hogar* (Angel in the House) in a wide range of social texts.[93] Women who did not conform to this ideal were portrayed as depraved, unnatural, and/or hysterical. The Spanish legal system also played its role in solidifying these social norms. Women's dependence on men was ensured by laws that made it nearly impossible for women to act independently. According to the Código Civil (Civil code) of 1889, within a marriage a woman was required to get approval from her husband before making any sort of monetary decisions, even if it involved assets that belonged to her before entering the marriage.[94] The Código Civil of 1889 actually made it a crime for a woman to disobey her husband on any matter.[95] While similar laws existed before the Código Civil of 1889, by redefining the subject as a free, rational individual who is proprietor of both his own body and property, and then denying women these very rights, the liberal regimes converted woman into an inferior and incomplete subject before the law.[96] Indeed, single women under twenty-five were not allowed to leave their father's home. Consequently, the greatest legal freedom was granted to the exceptional case of a single woman with wealth and over the age of twenty-five.[97] This happens to be precisely the position of Lina Mascareñas. However, this freedom was still greatly limited, as we have seen, by a society that viewed women who did not assimilate these new bourgeois values as deviants and hysterics.

It is in this social milieu that Lina attempts to redefine herself as a superior woman who is allowed to defy social conventions. Due to the death of her half-brother Diego, Lina, the illegitimate daughter of Doña Catalina Mascareñas y Lacunza de Céspedes, becomes the sole heir to her mother's fortune. Favored by her newly acquired economic status and her civil status as a single woman over twenty-five, Lina believes that she is immune to the discourses that define and control the married, middle-class woman. Toward the beginning of the novel she proclaims that "la mujer que posee un capital, debe considerarse tan fuerte como el varón" (136; a woman with capital should consider herself as powerful as a man).[98] She also makes it clear that for her, marriage is a social institution that has nothing to do with love and merely serves to imprison women. For Lina, marriage not only results in the male's usurpation of a woman's property, but also of her body and soul, the latter being of utmost importance to the novel's protagonist (178). When Don Antón de Polilla, an older male friend from the village in which Lina grew up, also tries to steer her toward marriage by proclaiming that love is women's biological destiny, she is quick to point out that love and marriage are not the same thing: "¿Y se ha enterado usted de que no hablábamos de amor, sino de matrimonio?" (136; Have you realized that we were not talking about love, but rather marriage?).

Having abandoned marriage and maternity as her life's goals, Lina embarks on a search for personal refinement and ideal love. Unlike society's understanding of love as a natural drive that leads to marriage and parenthood, Lina views love as an escape from the material world. Although she gets a taste of this love at a performance of Wagner's opera *Lohengrin*, her search for love, in the form of a real male companion, is fruitless (152).[99] Not only does she show herself to be intellectually superior to her male suitors but she also quickly recognizes that they are unable to view her as an equal. Her first suitor, Hilario Aparicio, lacks Lina's material refinement and reveals his mundane ideas about love by making it clear that for him, love is synonymous with the reproductive instinct. The second suitor is no better. As Lina soon finds out, her uncle Juan Clímaco wants her to marry his son, José María, so that he can have access to her wealth. But, even before Lina is made aware of her uncle's objectives, she views José María as her inferior. She points to his lack of intellect by portraying him as a stereotypical Andalusian man, whose "pensamiento no va más allá del sensualismo de su raza" (190; thinking does not go beyond the sensualism of his race). While Lina admits to the physical desire he arouses in her, she realizes that this allure, although powerful, is not the same as the ideal love she seeks. And her belief is affirmed when she sees her cousin coming out of her female servant's room. This sexual indiscretion proves to Lina that José María's attraction to her was the same physical attraction he feels toward women in general.

The third suitor, Agustín Almonte, is perhaps the most ingenious. Aware of Lina's aversion to marriage and sexual union, Almonte attempts to win Lina over by convincing her that they are bound together by friendship and their innate superiority. Lina is attracted by this idea and Almonte becomes her platonic companion. However, the nature of their relationship makes it difficult for Almonte to persuade Lina to marry him. He eventually begins to profess a passionate love for her, a love so selfless that he claims that he would give his life for her.

Not overly convinced by Almonte's words, Lina decides to test them by placing him in a situation where he would have to risk his life to save her. During a boat ride on their vacation in Switzerland, a storm sweeps the two of them into the treacherous waters of the lake. Almonte strikes Lina in the face and pushes her away in an attempt to save himself, rather than rescue her. His efforts to survive fail and he drowns in the lake, while Lina is pulled out of the water by the boatman. Lina thereby discovers that her suitor only paid lip service to her lofty ideals of love in order to marry her and take control of her purse. Lina comes to realize that, despite her education, refinement, civil status, and economic independence, she has been unable to find a male companion who truly considers her an equal. She also discovers the dangers of her over-exalted individualism as she comes to feel pangs of guilt for being largely responsible for Almonte's death.

Having failed to find satisfaction in egotism and romantic love, Lina begins a search for spiritual perfection following the hagiographical model provided by Saint Catherine of Alexandria. The novel opens with the story of the conversion and martyrdom of Saint Catherine, a female Christian saint renowned for her great erudition and thereby exemplifying many of Pardo Bazán's ideas on female emancipation, education, and Christianity. According to legend, Saint Catherine successfully debated the wisest philosophers in the region. Her fame as a great female intellectual appealed to Sor Juana Inés de la Cruz who dedicated a series of *villancicos* (lyric poems) to the Egyptian saint from the seventeenth century. The sixth *villancico* in particular celebrates her singular victory over the wisest men of Egypt as proof that God never intended for women to be excluded from intellectual pursuits, and that one's sex was of no importance when it came to the question of learning and intelligence:

De una Mujer se convencen
todos los Sabios de Egipto
para prueba de que el sexo
no es esencia en lo entendido[100]

One woman convinced
all the sages of Egypt
that to be female
does not mean to lack wisdom[101]

Sor Juana's *villancicos* to Saint Catherine, which were written a few months after her "Respuesta a Sor Filotea de la Cruz," (Answer to Sor Filotea de la Cruz) continue to build on the theme of "the equality of women with men in intellectual matters" and deliver the message strategically through the "unimpeachable figure" of a Catholic Saint.[102] The narrator/protagonist, Lina, and the author, Pardo Bazán, were clearly drawn to Saint Catherine for similar reasons: the Egyptian martyr was an example of a highly educated woman who defied society, yet her status as a Church heroine sanctioned her behavior. Moreover, her exceptional beauty and elegant attire made her something of a proto-decadent figure and therefore a model for the narrator/protagonist of *Dulce dueño*, and perhaps for Pardo Bazán herself. Indeed, Ezama Gil, citing passages from *La Quimera* (1905; The Chimera), asserts that Saint Catherine, with her combination of artistic elegance, superiority, and saintliness, was the ideal to which the author herself aspired.[103]

Lina listens to Saint Catherine's story in the first chapter of the novel and identifies with the saint's intellect, beauty, and overall sense of superiority. And later in the novel, once it becomes clear to Lina that she is not immune to succumbing to sin—her worst offense being her role in her last suitor's death—she decides to repent and to follow what she understands to be the hagiographical model of spiritual perfection provided by Saint Catherine. Yet, as Kathy Bacon points out, Lina's objective is still the same: her pursuit of saintliness is merely another attempt to distinguish herself as superior to others.[104]

It is unsurprising, then, that the beginnings of Lina's spiritual journey do not gain her the happiness she seeks. She renounces vanity by having a prostitute trample on her, resulting in the loss of one of her front teeth. She renounces her material wealth by telling her father to give her estate over to her uncle, Juan Clímaco. And despite her disdain for the common person, she attempts to rid herself of her pride by living with and helping two destitute women whom she finds repulsive. None of these actions, however, bring Lina the ecstasy she seeks, because her sense of superiority impedes her ability to feel compassion for others. As Lina goes through the motions of helping and caring for two beekeepers—Torcuata, a young teenager, and her blind grandmother—she admits that "en lo recóndito, en el escondrijo de la verdad, ningún afecto sentía por las dos mujeres" (279; in her depths, in the hiding place of truth, she had no feeling for the two women).

Only after Torcuata comes down with smallpox does Lina's transformation actually commence. It is then that Lina comes to feel love and compassion for another person for the first time: "La piedad al fin; la piedad humana, el reconocimiento de que alguien existe para mí, de que el dolor ajeno es el dolor mío" (285; Mercy at last; human mercy, the recognition that somebody exists for me, that another's pain is my pain). Not surprisingly, it is precisely at this moment that mystical ecstasy comes to Lina (285–86). Although Lina finally experiences spiritual fulfillment through self-renunciation and the practice of charity, she discovers that such a state does not require total abjection and self-denial. Lina experiences mystical union once she overcomes her most serious shortcoming: her lack of compassion for other human beings. In this way Lina's transformation is in keeping with technologies of the self that insisted self-mastery be a prerequisite for personal emancipation, as well as with Pardo Bazán's belief in the need for even select individuals to always exercise moral restraint so as to avoid a possible fall into egomania and vice.

Thus Lina learns that cultivation of the self must include a morality whose guiding tenet is empathy for others. Lina's mystical conversion and her new understanding of self also allow her to escape the scientific gaze and remove herself from the realm of the knowable. By proclaiming that her body and its actions do not reveal her interior experience of self, Lina can elude the scientific discourses of the time that held the essence of woman could be revealed by an empirical study of her body. Toward the end of the novel, Lina tells her father that she is happy despite the way things may look from the outside: "Mi felicidad tiene, para los que miran lo exterior (lo que no es), el aspecto de completa desventura" (286; My happiness has, to those that judge by exteriors (which isn't reality), the appearance of complete misfortune). This remark demonstrates the divide that Lina now recognizes between the exterior (materiality and language) and the interior (essence). Although throughout the novel Lina in effect rejects the materialist limitations that positivism imposed on women, it is only through her new understanding of mysticism and its affirmation of the invisible nature of reality that Lina can withdraw herself from the scientific gaze and the positivistic discourses that were controlling women at the time.

Conclusion

It must be pointed out that the mystical discourse in the text is far from being completely victorious in shaping Lina's identity. Scientific understandings of mysticism as hysteria render Lina an inmate in a mental institution. Just as many nineteenth- and twentieth-century doctors diagnosed religious experiences as forms of insanity, many novelists of the time used mystical discourse ironically to indicate the mental disorders of their characters. As we saw in Chapters 3 and 4, Eduardo López Bago and Leopoldo Alas undermined their female characters' romantic, or lyrical, aspirations by using their mystical language to signify their repressed sexuality and hysteria. Pardo Bazán's novel also plays with these ambiguities. Yet here an ironic, omniscient narrator does not undermine Lina's first-person unmediated account of events. Rather, Lina is able to present herself as a female *décadente* whose embrace of mysticism is validated by Torcuata and her grandmother, who have benefitted from Lina's charity and truly believe her to be a saint. What is more, the novel provides a validated model of sainthood in the figure of Saint Catherine of Alexandria, whose story is presented at length in the first chapter.

As indicated earlier, Lina's spiritual conversion has not sat well with many critics of the novel. Apart from appearing forced and overly moralistic and didactic, the nuptial metaphors, Lina's masochistic behavior, and her ultimate submission to a patriarchal god seem to reinscribe traditional gender hierarchies.[105] While these analyses problematize facile feminist readings of *Dulce dueño*, they do not invalidate an examination of the novel in terms of Pardo Bazán's ideas on the connection between mysticism and female emancipation, ideas that the author developed and elaborated throughout her writing career. Interestingly, Marina Mayoral criticizes the ending of the novel for its lack of verisimilitude, arguing that Lina's turn to mysticism is unconvincing and completely out of character: "Lina es muy dura, muy seca de corazón, a lo largo de su vida no ha querido a nadie. Su búsqueda de Dios parte del desprecio hacia las criaturas y no del amor" (Lina is very harsh, very dry-hearted, throughout her life she has not loved anyone. Her search for God is based on disdain for others and not on love).[106] This is a contradiction Mayoral also extends to the author herself: "Y otra contradicción muy llamativa se produce entre [su] defensa de los ideales cristianos (espíritu de sacrificio, ascetismo, desprecio de los bienes mundanos), que encontramos en gran parte de su obra, y su conducta personal, que nos parece movida por el deseo de triunfar y de disfrutar de todo cuanto la vida da de sí" (Another very striking contradiction is seen between her defense of Christian ideals (the spirit of sacrifice, asceticism, disdain of worldly goods) that we find in a large part of her work, and her personal conduct, which seems motivated by the desire to triumph and to enjoy all that life has to offer).[107]

It has been my contention, however, that these are the paradoxes the author is addressing in the works examined above, both on an intellectual and personal level. Moreover, reading these works in light of the reactionary messages on women, mysticism, and hysteria found in medical texts and male-authored literary works of the time problematizes assumptions about the "conservative" nature of Pardo Bazán's views on these same matters. Indeed, in terms of gender issues, her critiques of the antifeminist agenda of many scientists and liberals and her signaling of the ways religion, and specifically mysticism, provided models of successfully emancipated women demonstrated that Pardo Bazán was unquestionably more progressive than any of the other authors examined here.

CONCLUSION

THIS STUDY HAS attempted to explore the reasons why Spanish doctors and writers were so concerned with mysticism, particularly female mysticism, in nineteenth- and early twentieth-century Spain. Discussions of mysticism not only appear in the medical texts of the time but also in many literary works where female mystics are portrayed as hysterics. A close examination of these texts and the historical period in which they were created has suggested a twofold objective of diagnosing mysticism as hysteria in women. The first was to control female behavior. Modern, industrial society was attempting to uphold the restrictive domestic role of women despite the rise of liberalism, which promised to offer all free subjects equal rights regardless of gender. Traditional prejudices, as well as national campaigns to increase the size and genetic makeup of the population in order to fuel the growing industrial economy, were working against demands for female emancipation. Scientific and medical discourses were used to aid the State in this objective by creating a female subject naturally destined for marriage and motherhood and by pathologizing all behaviors on the part of women, including religious and mystical pursuits, that were contrary to these aims. The second objective of diagnosing mysticism as hysteria was to undermine the Church's authority. Anticlerical liberals were able to weaken the Church not only by depriving it of much of its wealth but also by establishing the superiority of "science" to "faith." These thinkers and politicians sought to reveal the weakness of Church teachings by diagnosing its canonized saints and mystics as hysterics. By asserting that liberal, scientific definitions of reality were more accurate than those proposed by the Church, anticlerical liberals sought to undermine ecclesiastical authority and usurp powers traditionally exercised by the Church.

For these reasons it is more accurate to view the battle waged between clergy and scientists on these questions as concerned less with ideology and more with political dominance. According to Noël Valis, "under liberalism, religion [was . . .] no longer the supreme authority governing men and institutions. The struggle over competing authorities was played out repeatedly [. . .] with no side really winning the big prize until, perhaps Franco."[1] This struggle for dominance becomes particularly clear when reading medical texts on sexuality. While doctors of the period presented themselves as compassionate and objective in their analyses of such matters, in many cases they were merely substituting the religious concept of sin for the medical concept of disease. However, whether homosexuality, for example, was a sin or a disease ultimately was of little consequence. In both cases the subject was encouraged to confess, either before a doctor or a priest, and correct the supposedly pernicious behavior. Thus, medical discourses, particularly in the form of hygiene, were merely redefining religious morality in medical terms and policing the population by converting sins and crimes into diseases and perversions. Moreover, many doctors and scientists reinforced traditional prejudices against women and racially and socially "undesirable" elements of society by affirming the polarization of the sexes and suggesting ways of improving the quality of the Spanish "race."

Regarding women, what is particularly striking is the way doctors redefined the female sexual response in order to make it better conform to medical theories that linked all sexual pleasure to reproduction. When scientists were able to prove that female orgasm played no role in reproduction, the clitoris was quickly pathologized as a disease-producing organ. Sexual practices that paid attention to this organ were said to make women more like men and thereby disrupt the "natural" polarization of the sexes. Not only could women, purportedly, lose their breasts, grow facial hair, turn to lesbianism, and/or become sterile, but they could also, through the acquisition of nymphomania, undermine male dominance in society, at least according to medical theories on seminal depletion that implied that oversexed women were a threat to male strength.

Medical discourses on female sexuality also sought to contain female mysticism because of its potential to undermine negative constructions of women and to provide models of emancipated women. The study of selected writings by Emilia Pardo Bazán in Chapter 5 develops this idea. In her essays, Pardo Bazán argues that, in regard to determining the essence of woman, metaphysical concepts of being were much more "scientific" than scientific theories claiming that anatomy was destiny. She insisted that, in terms of the inherent nature of the human subject, "science" was just as speculative as metaphysics and religion. In *Dulce dueño*, these ideas are given literary expression as Pardo Bazán inverts the hysteria/mysticism binary of the time. Taking her patron saint, Saint Catherine of Alexandria, as her model, the protagonist Lina Mascareñas eludes all the externally imposed concepts of who she is supposed to be by rejecting the idea that her body is able to signify her essence, and finds freedom through a mystical conversion.

The deployment of sexuality was used to suppress female mysticism in both the early modern and modern eras. In the sixteenth and seventeenth centuries, the Inquisition forced many self-proclaimed female mystics to produce confessions that recast their accounts of mystical union into narratives of sexual deviance, whereas in the nineteenth and early twentieth centuries doctors encouraged such women to confess to sexual aberrations that would translate into a hysteria diagnosis. In the modern era, doctors also reinterpreted past mystical texts, highlighting their supposedly sexual nature in order to transform them into evidence of hysteria. We see these same techniques in Eduardo López Bago's *Cura* trilogy and Leopoldo Alas's *La Regenta*. In these male-authored works, the narrators provide alternative, sexual interpretations of their female characters' mystical experiences in order to portray them as women afflicted by hysteria, nymphomania, or pseudo-hermaphroditism.

Alas's own views on mysticism and hysteria are brought into the discussion of *La Regenta*, since they give us some indication of the way the author was attempting to position the reader regarding his protagonist's mysticism. While embracing mysticism on a personal level, Alas was a strong critic of the institution of the Catholic Church. He also was strongly antifeminist. On several occasions he expressed his doubts about women's potential for authentic spirituality and their ability to transcend their material existence. While Alas admired Santa Teresa, he had misgivings about the authenticity of her mystical experiences. Alas's views indicate that he shared his narrator's ironic stance vis-à-vis Ana Ozores's mystical endeavors and reveal an antifeminist motivation for accepting the pathologization of religious experience in women. However, Alas's approach to the subject is still much more nuanced than the work of the radical naturalist López Bago, where scientific determinism negates all spiritual and psychological aspects of existence. In López Bago's work, women lack free will entirely and are presented as having no ambitions other than carrying out their reproductive function; anything that obstructs a woman's "natural" reproductive urges endangers her well-being.

Knowledge as a form of power also comes to the forefront in these debates. In both the early modern and modern periods, the desire for dominance and control was intricately tied to the determination of truth. In the sixteenth and seventeenth centuries, the Church held a monopoly on knowledge since it was in a position to dismiss, and even prosecute, as heresy any information that conflicted with its own teachings. The Church's desire and ability to control information even led the Inquisition to put the vernacular Bible on the index of prohibited books in 1559 because the circulation of this text was leading to alternative interpretations of Scripture. In the nineteenth and twentieth centuries, the situation had changed. The Catholic Church's power had been weakened and "science" had become the new authoritative discourse. Although scientists could not dismiss opposing knowledges as "heresy," they were able to establish the superiority of their conclusions to those of the Church by claiming to be able to substantiate them with empirical evidence. However, scientists' claims of being able to use the human body as empirical evidence for answers to metaphysical questions about the nature of human existence were faulty at best. In many cases, scientists were merely asserting as "scientific fact" that which conformed to preconceived notions and prejudices or that which served their own political objectives. Both religious leaders and scientists applied classifications (such as "orthodox" or "scientific") in order to authorize one form of power and knowledge over another.

This study also raises several issues that, although touched upon, are essentially left open for debate, such as the question of whether sexual and religious impulses arise from the same human instinct. The blurring of spiritual love and sexual love has a long literary history. Many trace it back to the Song of Songs in the Old Testament, where a collection of poems celebrating human love and marriage has been interpreted allegorically to represent the union between God and Israel in the Jewish tradition, and between Christ and the Church or between Christ and the individual soul in the Christian tradition.[2] The use of discourses on earthly love to represent divine love, and vice versa, can also be found in many medieval and renaissance literary works from Spain, such as *Milagros de Nuestra Señora* (Berceo, 2006; Miracles of the Our Lady), *El libro de buen amor* (Ruiz, 2006; The book of good love), courtly love poetry of the fifteenth and sixteenth centuries, and the mystical poetry of San Juan de la Cruz and Santa Teresa de Jesús. Does the frequent fusion of the language of divine and human love indicate that the nineteenth-century German doctor Richard von Krafft-Ebing was correct to assert that *agape* and *eros* derive from the same instinct and therefore often substitute one another?[3] Was he correct to equate religious penitence with sexual masochism? If religion and sexuality are indeed two manifestations of the same instinct, why do most religions insist on viewing them as separate and even antithetical, and why is the denial of one's sexuality often a necessary indication of true spirituality?

Also germane is the question surrounding the authenticity of mystical experiences themselves. I have argued that there were political consequences for viewing mysticism as either real or feigned: the authentication of female mysticism validated women's attempts to elude and defy misogynistic discourses, whereas a sexual-hysterical diagnosis resulted in a reaffirmation of these discourses. However, this argument does not address the question of whether any of these experiences were truly authentic. Recent scientific research has attempted to relate mystical experience to transformations in the brain. Neuroscientists have conducted studies that suggest that during mystical experiences one can observe a cessation of activity in the regions of the brain responsible for orienting us within space and time. Activity stops in that part of the brain that gives us a sense of being a separate self; our sense of where our body begins and ends ceases to function.[4] Yet this research does not necessarily help us determine whether the mystical experience is caused by anything external to the mind since, as Dr. Andrew Newberg, author of *Why God Won't Go Away*, points out, a neural correlate does not necessarily prove that there is no independent source of the sensation.[5]

I should perhaps conclude with a few words on my critique of nineteenth- and early twentieth-century science. In the last decades, there has been much criticism of cultural critics' attempts to analyze "science." Titles such as *Fashionable Nonsense: Postmodern Intellectuals' Abuse of Science* (Sokal and Bricmont, 1997, 1998),[6] *Higher Superstition: The Academic Left and Its Quarrels with Science* (Gross and Levitt, 1994), and *A House Built on Sand: Exposing Postmodernist Myths about Science* (Koertge, 1998), to name a few, attest to the negative reaction to humanist scholars' forays into science. Richard Dawkins, in *A Devil's Chaplain: Reflections on Hope, Lies, Science and Love* (2003), mocks cultural critiques of science's undisputed access to the truth when he writes that

> a scientist who has the temerity to utter the t-word ('true') is likely to encounter a form of philosophical heckling which goes something like this:
> "There is no absolute truth. You are committing an act of personal faith when you claim that the scientific method, including mathematics and logic, is the privileged road to truth. Other cultures might believe that truth is to be found in a rabbit's entrails,

or the ravings of a prophet up a pole. It is only your personal faith in science that leads you to favour your brand of truth."

That strand of half-baked philosophy goes by the name of cultural relativism.[7]

Dawkins goes on to add that science is true because it produces results. In other words, scientific theories and mathematical equations can make an airplane fly.[8] While in principle I agree with Dawkins's defense of the scientific method and scientific achievements, his arguments do not address the many falsehoods presented as "science" throughout history. How does one explain, for example, doctors' continued use of bloodletting as a treatment and prevention for disease up into the nineteenth century even though there were no empirical results supporting this three-thousand-year-old practice?[9] How does one account for a revision of the female sexual response in the mid-nineteenth century that lasted for over a hundred years despite empirical evidence to the contrary? One could argue that this was not truly "science." However, at the time it was called just that, and doctors and scientists insisted that empirical evidence supported it.

Philosophical and metaphysical speculation, particularly regarding the inherent nature of the human subject, can serve as an important check on the abuse of the name of "science," because it serves as a necessary reminder of science's limitations—that is, of what we, as human beings, do not and cannot comprehend empirically. When it comes to issues such as the "essence" or "purpose" of human existence, I agree with Pardo Bazán that there is no truly scientific answer to these questions.[10] Explanations of such matters, whether sought through faith or science, are bound to be speculative and imperfect. Had the Catholic Church in sixteenth-century Spain or the Spanish medical community in the nineteenth century been willing to recognize their ultimate ignorance about such issues, women's lives likely would have been very different. The refusal of scientific and religious institutions to accept the limitations of their definitions has often prevented, rather than facilitated, the universe from revealing its designs, whatever those may be.

NOTES

INTRODUCTION

1. Shortly after becoming a nun in 1829, Sor Patrocinio began "to have visions and revelations, followed by the development of [. . .] stigmata." Henry Charles Lea, *A History of the Inquisition of Spain*, 4 vols. (New York: Macmillan, 1906–1907), 4:92, Library of Iberian Resources Online, https://libro.uca.edu/lea4/lea4.htm; Arturo González and Miguel Diéguez, *Sor Patrocinio* (Madrid: Nacional, 1981), 175.
2. González and Diéguez, *Sor Patrocinio*, 221.
3. González and Diéguez, 250.
4. This and the following biographical information on Sor Patrocinio are taken from González and Diéguez, 39–71.
5. Andrea Graus, "Mysticism in the Courtroom in 19th-Century Europe," *History of the Human Sciences* 31, no. 3 (March 2018): 21–22, https://doi.org/10.1177/0952695118761499.
6. Andrea Graus, "'Wonder Nuns': Sor Patrocinio, the Politics of the Supernatural, and Republican Caricature," *Journal of Religious History* 42, no. 4 (November 2018): 569, https://doi.org/10.1111/1467-9809.12544.
7. Graus, "Mysticism in the Courtroom," 25.
8. Graus, 27, 31.
9. Graus, 34.
10. Jan Goldstein, "The Hysteria Diagnosis and Politics of Anticlericalism in Late Nineteenth-Century France," *Journal of Modern History* 54, no. 2 (June 1982): 236.
11. Goldstein, "The Hysteria Diagnosis," 239.
12. Janet Beizer, *Ventriloquized Bodies: Narratives of Hysteria in Nineteenth-Century France* (Ithaca: Cornell UP, 1993), 9.
13. Graus, "'Wonder Nuns,'" 589.
14. While specialists initially attributed the images to Gustavo and Valeriano Bécquer, the consensus now seems to be that the pseudonym SEM refers

to a group of anonymous artists. Isabel Burdiel, "El descenso de los reyes y la nación moral: A propósito de los *Borbones en pelota*," in *Los Borbones en Pelota*, ed. Isabel Burdiel (Zaragoza: Institución Fernando "El Católico," 2012), 10.

15. Isabel Burdiel, "*Los Borbones en pelota*: La pornografía política en la crisis del reinado isabelino," in *Los Borbones en pelota*, ed. Isabel Burdiel (Zaragoza: Institución Fernando "El Católico," 2012), 61.

16. Graus, "'Wonder Nuns,'" 569.

17. Lou Charnon-Deutsch, *Fictions of the Feminine in the Nineteenth-Century Spanish Press* (University Park: Pennsylvania State University Press, 2000), 124.

18. Maite Zubiaurre, *Cultures of the Erotic in Spain, 1898–1939* (Nashville, TN: Vanderbilt University Press, 2012), 47.

19. Angela King, "The Prisoner of Gender: Foucault and the Disciplining of the Female Body," *Journal of International Women's Studies* 5, no. 2 (March 2004): 29, https://vc.bridgew.edu/jiws/vol5/iss2/4; Monique Deveaux, "Feminism and Empowerment: A Critical Reading of Foucault," *Feminist Studies* 20, no. 2 (Summer 1994): 224, http://www.jstor.org/stable/3178151.

20. Dominique D. Fisher, "Should Feminists Forget Foucault?," *Studies in 20th Century Literature* 22, no. 1 (January 1998): 1–18, https://doi.org/10.4148/2334-4415.1440.

21. Fisher, "Should Feminists Forget Foucault?," 10–11.

22. King, "The Prisoner of Gender," 29.

23. Richard Cleminson and Francisco Vázquez García, *Hermaphroditism, Medical Science and Sexual Identity in Spain, 1850–1960* (Cardiff: University of Wales Press, 2009), 17–18.

24. Cleminson and Vázquez García, *Hermaphroditism*, 29.

25. Catherine Jagoe, "Sexo y género en la medicina del siglo XIX," in *La mujer en los discursos de género: Textos y contextos en el siglo XIX*, eds. Catherine Jagoe, Alda Blanco, and Cristina Enríquez de Salamanca (Barcelona: Icaria, 1998): 305–67.

26. Jesús Cruz, *The Rise of Middle-Class Culture in Nineteenth-Century Spain* (Baton Rouge: Louisiana State University Press, 2011), 3.

27. Cleminson and Vázquez García, *Hermaphroditism*, 82.

28. Ricardo Campos Marín, *Monlau, Rubio, Giné: Curar y gobernar: Medicina y liberalismo en la España del siglo XIX* (Madrid: Nivola, 2003), 42–43, 60, 62.

29. Campos Marín, *Monlau, Rubio, Giné*, 60, 62.

30. Joshua Goode, *Impurity of Blood: Defining Race in Spain: 1879–1939* (Baton Rouge: Louisiana State University Press, 2009), 4.

31. Goode, *Impurity of Blood*, 3, 13.

32. Ricardo Campos Marín, Rafael Huertas García-Alejo, and José Martínez Pérez, *Los ilegales de la naturaleza: Medicina y degeneracionismo en la España de la Restauración (1876–1923)* (Madrid: Consejo Superior de Investigaciones Científicas, 2000), 164.

33. Richard Cleminson and Teresa Fuentes Peris, "'La mala vida': Source

and Focus of Degeneration, Degeneracy and Decline," *Journal of Spanish Cultural Studies* 10, no. 4 (December 2009): 385–97, https://doi.org/10.1080/14636200903400173.

34. Francisco Vázquez García, *La invención del racismo: Nacimiento de la biopolítica en España, 1600–1940* (Madrid: Akal, 2011): 13.
35. Vázquez García, *La invención del racismo*, 13.
36. Bridget A. Aldaraca, *El ángel del hogar: Galdós and the Ideology of Domesticity in Spain* (Chapel Hill: North Carolina Studies in the Romance Languages and Literatures, 1991), 64.
37. Campos Marín, García-Alejo, and Martínez Pérez, *Los ilegales*, 175.
38. Erika Rodríguez, "Crip Time in Fin-de-siècle Spain: Disability, Degeneration, and Eugenics." (PhD diss., Washington University in Saint Louis 2019), 2. According to Rodríguez, "Commonly used terms in medical, legal, and popular texts identified people by their specific impairments, such as *inválido* (invalid), *ciego* (blind), *manco* (one-armed), *idiota* (idiot), *demente* (mad), and later, more broadly as *anormales* (abnormal)." ("Crip Time," 2).
39. Anna Mollow, "Chriphystemologies: What Disability Theory Needs to Know about Hysteria," *Journal of Literary & Cultural Disability Studies* 8, no. 1 (2014): 185–86, https://www.muse.jhu.edu/article/548850.
40. Mollow, "Chriphystemologies," 185–87.
41. Judith Butler, *Bodies That Matter: On the Discursive Limits of "Sex"* (London: Routledge, 1993), 10.
42. Robert Dale Parker, *How to Interpret Literature: Critical Theory for Literary and Cultural Studies*, 3rd ed. (New York: Oxford University Press, 2015), 281–82.
43. Parker, *How to Interpret Literature*, 260.
44. Jagoe, "Sexo y género" 306.
45. Janet Beizer, in regard to hysteria, notes that "While the writer [. . .] sees himself as literary experimenter injecting an exotic pathological strain into the novel, the physician, at roughly the same time, finds considerable traces of hysteria in the novel" (*Ventriloquized Bodies*, 16).
46. *Nazarín* (1907) and *Ángel Guerra* (1891) also deal with questions of saintliness and mysticism, but in men. The Galdós novel perhaps most related to the study here is *La fontana de oro* which deals with questions of mysticism and hysteria in women and uses Santa Teresa de Jesús as an intertext to develop the topic. See Bienvenido Morros Mestres, "La histeria de Paulina Porreño en *La fontana de oro* de Galdós," *Bulletin Hispanique* 110, no. 1 (June 2008): 333–70, https://doi.org/10.4000/bulletinhispanique.664.
47. Denise DuPont, *Writing Teresa: The Saint from Avila at the fin-de-siglo* (Lewisburg, PA: Bucknell University Press, 2011), 61–63.

CHAPTER 1

1. Esteban Rodríguez Ocaña, *La constitución de la medicina social como disciplina en España (1882–1923)* (Madrid: Ministerio de Sanidad y Consumo, 1987), 17.

2.   José Martínez, "Sexualidad y orden social: La visión médica en la España del primer tercio del siglo XIX." *Asclepio* 2, no. 2 (1990): 120, http://hdl.handle.net/10261/26237.

3.   Martínez, "Sexualidad y orden social," 120.

4.   Juan Casco Solís, "La higiene sexual en el proceso de institucionalización de la sanidad pública." *Asclepio* 2, no. 2 (1990): 224.

5.   Rodríguez Ocaña, *La constitución*, 17–18.

6.   Casco Solís, "La higiene sexual," 238.

7.   Jo Labanyi, *Gender and Modernization in the Spanish Realist Novel* (New York: Oxford University Press, 2000), 71.

8.   Thomas W. Laqueur, *Making Sex: Body and Gender from the Greeks to Freud* (Cambridge, MA: Harvard University Press, 1990), 194.

9.   Laqueur, *Making Sex*, 196.

10. Pedro Felipe Monlau, *Higiene del matrimonio, o, El libro de los casados*, 2nd ed. (Madrid: M. Rivadeneyra, 1858), 15. According to Richard Cleminson, Monlau's best-selling hygiene manuals made him "the first to provide a systematic, in-depth marriage and health guide for couples" in Spain. Richard Cleminson, *Anarchism, Science, and Sex: Eugenics in Eastern Spain, 1900–1937* (New York: Lang, 2000), 65.

11. Laqueur, *Making Sex*, 6, 196–97.

12. Joan Cadden, *Meanings of Sex Difference in the Middle Ages: Medicine, Science, and Culture* (Cambridge, UK: Cambridge University Press, 1993), 3; Lorraine Daston and Katherine Park, "The Hermaphrodite and the Orders of Nature: Sexual Ambiguity in Early Modern France," in *Premodern Sexualities*, edited by Louise Fradenburg and Carla Freccero (New York: Routledge, 1996), 118; cited in Cleminson and Vázquez García, *Hermaphroditism*, 6.

13. Jagoe, "Sexo y género," 314–33.

14. For example, Monlau describes the "polarization of the sexes" in the following way: "El hombre y la mujer no solo se distinguen entre sí por la diversa configuracion ó situacion y uso de los órganos de la generacion, sino tambien por otros varios caracteres especiales (anatómicos, fisiológicos y psicológicos) que completan la sexualidad separada, constituyendo la mas admirable armonía de oposicion, ó lo que algunos naturalistas llaman tambien la *polarizacion de los sexos*" (*Higiene*, 113; italics in the original; Man and women are not only different from each other in the unique configuration and condition of their reproductive organs, but also in other very special characteristics (anatomical, physiological, and psychological) that complement a separate sexuality, consisting of the most admirable harmony of opposition, or what some naturalists also call the *polarization of the sexes*).

15. According to Monlau, for example,

> La mujer está dotada de una sensibilidad mayor; sus sentidos son mas delicados y finos. Predominan en la mujer las facultades afectivas, así como en el hombre las intelectuales. El destino de la mujer, dice

Cabanis, no es figurar en el liceo ni en el pórtico, en el gimnasio ni el hipódromo. Por esto, dice otro observador, las mujeres no han creado religion alguna, ni compuesto ningun poema épico, ni hecho grandes descubrimientos. Su destino es fundar las delicias y el amor de la familia. (*Higiene*, 115)

Woman is endowed with a greater sensitivity; her senses are more delicate y refined. Emotional faculties dominate in women. Woman's destiny, Cabanis says, is not to have a role in the lyceum or in the great institutions, or at the gymnasium, or at the racetrack. That's why, as another observer states, women have not created any type of religion, have not written any epic poems, have not made great discoveries. Their destiny is to establish the delights and love of the home.

16. Busto, Andrés del. "Problemas morales y sociales que resuelve el estudio médico de la mujer," in *Discursos leídos en la solemne sesión inaugural del año de 1892 de la Real Academia de Medicina* (Madrid: Enrique Teodoro, 1892), 23. All translations by the author unless otherwise indicated.

17. Monlau argues that

El matrimonio constituye, por consiguiente, un sér nuevo, con órganos exteriores dobles para las dos individualidades corpóreas, pero con estas confundidas en un solo amor, en un solo pensamiento y en una sola voluntad. [. . .] El alma del que hemos llamado *sér humano* se manifiesta por uno de sus órganos, por el mas inteligente (el varon), y fuera ridículo pedir dos votos al sér que no debe tener mas que una voluntad" (*Higiene*, 3–4)

The married couple constitutes, accordingly, a new being, with double external organs for two corporal individualities, but with these confused in only one love, one way of thinking, and one will. [. . .] The soul of the one we have called a human being, is shown by one of its parts, by the most intelligent part (the man), and it would be ridiculous to ask for voting rights for the other part who should not have a separate will.

18. María José Ruiz Somavilla, "La legitimación de la ideología a través de la ciencia: La salud y la enfermedad de la mujer en el *Siglo Médico*," in *De la ilustracion al romanticismo, VII Encuentro: La mujer en los siglos XVIII—XIX*, ed. Cinta Canterla González (Cádiz, Spain: Universidad de Cádiz, 1994), 110.

19. Pulido writes that "La lectura continuada de ciertos libros, y las grandes tareas mentales, son causas muy abonadas que facilitan el desarrollo de la locura" (Regularly reading certain books, and engaging in challenging mental tasks, are well substantiated causes of the development of insanity). Ángel Pulido Fernández, *Bosquejos medico-sociales para la mujer* (Madrid: Víctor Saiz, 1876), 336.

20. Monlau, *Higiene*, 205, 240–41.

21. Raymond Carr, *Modern Spain: 1875–1980* (Oxford, UK: Oxford University Press, 1980), 39.

22. Michel Foucault, *History of Sexuality. Volume 1: An Introduction*, trans. Robert Hurley, (New York: Random House, 1978), 92–102.

23. Foucault, *History of Sexuality*, 104–5.

24. While I do not discuss the second technology, the pedagogization of children's sex, its central theme, masturbation, will be discussed in relation to women under the category of the psychiatrization of perverse pleasure.

25. In his introduction to the volume *La sexualidad en la España Contemporánea: 1800–1950* (2011; Sexuality in contemporary Spain: 1800–1950) Jean-Louis Guereña summarizes the current research on the history of sexuality in Spain. He asserts that a once neglected field of study has received deserved attention in the last two decades, thanks to the increasing prominence of feminist studies and queer studies in the English-speaking academic world, the three volumes that comprise Foucault's *History of Sexuality*, Spanish journals such as *Asclepio, Dynamis, Gimbernat*, and *Revista de Sexología*, and a series of articles and monographs by authors such as Francisco Vázquez García, Andrés Moreno Mengíbar, Rafael Huertas García-Alejo, Richard Cleminson, José Benito Seone Cegarra and Eduardo Balbo, among others. Jean-Louis Guereña, introduction to *La sexualidad en la España contemporánea: 1800–1930*, ed. Jean-Louis Guereña (Cádiz: Universidad de Cádiz, 2011), 12–15. Another indispensable resource on the history of sexuality in Spain is Maite Zubiaurre's *Cultures of the Erotic in Spain, 1898–1939* (Nashville, TN: Vanderbilt University Press, 2012).

26. An earlier version of this chapter was initially published as Jennifer Smith, "Women and the Deployment of Sexuality in Nineteenth-Century Spain," *Revista de Estudios Hispánicos* 40, no. 1 (January 2006): 145–70. For other articles that deal with the treatment of women in nineteenth-century medical texts see María Pilar Simón Palmer, "La higiene y la medicina de la mujer española a través de los libros (S.XVI a XIX)," in *La mujer en la historia de Espana (Siglos XVI–XX): Actas de las II jornadas de investigacion interdisciplinaria sobre la mujer*, ed. Cinta Canterla González (Madrid: Universidad Autónoma de Madrid, 1982), 71–84; Josette Borderies-Guereña, "El discurso higiénico como conformador de la mentalidad femenina (1864–1915)," in *Mujeres y hombres en la formacion del pensamiento occidental*, ed. Virginia Maquieira D'Angelo et al. (Madrid: Universidad Autónoma de Madrid, 1989), 2:299–309; Bridget Aldaraca, "The Medical Construction of the Feminine Subject in Nineteenth-Century Spain," in *Cultural and Historical Grounding for Hispanic and Luso-Brazilian Feminist Literary Criticism*, ed. Hernan Vidal (Minneapolis, MN: Institute for the Study of Ideologies and Literature, 1989), 395–413; Jesús Castellanos, Isabel Jiménez Lucena, and María José Ruiz Somavilla, "La ciencia médica en el siglo XIX como instrumento de reafirmación ideológica: La defensa de la desigualdad de la mujer a través de la patología femenina," in *La mujer en Andalucia: Actas del I encuentro interdisciplinar de estudios de la mujer*, ed. Pilar Ballarín and Teresa Orti (Granada: Universidad de Granada, 1990), 2:879–88. Consuelo Flecha

García, "La mujer en los discursos médicos del siglo XIX," in *Las mujeres en Andalucia: Actas del 2° encuentro interdisciplinar de estudios de la mujer en Andalucia* (Málaga: Diputación Provincial de Malaga, 1993), 1:189–202; María José Ruiz Somavilla, "La legitimación." Also of interest is chapter 4 of Francisco Vázquez García and Andrés Moreno Mengíbar, *Sexo y razón: Una genealogia de la moral sexual en España (Siglos XVI–XX)* (Madrid: Akal, 1997), and chapters 7 and 8 of Catherine Jagoe, Alda Blanco, and Cristina Enríquez de Salamanca eds., *La mujer en los discursos de género: Textos y contextos en el siglo XIX* (Barcelona: Icaria, 1998). While other critics have already discussed the ways particular nineteenth-century medical discourses constructed the female subject, my objective here is to show how this process functioned specifically within Foucault's concept of the hysterization of the female body.

27. Jagoe, "Sexo y género," 317.
28. Foucault, *History of Sexuality*, 104.
29. Baltasar Viguera, *La fisiología y patología de la mujer* (Madrid: Ortega, 1827), 1:13.
30. Ruiz Somavilla, "La legitimación," 104–5.
31. Monlau, *Higiene*, 103. *Higiene del matrimonio* went through fourteen editions. Efigenio Amezcúa, "Cien años de temática sexual en España, 1850–1950: Repertorio y análisis. Contribución al estudio de materiales para una historia de la sexología," *Revista de Sexología* 48 (1991): 136. According to Zubiaurre, it became "the leading model of subsequent works on marital sex and hygiene" (*Cultures*, 44).
32. Viguera, *La fisiología*, 2:67.
33. Viguera 1:17.
34. Pulido Fernández, *Bosquejos*, 335.
35. Jagoe, "Sexo y género," 339.
36. Mark S. Micale, *Approaching Hysteria: Disease and Its Interpretations* (Princeton, NJ: Princeton University Press, 1995), 19.
37. Micale, *Approaching*, 23.
38. Micale, 23.
39. Micale, 24–25.
40. Jagoe, "Sexo y género," 341–42.
41. Elaine Showalter, *The Female Malady: Women, Madness and English Culture: 1830–1980* (New York: Penguin, 1985): 148.
42. Jagoe, "Sexo y género," 342.
43. Micale, *Approaching*, 25.
44. Jagoe, "Sexo y género," 338–39.
45. Micale, 24.
46. Jagoe, "Sexo y género," 344.
47. Because hysteria was often diagnosed in women who contravened conventional gender norms, feminist critics such as Carroll Smith-Rosenberg and Elaine Showalter have interpreted hysteria as both an act of defiance on the part of women and as a negative diagnosis applied by medical

doctors to contain such behavior. Carroll Smith-Rosenberg, *Disorderly Conduct: Visions of Gender in Victorian America* (New York: Knopf, 1985); Showalter, *The Female Malady*.

48. Jagoe, "Sexo y género," 343.
49. Ángel Pulido Fernández, *Anales de la Sociedad Ginecológica Española* 2 (1876), 343. Pulido Fernández summarizes the various talks on discontinuous pages of volume 2 (1876) of the *Anales de la Sociedad Ginecólogica Española*.
50. Pulido Fernández, *Anales*, 53–54.
51. Pulido Fernández, 53.
52. Pulido Fernández, 79.
53. Laqueur, *Making Sex*, 8, 163.
54. Peratoner, *Fisiología de la noche de bodas: misterios del lecho conyugal* (Barcelona: N. Curriols, 1892),142. While Amancio Peratoner's work was clearly influenced by Monlau's, he branched out by giving more space to the so-called perversions (Amezúa, "Cien años," 137; Zubiaurre, *Cultures*, 43).
55. Monlau, *Higiene*, 146.
56. Foucault, *History of Sexuality*, 104–5.
57. Peratoner, *Fisiología*, 11.
58. Juan Giné y Partagas, *Curso elemental de higien eprivada y publica*, 4th ed. (Barcelona: Juan y Antonio Bastinos, 1880), 3:442–43.
59. Foucault, *History of Sexuality*, 105.
60. Raquel Alvarez Peláez explores the role of Malthusianism, neo-Malthusianism, and eugenics in the debates on birth control and women's reproductive role in society in early twentieth-century Spain. Raquel Alvarez Peláez, "La mujer española y el control de natalidad en los comienzos del siglo XX," *Asclepio* 42 (1990): 175–200.
61. Thomas Robert Malthus, *An Essay on the Principle of Population*, ed. Philip Appleman (New York: Norton, 1976), 20.
62. Malthus, *An Essay*, 132.
63. Rodríguez Ocaña, *La constitución*, 10.
64. Rodríguez Ocaña, 20.
65. Pulido Fernández, *Bosquejos*, 36.
66. Monlau, *Higiene*, 263.
67. Francisco Vázquez García notes that Monlau's argument went against his own dictum that what is not moral is also not hygienic; in other words, chastity could not be hygienic and morally good for some and not for others. Francisco Vázquez García, "Patologización del celibato en la medicina española (1820–1920)," *Asclepio* 70, no. 2 (June-December 2018): 6.
68. Giné y Partagas, *Curso*, 3:397.
69. Peratoner, *Fisiología*, 146.
70. Peratoner, 14.
71. Foucault, *History of Sexuality*, 105.
72. Jagoe, "Sexo y género," 326.
73. This method was not particularly effective since, as Alvarez Peláez points out, it was not until 1923 that doctors finally understood exactly how the

menstrual cycle and ovulation worked. Alvarez Peláez, "La mujer," 189.

74. Suárez Casañ, *Enciclopedia médica*, 2:40–41. Zubiaurre lists Vicente Suárez Casañ, alongside Felipe Monlau and Amancio Peratoner, as the most influential early nineteenth-century sexologists (*Cultures*, 43).

75. Monlau, *Higiene*, 258.

76. Suárez Casañ, *Enciclopedia médica*, 2:131–35.

77. Monlau, *Higiene*, 475.

78. Quoted in Rodríguez Ocaña, *La constitución*, 30.

79. Foucault, *History of Sexuality*, 124.

80. Foucault, 123–24.

81. Monlau, *Higiene*, 139; Peratoner, *La fisiología*, 47.

82. Suárez Casañ, *Enciclopedia médica*, 2:161.

83. Suárez Casañ, 2:287.

84. *La vida de Lazarillo de Tormes*, 4th ed. (Madrid: Castalia, 1984), 107.

85. Monlau, *Higiene*, 430.

86. Monlau, 430.

87. Monlau, 431.

88. Pulido Fernández, *Bosquejos*, 26.

89. Busto, "Problemas," 51.

90. Laqueur, *Making Sex*, 8, 163.

91. Jagoe, "Sexo y género," 318–19, 327.

92. Viguera writes,

> En el vértice de la vulva preside y corona a las ninfas el clitoris, órgano en miniatura muy semejante al miembro viril, y que goza de algunas de sus calidades, pues que es en la muger el foco irradiante de la sensualidad, así como la glande lo es en el hombre. . . . La sensibilidad de este órgano es del mas esquisito témple, y su influencia de la mayor importancia para la concepción. (*La fisiología*, 1:94)
>
> *At the crown of the vulva, the clitoris presides and crowns the labia, it is a miniature organ very similar to the male member, and enjoys some of its qualities, since in women it is the radiating focal point of sensuality, just as the glans is in the male. [. . .] The sensitivity of this organ is of the most exquisite temperament, and its influence is of the greatest importance in conception.*

93. Monlau, *Higiene*, 206.

94. Monlau, 206.

95. Peratoner, *Fisiología*, 43.

96. Giné y Partagás, *La fisiología*, 1:563.

97. Busto, "Problemas," 49.

98. Sigmund Freud, "Femininity," in *New Introductory Lectures on Psychoanalysis*, edited and translated by James Strachey (New York: Norton, 1965), 112–35.

99. Foucault, *History of Sexuality*, 105.

100. For more on the concept of perversion in nineteenth-century medicine see Eduardo A. Balbo, "El concepto de perversión en la psiquiatría dinámica,"

Asclepio 42, no. 2 (1990): 101–9; Rafael Huertas García Alejo, "El concepto de 'perversion' sexual en la medicina positivista," *Asclepio* 42, no. 1 (1990): 89–99.

101. Butler, *Bodies*, 3.
102. Carol Groneman, *Nymphomania: A History* (New York: Norton, 2000), xvii–xviii.
103. Thomas Laqueur, *Solitary Sex: A Cultural History of Masturbation* (Brooklyn, NY: Zone Books, 2003), 215.
104. Laqueur, *Solitary Sex*, 13–15.
105. Laqueur, 13–14.
106. Laqueur, 38–40.
107. Laqueur, 40–41. Vázquez García and Seoane Cegarra analyze the campaign against masturbation specifically in nineteenth-century Spain. Francisco Vázquez García and José Benito Seoane Cegarra, "España y la cruzada médica contra la masturbación (1800–1900): Elementos para una genealogía," *Hispania* 64, no. 218 (2004), 835–67.
108. Foucault, *History of Sexuality*, 104.
109. Viguera, *La fisiología*, 2:116.
110. Jagoe, "Sexo y género," 338.
111. Peratoner, *Fisiología*, 167.
112. Juan Cuesta y Ckerner, *Enfermedades de las mujeres: Extracto de las asignaturas que tienen que estudiar los cirujanos de segunda clase que aspiran al titulo de Facultativo habilitados por medio de estudios privados* (Madrid: Tomas Alonso, 1868), 7.
113. Doctors also linked prostitution to masturbation and large clitorises. Carol Groneman, "Nymphomania: The Historical Construction of Female Sexuality," *Signs* 19, no. 2 (Winter 1994): 355–56. For more on prostitution in late nineteenth-century Spain see Pura Fernández, *Mujer pública y vida privada: Del arte eunuco a la novela lupanaria* (London: Tamesis, 2008); Akiko Tsuchiya, *Marginal Subjects: Gender Deviance in Fin-de-siècle Spain* (Toronto: University of Toronto Press, 2011); Akiko Tsuchiya, "Taming the Deviant Body: Representations of the Prostitute in Nineteenth-Century Spain," *Anales Galdosianos* 36 (2001): 255–67.
114. Cleminson and Vázquez García, *Hermaphroditism*, 2.
115. Cleminson and Vázquez García, 85.
116. Monlau, *Higiene*, 107–8.
117. Monlau, 238–39.
118. V. Suárez Casañ, *El amor lesbio*, vol. 9 of *Conocimientos para la vida privada*, 2nd ed., ed. Pío Arias Carvajal (Barcelona: Maucci, [189-?]).
119. Peratoner, *Fisiología*, 111.
120. Freud, "Femininity," 129–30.
121. Viguera, *La fisiología*, 2:116.
122. Viguera, 2:135.
123. Francisco Vázquez García, "Ninfomanía y construcción simbólica de la femineidad (España, siglos XVIII-XIX)," in *De la ilustracion al romanti-*

cismo, VII encuentro: La mujer en los siglos XVIII–XIX, ed. Cinta Canterla González (Cadiz: Universidad de Cadiz, 1994), 131.

124. G. S. Rousseau, "Nymphomania, Bienville and the Rise of Erotic Sensibility," in *Sexuality in Eighteenth-Century Britain*, ed. Paul-Gabriel Bouce (Manchester: Manchester University Press, 1982), 98.

125. Pulido Fernández, *Bosquejos*, 59.

126. Pulido Fernández, 63.

127. Pulido Fernández, 64.

128. Viguera, *La fisiología*, 2:122.

129. Foucault, *History of Sexuality*, 139–40.

130. Foucault, 140–41.

131. Laqueur, *Making Sex*, 152.

CHAPTER 2

1. Tomás Álvarez, *Santa Teresa a contraluz: La santa ante la crítica* (Burgos: Monte Carmelo, 2004), 10–13. Mainez was director of the *Crónica de los Cervantistas* (The chronicle of Cervantistas), and the author of works such as *Vida de Miguel de Cervantes Saavedra* (The life of Miguel de Cervantes Saavedra), *Cervantes y los críticos* (Cervantes and the critics), and *Los continuadores del* Quijote (The continuers of *The Quixote*) (Álvarez, *Santa Teresa*, 10). Juan Bosco Sanramón describes Mainez as "el engendro antiteresiano quizá más desaforado y satánico de todos los tiempos" (perhaps the most outrageous and satanic anti-Teresa freak of all times). Juan Bosco Sanromán, "Anteriores centenarios de la muerte de Santa Teresa," in *Pérfil histórico de Santa Teresa*, edited by Teófanes Egido Martínez, 2nd ed. (Madrid, Editorial de Espiritualidad, 1981), 181.

2. Not all liberals shared Mainez's view. Many of the liberals on the organizing committee for the tricentennial celebration of the death of Santa Teresa sought to highlight the literary and humanistic value of her writings. This approach, however, was rejected by those who hoped to use the celebration as a means of strengthening the Catholic faith (Bosco Sanramón, "Anteriores," 181).

3. Álvarez, *Santa Teresa*, 15–16.

4. Álvarez, 15–21.

5. Álvarez, 23–24. The jury in Salamanca initially awarded Hahn first prize for the topic cited above. Yet, when the Bishop of Salamanca objected that Hahn's essays did not directly address the proposed topic, the jury decided to give him *la medalla de oro* (the gold medal) for one of the other proposed topics (Álvarez, 23–24). Only a few months later, at the beginning of 1883, Hahn's essay would be published by the *Revue des question scientifiques* (Journal of scientific questions), and shortly thereafter, as a separate publication (Álvarez, 27).

6. Álvarez, 27.

7. Álvarez, 55. Topic 5 read as follows: "Los éxtasis y arrobamientos de santa Teresa de Jesús, según ella los describe, tampoco son efecto de la enfermedad o accidente natural alguno, sino únicamente de la gracia de Dios" (Álvarez, 17; The ecstasies and raptures of Santa Teresa de Jesús, according to how she describes them, are not the effect of illness or any natural accident, but rather solely of the grace of God).

8. Álvarez, 56.

9. Álvarez, 59–61. As a result of the Church's condemnation of his work and the fallout that ensued, in 1887 G. Hahn withdrew from the Jesuit order so that the Church would no longer be associated in any way with his writings (Álvarez, 40).

10. Álvarez, 14–15.

11. Eduardo Ovejero y Maury was a famous translator at the time, best known for his Spanish translations of philosophical works by Arthur Schopenhauer, Friedrich Nietzsche, and John Stuart Mill, amongst others. *Filosofía en español*, s.v. "Eduardo Ovejero Maury," accessed August 28, 2019, http://www.filosofia.org/ave/001/a444.htm. Auguste Armand Victor Marie was doctor and chief of the Seine asylums. "Auguste Marie. Mysticisme et folie. Partie I. Extrait des 'Archives de Neurologie,' (Paris)," *Histoire et folie*, accessed August 26, 2019, http://www.histoiredelafolie. fr/psychiatrie-neurologie/auguste-marie-mysticisme-et-folie-partie-1-extrait-des-archives-de-neurologie-paris-deuxieme-serie-tome-vii-n40-avril-1899-pp-257-278. The prologue was written by Dr. Henri Thulié, a well-known doctor and anthropologist who specialized in mental illness.

12. Thomas Mautner, "Positivism," in *Dictionary of Philosophy* (New York: Penguin, 1997), 437–38.

13. Thomas Mautner, "Comte," in *Dictionary of Philosophy* (New York: Penguin, 1997), 102; Arline Reilein Standley, *Auguste Comte* (Boston: Twayne, 1981), 31.

14. Stanely G. Payne. *Spanish Catholicism: An Historical Overview* (Madison: University of Wisconsin Press, 1984), 118.

15. Payne, *Spanish Catholicism*, 76–77. The liberal restoration of the constitution in 1820 brought about the second abolition of the Inquisition (Payne 76). Although Fernando VII overturned the liberal reforms when he returned to power in 1823, he did not reinstate the Inquisition. Rather, he set up *juntas de fe* (faith committees) that served similar purposes. Adrian Shubert, *A Social History of Modern Spain* (London: Unwin Hyman, 1990), 147. Under the regency of María Cristina, the Inquisition was officially abolished by decree in 1834 (Lea, *A History*, 4:468). This is why 1834 is given as the date of the abolition of the Inquisition, even though the Inquisition had ceased to function in 1820. The following year, 1835, the *juntas de fe* were also abolished by decree (Lea 4:468).

16. Lea, *A History*, 4:82.

17. Shubert, *A Social History*, 167.

18. Carr, *Modern Spain*, 42.
19. Grace Jantzen, *Power, Gender and Christian Mysticism* (Cambridge, UK: Cambridge University Press, 1995), xv.
20. Pamela Beth Radcliff, *Modern Spain: 1808 to the Present* (Hoboken, NJ: John Wiley and Sons, 2017), 139.
21. Emilia Pardo Bazán, "La mujer española," in *La mujer española y otros escritos*, ed. Guadalupe Gómez Ferrer (Madrid: Cátedra, 1999), 90.
22. Quoted in Shubert, *A Social History*, 63.
23. Shubert, 55, 150–51.
24. Pardo Bazán, "La mujer," 89–91.
25. Pardo Bazán, 92.
26. A. Marie, *Misticismo y locura: Estudio de psicología normal y patológica comparadas*, trans. Eduardo Ovejero (Madrid: España Moderna, [1907?]), 143.
27. Eduardo Zamacois, *El misticismo y las perturbaciones del sistema nervioso* (Madrid: Imprenta Popular, 1893), 16.
28. Viguera, *La fisiología*, 1:19.
29. Ramón León Mainez Fernández, *Teresa de Jesús ante la crítica* (Madrid: Aurelio J. Alaria, 1880), 6.
30. Mainez Fernández, *Teresa de Jesús*, 26.
31. Cristina Mazzoni, *Saint Hysteria: Neurosis, Mysticism and Gender in European Culture* (Ithaca, NY: Cornell University Press, 1996), 37.
32. Mazzoni, *Saint Hysteria*, 90–91, 40–42, 31–36, 42–44.
33. Zamacois, *El misticismo*, 99.
34. Foucault, *History of Sexuality*, 62–64.
35. Foucault, 47.
36. Jeremy Tambling, *Confession: Sexuality, Sin, the Subject* (Manchester, UK: Manchester University Press, 1990), 2.
37. Alastair Hamilton, *Heresy and Mysticism in Sixteenth-Century Spain: The "Alumbrados."* (Toronto: University of Toronto Press, 1992), 25; Alison Weber, *Teresa of Ávila and the Rhetoric of Femininity* (Princeton, NJ: Princeton University Press, 1990), 22.
38. Hamilton, *Heresy*, 16; María Palacios Alcalde, "Las beatas ante la Inquisición," in *HispaniaSacra* 40, no. 81 (1988): 11–12, 129; Weber, *Teresa of Ávila*, 22.
39. Álvaro Huerga, *Historia de los Alumbrados* (Madrid: Fundación Universitaria Española, 1978–1994), 5:203.
40. Palacios Alcalde, "Las beatas," 123.
41. Palacios Alcalde 123; Huerga, *Historia*, 5:195–98.
42. Huerga 5:198–99.
43. Palacios Alcalde, "Las beatas," 112.
44. Palacios Alcalde, 113.
45. Huerga, *Historia*, 5:194.
46. *Dejamiento* was a form of mental prayer in which the individual surrendered his/her will to God (Hamilton, *Heresy*, 29; Weber, *Teresa of Ávila*, 24).
47. Weber, 24, n. 15; Jacqueline Holler, "More Sins than the Queen of England: Marina de San Miguel before the Mexican Inquisition," in

Women in the Inquisition: Spain and the New World, ed. Mary E. Giles (Baltimore, MD: Johns Hopkins University Press, 1999), 223–28.

48. Holler, "More Sins," 223.

49. Jacobus Sprenger and Heinrich Kramer, *Malleus Maleficarum*, trans. Montague Summers (London: Folio Society, 1968).

50. Mannarelli writes "Es posible percibir—en los procesos de beatas sospechosas de herejía—a través de las preguntas de los inquisidores y de las observaciones de los testigos, un especial interés por auscultar el presunto desacato sexual de las implicadas en esa clase de transgression." (It is possible to perceive—in the trials of *beatas* suspected of heresy—through the inquisitors' questions and the witnesses' observations, a special interest in investigation of the presumed sexual irreverence of the women implicated in that type of transgression). María Emma Mannarelli, *Hechiceras, beatas y expósitas: Mujeres y poder inquisitorial en Lima* (Lima, Congreso del Perú, 1998), 17.

51. Holler, "More Sins," 222–23.

52. Huerga, *Historia*, 5:204.

53. Huerga, 5:14.

54. According to Stanley G. Payne, the practice of living together outside of wedlock was so prevalent among both lay people and clergy that when Cardinal Cisneros tried to reform the situation in 1480, physical violence erupted and many friars moved to Morocco and converted to Islam rather than remain chaste (*Spanish Catholicism*, 39). Even the Counter-Reformation did not necessarily put an end to such practices since, as Payne states, "fornication between unmarried consenting adults was widely accepted and even considered unsinful during the sixteenth century" (50). Thus, we must remember that the sexual activities of the *alumbrados* were not necessarily an anomaly, because other members of society, including the clergy, engaged in such practices.

55. Hamilton, *Heresy*, 122.

56. Weber, *Teresa of Ávila*, 158–59.

57. Zamacois, *El misticismo*, 41.

58. Mainez Fernández, *Teresa de Jesús*, 26.

59. H. Thulié, prologue to *Misticismo y locura: Estudio de psicología normal y patológica comparadas*, trans. by Eduardo Ovejero (Madrid: España Moderna, [1907?]), 6.

60. According to Richet, "Cette hystérie légère n'est pas une maladie véritable. C'est une des variétés du caractère de la femme. On peut même dire que les hystériques sont femmes plus que les autres femmes: elles ont des sentimen[t]s passagers et vifs, des imaginations mobiles et brillantes, et parmi tout cela l'impuissance de dominer par la raison et le jugement ces sentimen[t]s et ces imaginations" (This mild hysteria is not a true disease. It is one type of female character. One can even say that hysterics are more female than other women: they have vivid and short-lived feelings, agile and brilliant imaginations, and in combination with all that

the inability to dominate these feelings and fantasies with reason and judgment). Charles Richet, "Les démoniaques d'aujourd'hui," *Revue des Deux Mondes* (1880): 346.

61. Mazzoni, *Saint Hysteria*, 34.

62. G. S. J. Hahn, "Les phénomènes hystériques et les révélations de Sainte Thérèse," *La Revue des Questions Scientifiques* 13–14 (1883): 24.

63. Richet argued that giving women an education superior to their social class was often the cause of hysteria ("Les démoniaques," 346).

64. Hahn writes, "On sait combien les hystériques sont portés à la simulation; aussi a-t-on recours aux précautions les plus attentives pour se mettre à l'abri de leurs ruses" ("Les phénomènes," 19; We know how much hysterics are prone to faking; so one should take the most careful precautions so as not to be taken in by their tricks).

65. For example, according to Richet, "Rien n'est plus commun en effet que de voir une jeune femme, jusque-là tendre à son mari et à ses enfan[t]s, les prendre subitement en disaffection, puis en haine" ("Les démoniaques," 347; Indeed, nothing is more common than seeing a young woman, who until then was affectionate toward her husband and children, suddenly show dislike, and even hatred for them).

66. Jagoe, "Sexo y género," 345.

67. Showalter makes this argument in *The Female Malady: Women, Madness, and English Culture*, and Smith-Rosenberg in *Disorderly Conduct: Visions of Gender in Victorian America*.

68. Marie, *Misticismo*, 153.

69. Mainez Fernández, *Teresa de Jesús*, 14–15.

70. Marie, *Misticismo*, 151–53.

71. V. Suárez Casañ, *Los vicios solitarios*, vol. 5 of *Conocimientos para la vida privada*, 2nd ed., edited by Pío Arias Carvajal. Barcelona: Maucci, [189-?], 68.

72. Francisco de Cortejarena y Aldebó, *Memoria presentada a la Academia de Medicina de Madrid: ¿Son hoy mas frecuentes que en otros tiempos las enfermedades de la matriz?* (Madrid: T. Fortanet, 1869), 8. This talk was given in 1867, but the publication date of the printed text is 1869.

73. Leopoldo Alas, *Solos de Clarín*. 4th ed. (Madrid: Librería de Fernando Fe, 1891), 83.

74. Leopoldo Alas, *Preludios de "Clarín,"* ed. Jean-François Botrel (Oviedo, Spain: Instituto de Estudios Asturianos, 1972), 28.

75. Pardo Bazán, "La mujer," 91.

76. Álvarez, Santa Teresa, 10.

77. Mainez Fernández, *Teresa de Jesús*, 30.

78. Zamacois, *El misticismo*, 50.

79. Richard von Krafft-Ebing, *Psychopathia Sexualis*, trans. Franklin S. Klaf (New York: Stein and Day, 1965), 4.

80. Viguera, *Fisiología*, 2:76–81.

81. Zamacois, *El misticismo*, 51–52.

82. Marie, *Misticismo*, 170.
83. Marie, 171.
84. Jacqueline Holler, ed. and trans., "The Spiritual and Physical Ecstasies of a Sixteenth-Century *Beata*: Marina de San Miguel Confesses before the Mexican Inquisition," in *Colonial Lives: Documents on Latin American History, 1550–1850*, ed. Richard Boyer and Geoffrey Spurling (Oxford, UK: Oxford University Press, 2000), 87.
85. Thesée Pouillet, *Del onanismo en la mujer (Placeres ilícitos)* (Madrid: A. Pérez, 1883), 75.
86. Pouillet, *Del onanismo*, 140.
87. According to Suárez Casañ, "Cuando más se masturba, tanto más crece la irritación de sus órganos genitales, y tanto mayor es su furor erótico y su lascivos deseos" (*Los vicios*, 62; When one masturbates more, the irritation of the sexual organs grows even more, and even more is their erotic fury and lascivious desires).
88. Mainez states that, "Perturbada la imaginacion de Teresa con sus lecturas amorosas, irreflexivas, inexpertas, ¿qué podia esperarse de aquel choque continuo de voluntades sobreexcitadas sino locas imprudencias?" (*Teresa de Jesús*, 16; Teresa's imagination perturbed by her thoughtless, inexperienced, romantic readings, what could one expect from that continuous clash of overly aroused desires but crazy indiscretions). Although the "crazy indiscretions" caused by Santa Teresa's overly excited imagination seem to refer to many of her behaviors, the nineteenth-century reader, most likely familiar with a number of the hygiene manuals circulating during the time, would have made the connection between Santa Teresa's overly active imaginative faculties and the solitary vice that was said to attack women who were fond of reading novels.
89. Palacios Alcalde, "Las beatas," 126–27.
90. Mazzoni, *Saint Hysteria*, 38.
91. Micale, *Approaching*, 25.
92. Viguera, *Fisiología*, 2:86.
93. Viguera, 2:86.
94. Viguera 2:85.
95. Monlau, *Higiene*, 140.
96. Richet, "Les démoniaques," 356.
97. Monlau, for example, warns his male readers of this fact:

    > No olviden esta regla los lectores, y sepan que toda emision seminal extenúa el cuerpo, ya á causa de la sustraccion del líquido espermático, que es la quinta esencia de la sangre, elaborado con prolijidad por la naturaleza, ya tambien á causa del sacudimiento que acompaña á su eyaculacion. [. . .] Todo animal, y todavía mas el hombre, después del cóito, ha dado con esfuerzos convulsivos una porcion de su vida: el resto toca ya á la muerte. (*Higiene*, 135)

    > *Do not forget this rule readers, and know that every seminal emission drains the body, whether because of the loss of the spermatic fluid,*

which is the fifth essence of the blood, manufactured with laboriousness by nature, or also because of the spasms that accompany its ejaculation. [. . .] Every animal, especially man, after coitus, has given away part of his life through the convulsive force: the rest now remains for death.

98. Suárez Casáñ, *Los vicios*, 63.
99. Richet, "Les démoniaques," 354.
100. Jacqueline Carroy-Thirard, "Possession, extase, hystérie au 19ᵉ siècle," *Psychanalyse à l'université* 5, no. 19 (June 1980): 507.
101. For an analysis of visual representations of the mystic/hysteric, see Nuria Godón, "Las poseídas: Cuadros histéricos de la mística en el imaginario decimonónico," in *Baroque Projections: Images and Texts in Dialog with the Early Modern Hispanic World*, ed. Frédéric Conrod and Michael Horswell (Newark, DE: Juan de la Cuesta, 2016), 109–32.
102. Hahn "Les phénomènes," 32–33.
103. John Stuart Mill, *"On Liberty" and Other Essays*, ed. John Gray (Oxford, UK: Oxford University Press, 1998), 536.
104. Foucault, *History of Sexuality*, 135–45.
105. Carroy-Thirard, "Possession," 500.
106. Emilia Pardo Bazán, *San Francisco de Asís* (Mexico City: Porrúa), 1994, 184–85.
107. Luce Irigaray, *Speculum of the Other Woman*, trans. Gillian C. Gill (Ithaca, NY: Cornell University Press, 1985), 191.
108. Kathy Bacon, *Negotiating Sainthood: Distinction, Cursilería and Saintliness in Spanish Novels* (London: Legenda, 2007), 2.
109. DuPont, *Writing Teresa*, 9.
110. Carolina Coronado, *Jarilla: Novela original, Los genios gemelos* (Badajoz, Spain: Dip. Prov. de Badajoz, 2001), 299.
111. Susan Kirkpatrick, *Las Románticas: Women Writers and Subjectivity in Spain* (Berkeley: University of California Press, 1989), 296.
112. Ángeles Ezama Gil, "Ana Ozores y el modelo teresiano: Ejemplaridad y escritura literaria," in *Leopoldo Alas, un clásico contemporáneo (1901–2001): Actas del congreso celebrado en Oviedo (12–16 de noviembre de 2001)*, ed. Araceli Iravedra Valea, Elena de Lorenzo Álvarez, and Álvaro Ruiz de la Peña (Oviedo, Spain: Universidad de Oviedo, 2002), 2:779, 782.

CHAPTER 3

1. Pura Fernández, *Eduardo López Bago y el naturalismo radical: La novela y el mercado en el siglo XIX* (Amsterdam: Rodopi, 1995), 5.
2. As Maite Zubiaurre notes, López Bago's novels were best sellers in spite of their being labeled obscene. Maite Zubiaurre, introduction to *El cura (Caso de incesto): Novela médico-social*, by Eduardo López Bago, ed. Maite Zubiaurre and Luis Cuesta (Doral, FL: Stockcero, 2013), xiii.
3. Fernández, *Eduardo López Bago*, 73.

4. Fernández, *Eduardo López Bago* 72.

5. For example, toward the end of *El cura* (The priest), the protagonist hears voices that tell him, "La materia y las cosas físicas, los cuerpos y sus cualidades, eso es lo que analiza [la escuela de la sensación]. Fuera de esto, el hombre no sabe nada. La naturaleza es su todo. Puede analizarla, someterla al escalpelo, sondarla, medirla, pesarla, calcular sus leyes; pero nada más; no puede penetrar hasta la fuerza viva: el alma no la concibe, no tiene datos que la revelen. No existe" (Matter and physical things, bodies and their qualities, that is what [the study of sensations] analyzes. Apart from that, man knows nothing. Nature is his entire existence. He can analyze it, operate on it, probe it, measure it, weigh it, calculate its laws; but nothing else; he cannot penetrate the living force: he cannot comprehend the soul; he does not have the data to reveal it. It does not exist). Eduardo López-Bago, *El cura (Caso de incesto): Novela médico-social* (Madrid: Juan Muñoz Sánchez, 1885), 250–52.

6. Fernández writes, "La entusiasta militancia en el polémico movimiento convierte a López Bago en un mesiánico discípulo que raya en el fanatismo. Nuestro novelista no reconoce más autoridad y fe que la ciencia y la única fuerza que rige los destinos de sus personajes es la del determinismo férreo aliado con el fatalismo, que convierte a los protagonistas en seres agónicos impelidos hacia la destrucción" (*Eduardo López Bago*, 68; His militant enthusiasm for the polemical movement converts López Bago into a messianic disciple who verges on fanaticism. Our novelist does not acknowledge any authority or faith other than science, and the only force that governs the destiny of his characters is one of fierce determinism and fatalism that converts his protagonists into moribund beings propelled toward destruction).

7. The secular-minded priest in *El cura*, Don Fermín, tells the protagonist that "las pasiones no son facultades ni elementos de la voluntad, sino estados exagerados de las aptitudes, instintos y sentimientos del hombre que necesitan vivamente ser satisfechos; y que si no lo son causan dolor y hacen sufrir: por eso son pasiones" (102; the passions are not faculties nor elements controlled by one's will, but rather exaggerated states of man's aptitudes, instincts, and feelings that strongly need to be satisfied; and if they are not, they cause pain and suffering: that is why they are passions).

8. In the appendix to the novel, titled "Vosotros y yo" (You and me) López Bago writes that by insisting on the chastity vows of its clergy "la Iglesia decreta la guerra á la sociedad y á la familia, menosprecia lo infalible de la ciencia y ataca á la razón natural" (the Church declares war on society and the family, it disdains the infallibility of science and attacks natural reason). Eduardo López-Bago, "Vosotros y yo," in *El cura (Caso de incesto): Novela médico-social*, by Eduardo López Bago (Madrid: Juan Muñoz Sánchez, 1885), 260.

9. Echoing this idea, the narrator of his novel *El preso* (The prisoner) states, "Mientras el derecho obre a espaldas de la ciencia, el Código penal no será

justo ni razonado, ni completo. Todo aquello que con la humanidad se relaciona tiene que buscar su cimento y base en el conocimiento de la naturaleza y del organismo humano" (As long as the law operates independently of science, the legal Code will not be just nor reasonable nor complete. All that relates to humanity has to find its support and basis in the knowledge of nature and the human organism). Eduardo López-Bago, *El preso: Novela médico-social* (Madrid: José Góngora, 1880), *Biblioteca Digital Hispánica. Biblioteca Nacional de España*, 115–16, http://bdh-rd.bne. es/viewer.vm?pid=d-3488426.

10. Sharon L. Reeves, "El anticlericalismo en la novela naturalista española de Eduardo López Bago," in *Ensayos sin frontera (Estudios sobre literatura hispano-americana)*, ed. Carlos Aguasaco et al. (New York: Sin Frontera: 2005), 107.

11. Fernández, *Eduardo López Bago*, 107, 48.

12. Fernández, 182–83.

13. Erika Sutherland, "Death in the Bedroom: Eduardo López Bago and His Suspect Syphilitics," *Excavatio* 18, nos. 1–2 (2003): 278–79.

14. Yvan Lissorgues, "'El naturalismo radical': Eduardo López Bago (y Alejandro Sawa)," *Biblioteca Virtual Miguel de Cervantes*, n. pag., http://www. cervantesvirtual.com/nd/ark:/59851/bmcrv128.

15. Fernández writes, "El dogma científico sustituye a la revelación religiosa y se enarbola como una teoría absoluta de la causalidad universal inmanente e inmutable, paradoja sorprendente que contradice las bases teóricas del método experimental" (*Eduardo López Bago*, 191, 71; Scientific dogma substitutes religious revelation and is held up as an absolute theory of universal circumstances that are immanent and immutable, a surprising paradox that contradicts the theoretical bases of the experimental method).

16. Zubiaurre, Introduction to *El cura*, xix.

17. Juan Ignacio Ferreras, introduction to *El cura (Caso de incesto): Novela médico social*, by Eduardo López Bago, ed. Juan Ignacio Ferreras (Madrid: Vosa, 1996), 14.

18. Zubiaurre, introduction to *El cura*, xxix.

19. Akiko Tsuchiya, "Entre la ciencia y la pornografía: Masculinidades abyectas y perversiones femeninas en la serie *El Cura* (1885) de Eduardo López Bago," in *Sexualidades periféricas: Consolidaciones literarias y fílmicas en la España de fin de siglo XIX y fin de milenio*, ed. Nuria Godón and Michael J. Horswell (Madrid: Fundamentos, 2016), 36, 41.

20. Zubiaurre, Introduction to *El cura*, xxix.

21. Zubiaurre, xxxiv.

22. Gracia's hysteria is discussed in detail later in this chapter.

23. For an excellent analysis of López Bago's representation of syphilis in *La prostituta* (1894; The prostitute) and *La pálida* (1894; The pale woman), see Sutherland, "Death."

24. "En *El cura* empiezo una nueva serie de estudios dedicados á combatir el celibato eclesiástico en lo que tiene de peligroso y bajo el punto de vista

médico-social" (López Bago, *El cura*, 259; In *El cura*, I begin a new series of studies dedicated to combatting ecclesiastical celibacy for the ways in which it is dangerous, and from a socio-medical perspective).

25. Zubiaurre, introduction to *El cura*, viii.
26. Isaac García Guerrero, "The Perverted Doctor Bago: The Paradox of Modernity in Eduardo López Bago's *El Cura*," in *Perversiones decimonóni-cas: Literatura y parafilia en el siglo XIX*, ed. Jorge Avilés (Valencia: Albatros, 2018), 302.
27. Collin McKinney, "'Enemigos de la virilidad': Sex, Masturbation, and Celibacy in Nineteenth-Century Spain," *Prisma Social* 13 (December 2014–May 2015): 81–82, 87, http://www.isdfundacion.org/publicaciones/revista/numeros/13/secciones/tematica/t_03_enemigos_virilidad.html.
28. Nicholas Wolters, however, notes that despite the fact that *El cura* was a best seller it "received mixed reviews even from liberal audiences." Nicholas Wolters, "Unholy Perversions: Clerical Deviance and Precarious Youth in Nakens, Sawa, and López Bago," in *Literatura y parafilia en el siglo XIX*, ed. Jorge Avilés-Diz (Madrid: Albatros Ediciones, 2018), 284.
29. Ferreras, introduction to *El cura*, 15–16.
30. Zubiaurre, introduction to *El cura*, xxii–xxiii. The ending of the novel does not strike me as celebratory, and even less so when read in relation to Gracia's death and Román's fall into complete depravity in *El confesionario*. As Sharon Reeves points out, "The anguished priest of *El cura* disappears in *El confesionario* and *La monja*. Whereas Román inspired compassion in the first novel, he becomes a dehumanized monster in the last two; cold, vicious, sadistic and calculating." Sharon L. Reeves, "Behind the Convent Walls: Anticlericalism in Eduardo López Bago's *La Monja*," in *Aportaciones eruditas y literarias en homenaje a Gregorio C. Martín*, ed.Juan Fernández Jiménez et al. (Erie, PA: School of Humanities and Social Sciences, Penn State Erie, the Behrend College, 2016), 221–24. To my mind, all three novels end with disturbing events: *El cura* with the consummation of incest, *El confesionario* with Gertrudis's rape, and *La monja* with Melita's and Soledad's gruesome deaths.
31. Fernández, *Eduardo López Bago*, 173–75.
32. Tsuchiya, "Entre la ciencia," 39–40.
33. Tsuchiya, 36.
34. Pura Fernández, "*Scientia sexualis* y saber psiquiátrico en la novela naturalista decimonónica," *Asclepio* 9, no. 1 (1997): 230, http://dx.doi.org/10.3989/asclepio.1997.v49.i1.389.
35. García Guerrero, "The Perverted Doctor Bago," 305–6.
36. For example, in his summation of a session on hysteria at the Sociedad Ginecológica Española (The Spanish Society of Gynecology) in 1876 Ángel Pulido Fernández writes that Sr. Castillo de Piñeyro took note of the frequency with which the affliction occurs during puberty. He writes "siguió ocupándose de las causas [del histerismo] y lo hizo de la pubertad haciendo notar la gran frecuencia de la afección que le ocupaba en un

período de la vida, al que consideró como uno de los más borrascosos que corre la mujer" (*Anales*, 53; continued discussing the causes [of hysteria] and making puberty one of them, noting the great frequency of the disease he was dealing with during a certain period of life, which he considered one of the most stormy that a woman undergoes).

37. "Gracia era una niña, una verdadera niña, que recibía siempre con susto las revelaciones del organismo, llegando á desesperarse y á tener ira contra su propia carne, porque se redondeaba abultando los pechos, y con las pródigas hemorragias de su exuberante sexo, que la producían estado de sensibilidad exquisita, una verdadera neurosis, en que el menor ruido era su sobresalto, y el roce más leve un cosquilleo de la piel que la estremecía poderosamente." (López Bago, *El cura*, 26–27; Gracia was a girl, truly just a girl, she always reacted with fear to the changes in her body, falling into despair and becoming angry at her own flesh, because she was acquiring curves and breasts, and with the prodigious bleeding of her exuberant genitals, that produced in her an exquisite state of sensitivity, a veritable neurosis, in which the slightest noise produced a shock, or in which the faintest tickling sensation caused powerful tremors). Echoing scientific discourses on the highly sensitive nature of the female body, this scene suggests that becoming a woman is a physically produced "neurosis."

38. Román was "casi tan desmayado como la paciente, casi convulsivo, casi epiléptico" (183; almost as unconscious as the patient, almost convulsive, almost epileptic).

39. Rachel P. Maines, *The Technology of Orgasm: "Hysteria," the Vibrator, and Women's Sexual Satisfaction* (Baltimore, MD: Johns Hopkins University Press, 1999), 3.

40. He also reaffirms very traditional notions of the disease arguing that only women are affected by it (López Bago, 186). This suggests that López Bago did not subscribe to Jean-Marie Charcot's theory that men could also be affected by hysteria.

41. Harold and Susan J. Merskey, "Hysteria or 'Suffocation of the Mother,'" *History of Medicine* 148, no. 3 (February 1993): 399.

42. Soledad says,

> Me irrita oírlas decir que buscan en tales porquerías el éxtasis. Que son extáticas. Yo no vine al convento en estado de inocencia. A mí, como á otras novicias, no pudieron engañarme. Así que soy aquí la víctima de todas. [. . .] no caeré nunca; pero han hecho que mi castidad desaparezca, y que tenga fijo mi pensamiento en el hombre. No es mía la culpa. No lo puedo evitar. Monja soy, pero también soy hembra, muy hembra.
>
> *It irritates me to hear them say they are looking for ecstasy in such disgusting activities. [To hear them say] that they are ecstatic. I did not come to this convent in a state of innocence. They could not deceive me the way they did with other novitiates. For this reason, here I am the vic-*

tim of all of them. [. . .] I will never fall; but they have made my chastity disappear and turned my thoughts constantly on men. It's not my fault. I can't help it. I'm a nun, but I'm also female, very female.

Eduardo López-Bago, *La monja: Novela médico-social* (Madrid, Mariano Núñez Samper, 1904), 131.

43. "Sus noches eran de insomnio y fiebre, agitándose en el camastro el cuerpo" (*La monja*, 164–65; her nights were filled with fever and insomnia, her body shaking in her rickety old bed).

44. Tsuchiya, "Entre la ciencia," 54.

45. Freud, "Femininity," 129–30.

46. Suárez Casañ, *El amor lesbio*, 72.

47. "Ya no continuaron desarrollándose aquellas curvas suaves de la forma que iban á caracterizar y hermosear su incipiente sexo" (*La monja*, 225; Those soft curves no longer continued to develop in a way that would characterize and beautify her incipient sex). Even though Melita is sixteen years old at the beginning of the novel, she still looks prepubescent (19). In fact, Román wants her to profess before she completes puberty, and while she is still totally sexually naïve (22). However, the unhygienic conditions of the convent make her succumb to tuberculosis before her full transition into adulthood.

48. Labanyi, *Gender and Modernization*, 117; Collin McKinney, "'Enemigos de la virilidad': Sex, Masturbation, and Celibacy in Nineteenth-Century Spain," *Prisma Social* 13 (December 2014–May 2015): 87. http://www. isdfundacion.org/publicaciones/revista/numeros/13/secciones/tematica/ t_03_enemigos_virilidad.html; Jennifer Smith, "Female Masculinity in *La Regenta*," *Modern Spanish Women as Agents of Change: Essays in Honor of Maryellen Bieder*, ed. Jennifer Smith (Lewisburg, PA: Bucknell University Press, 2018), 192–93.

49. Peter Brooks, *Body Work: Objects of Desire in Modern Narrative* (Cambridge, MA: Harvard University Press, 1993), 22.

50. The description reads,

Allí estaba Gracia, vidriados ya los ojos y hundidos, arrugadas las sienes, perdido el conocimiento, abriendo y cerrando las manos para coger *á puñados* las sábanas que la cubrían.

Estaba con el estertor. No se oía otra cosa en el gabinete. Un hervor de flemas que ensordecía á Román, *al futuro Papa.*
Lo escuchaba atontado. (italics in the original)

There was Gracia, her eyes already glassy and sunken, her temples wrinkled, unconscious, opening and closing her hands in order to grab by handfuls the sheets that covered her.
She had the death rattle. You could not hear anything else in the room. A fervor of phlegm that deafened Román, the future Pope.
He listened to it stunned.

Eduardo López-Bago, *El confesionario (Satiriasis): Novela médico-social* (Madrid: Juan Muñoz y Compañía, 1885), 234.

51. The narrator of *El confesionario* informs us that Gertrudis is beautiful and youthful (53). She herself reveals her age, thirty, in her first confession with Román (60).

52. At the beginning of *La monja*, the narrator makes clear that if Melita's taking of the habit ends badly, it is entirely Román's and Gertrudis's fault (22).

53. The narrator of *La monja*, seemingly aware of the lack of verisimilitude in the quick and early progression of Gertrudis's menopause, informs us that it was probably premature for her age (115).

54. As we saw in Chapter 1, women with same-sex proclivities were generally referred to as pseudo-hermaphrodites, *tribadas* (tribades), *marimachos* (butch women), or *viragines* or *viragos* (mannish women). J. Halberstam confirms this usage when she writes that in the early nineteenth century masculine women who desired other women would have been referred to as "tribades," "hermaphrodites," or "female husbands" rather than "lesbians." Judith Halberstam, *Female Masculinity* (Durham, NC: Duke University Press, 1998), 50. Ciro Bayo even makes use of the term *tortillera* (dyke) in his description of Sappho. Ciro Bayo, *Higiene sexual del soltero*. (Madrid: A. Marzo, n.d.), 104. Since "tribade" is one of the most common terms in the hygiene manuals studied here, it is the term I have chosen to use, rather than the less historical term "lesbian." However, as was noted earlier, V. Suárez Casañ, anticipating contemporary terminology, refers to lesbianism as "amor lesbio" (lesbian love), and to women who engage in same-sex activities as "lesbias" (lesbians) (*El amor lesbio*, 13).

55. Suárez Casañ, *El amor lesbio*, 56.

56. *El amor lesbio* is volume nine of Suárez Casañ's multi-volume work *Conocimientos para la vida privada* (Knowledge for private life). Richard Cleminson, and Francisco Vázquez García, *"Los invisibles": A History of Male Homosexuality in Spain: 1850–1940* (Cardiff: University of Wales Press, 2007), 58. This series went through at least twenty editions, which, as Cleminson and Vázquez García note, attests to its popularity with the reading public (*"Los invisibles,"* 58). The earliest edition of *El amor lesbio* in the National Library of Spain has a publication date of 1892, which would postdate the publication of the *Cura* trilogy. However, even if it was not published until seven years later, it still serves as a representation of ideas circulating at the time.

57. Suárez Casañ, 53.

58. Suárez Casañ, 54.

59. Suárez Casañ, 56–57.

60. Fernández, *Eduardo López Bago*, 49.

61. The similarities between Eduardo López Bago's *La monja* and Denis Diderot's *La religieuse* (completed in 1780, but not published until 1796, after Diderot's death) on the portrayal of lesbianism in the convent has already been noted by Pura Fernández (*Eduardo López Bago*, 184). Although Dide-

rot's novel is from the Enlightenment era and precedes López Bago's work by nearly a century, the late nineteenth-century Spanish anticlerical magazine *El motín* included advertisements for the novel in Spanish translation, suggesting that it was still being read by those with strong anticlerical sympathies. My thanks go to Nicholas Wolters for informing me of these ads. Also worthy of note is the fact that the 1886 Spanish translation omitted the homoerotic passages from Diderot's novel because they were considered obscene. David Marín Hernández and Fernando José Hidalgo Moreno, "La recepción de Diderot en la España del XIX: La traducción de *La religiosa* de Ángel Rodríguez Chaves," *Hispania Nova* 14 (2006): 271, https://e-revistas.uc3m.es/index.php/HISPNOV/article/view/2976.

62. Sor María Josefa tells Melita that "Todas gozamos ya hace tiempo del tercer periodo, del *unitivo*. Todas somos *extáticas*" (106; We have all been enjoying the third period, the *unitive* period. We are all *ecstatic*).

63. Suárez Casañ, *El amor lesbio*, 58.

64. Román is referred to as a faun in *La monja* 84, 87, and *El confesionario* 229–30. Moreover, Román's neighbor and fellow lecherous priest, Don Fermín, is also referred to as a faun in *El cura*, 212, and *El confesionario*, 121, and is even compared to Mephistopheles in *El cura*, 95. Nicholas Wolters also notes that Alejandro Sawa's priests in *El criadero de curas* (2014; The priests' breeding ground) are referred to as satyrs and "macho cabríos" (he-goats/devils) ("Unholy Perversions," 283).

65. The rape of Gertrudis in *El confesionario* is described using very similar language: "sintió el contacto duro del *fauno*: los brazos la estrecharon, no como caricia, sino como agresión: dos *zarpazos de fiera* que desgarraron los encajes, el raso" (229–30, emphasis mine; she felt the hard contact of the *faun*: his arms held her, not in an embrace, but rather as aggression: two *clawings of a wild beast* that tore the lace, the satin).

66. According to Sharon Reeves, "While the focus of the evil acts committed in the trilogy has been concentrated on the diabolical Román Acevedo, López Bago delivers a coup de main by choosing the nuns as the insidious perpetrators of the greatest crime against nature, the law and religion in the trilogy: coldblooded premeditated murder" ("Behind Convent Walls" 227).

67. Jules Michelet, *La Sorcière: The Witch of the Middle Ages*, trans. L. J. Trotter (London: Simpkin Marshall, 1863), 153–54.

68. Only a few years after the publication of *La monja*, Joris-Karl Huysmans would make satanism and the black mass the subjects of his 1891 novel *Là-bas* (Down there), clearly signaling the presence of such ideas in the cultural imaginary of the time.

69. Peter Ward, *The Clean Body: A Modern History* (Montreal: McGill-Queens University Press, 2019), 33.

70. Ward, *The Clean Body*, 35.

71. The description reads,

No se estaba quieta un minuto. ¡Bueno! Ahora se había puesto boca abajo, se agitaba con una actividad muscular que parecía convulsiva [. . .] Gracia sofocó un grito mordiendo la almohada. Fue una exhalación de sorpresa inaudita y al mismo tiempo de placer intenso. Quedó como desmayada, inmóvil un rato. ¡Ah! Nunca, nunca, desde que padecía su mal, le había sucedido aquello. Había sido, sin duda, el roce de las sábanas. El roce, que otras veces la cosquilleaba tan sólo, ahora . . ., ahora no supo explicarse el nuevo fenómeno. (117)

She could not remain still for a minute. Well! Now she had turned over face down and shook with a muscular activity that appeared convulsive [. . .] Gracia silenced a scream by biting her pillow. It was an exhalation of strange surprise and at the same time of intense pleasure. She was still for a while, motionless, as if she had fainted. Oh! Never, never, since she had suffered from her illness, had that happened. It had been, without a doubt, the contact with the sheets. A contact that on other occasions only produced a tickle, now . . ., now she didn't know how to explain the new phenomenon.

The pleasure this experience produces leads Gracia to simultaneously fear and long for its reoccurrence (118).

72. Manuel Durán, *Luis de León* (New York: Twayne, 1971), 90–91.
73. The fact that Gertrudis is also the name of the woman Román has seduced mystically is suggestive. (López Bago, 59).
74. Marie, *Misticismo*, 170.
75. Denise DuPont, "Teresa de Jesús and the Creation of Gender Communities in Eduardo López Bago's *El Cura* Trilogy," *Revista de Estudios Hispánicos* 41, no. 3 (October 2007): 345.
76. DuPont, "Teresa de Jesús," 352–53.
77. DuPont, "Teresa de Jesús," 349.
78. DuPont, 349.
79. DuPont, 357.
80. DuPont, 358.
81. Tsuchiya, "Entre la ciencia," 56.
82. Suárez Casañ, 44–45. Referred to as *pederastia* (pederasty) since *homosexuality* was not yet a term employed at the time.

CHAPTER 4

1. See Noël Valis, "Hysteria and Historical Context in *La Regenta*," *Revista Hispánica Moderna* 52, no. 2 (December 2000): 325–51; Nicholas Wolter, "Unholy Perversions"; Maite Zubiaurre, introduction to *El cura (Caso de incesto): Novela médico-social*; Maite Zubiaurre, introduction to *La Regenta*, by Leopoldo Alas (Clarín), ed. Maite Zubiaurre and Eilene Powell (Doral, FL: Stockcero, 2012), vii–xliii.

2. While Fermín de Pas from *La Regenta* most closely resembles Román Acebedo of the *Cura* trilogy, there are also similarities between Fermín the protagonist of *La Regenta* and Fermín the lecherous priest and secondary character of *El cura* and *El confesionario*, as has been noted by critics such as Valis and Zubiaurre (Valis "Hysteria," 340; Zubiaurre, introduction to *El cura*, xxvi).

3. Leopoldo Alas, *La Regenta*, edited by Gonzalo Sobejano (Madrid: Clásicos Castalia, 1981), 1:94; López Bago, *La monja*, 51. As Nicholas Wolters notes, Fermín's turn to the Church as a way of escaping his working-class origins brings the question of social class and social mobility to the fore. Nicholas Wolters, "Debajo de la sotana: (Re)Dressing Clerical Masculinity in Alas's *La Regenta*," *Revista de Estudios Hispánicos* 53, no. 1 (March 2019): 336. This is in contrast with the *Cura* trilogy where Román hails from the upper class, his parents being wealthy farmers from Tudela (López Bago, *El cura*, 30).

4. Neither priest wants to consummate their relationship with his confessant: Fermín because he doesn't want to spoil his idealistic love or lose Ana's respect, Román because he doesn't want to lose his superior standing vis-à-vis Gertrudis. However, Román, unlike Fermín, gives in to his physical desires for Gertrudis by the end of the second novel.

5. There are rumors that Don Fermín has had many lovers, and we also know he had an affair of some sort with the Brigadiera, and that he gives into his desires for Petra. Moreover, there is a suggestion of pedophilia in the scene in which Fermín visits the all-girl Catholic school and is sexually aroused by the young girls there (Alas, *La Regenta*, 2:199–204).

6. Despite Robustiano Somoza's conservative politics, he is strongly anticlerical and is therefore referred to as a *volteriano* even though we are told he never actually read any Voltaire (Alas, 1:426–27). He is portrayed as somewhat of a fool who gives all his patients the same diagnosis: initially it was "flato" (flatulence), later a "cuestión de nervios" (1:427; a matter of nerves). Nevertheless, his diagnosis of Ana's problems as a case of nerves, even if it's just a guess, is in keeping with the apparent intent of the novel.

7. Alas, 2:428–59. He also argues that young women who become nuns right away really do not do so freely because they are too young to know what they are committing themselves to (1:430–31). We see this theme in *La monja* as Román wants Melita to profess before she truly realizes what she is committing herself to (22).

8. Benítez is only referred to by his last name in the novel. For insightful analyses on the representation of the doctor in *La Regenta* see Peter Bly, "The Physician in the Narratives of Galdós and Clarín," in *Imagined Truths: Realism in Modern Spanish Literature and Culture*, edited by Mary L. Coffey and Margot Versteeg (Toronto: University of Toronto Press, 2019), 111–43; Anne Gilfoil, "Doctor vs. Priest: Urban Planning and Reform in Vetusta," *Decimonónica* 6, no. 1 (Winter 2009): 34–45, http://www.decimononica.org/wp-content/uploads/2013/01/Gilfoil_6.1.pdf.

9. Catherine Jaffe, "In Her Father's Library: Women's Reading in *La Regenta*," *Revista de Estudios Hispánicos* 39, no. 1 (January 2005): 7.

10. As was discussed in a previous note, Somoza, unlike Benítez, is not very up to date on the scientific knowledge of his day. Yet, to his credit, he seems to acknowledge his inability to effectively treat Ana, and he consequently hands her over to the more capable Benítez.

11. Maite Zubiaurre has explored the similarities in the representation of Ana's hysteria in *La Regenta* and Gracia's hysteria in *El cura* (introduction to *El cura*, xxx–xxxiv).

12. Valis, "Hysteria," 340.

13. The first volume of Alas's novel was published at the end of 1884 or the beginning of 1885, and the second volume appeared a few months later in June of 1885. Juan Oleza, introduction to *La Regenta*, by Leopoldo Alas Clarín (Madrid: Cátedra, 1989), 1:40. López Bago published *El cura* and *El confesionario* in 1885 and *La monja* in 1886.

14. Valis, "Hysteria"; Zubiaurre, introduction to *El cura*; Lou Charnon-Deutsch, "Between Agency and Determinism: A Critical Review of Clarín Studies," *Hispanic Review* 76, no. 2 (Spring 2008): 135–53.

15. Simone Saillard, "Ana Ozores, de la mystique à l'hystérie," *Co-Textes* 18 (1989): 65–131; Bridget Aldaraca, "El caso de Ana O.: Histeria y sexualidad en *La Regenta*," *Asclepio* 42 (1990): 51–61; Joan Ramon Resina, "Ana Ozores's Nerves," *Hispanic Review* 71 (Spring 2003): 229–52; Maria Giovanna Tomsich, "Histeria y narración en *La Regenta*," *Anales de Literatura Española* 5 (1986–87): 494–517; Jo Labanyi, "Mysticism and Hysteria in *La Regenta*: The Problem of Female Identity," in *Feminist Readings on Spanish and Latin American Literature*, ed. by Lisa P. Condé and Stephen Hart (Lewiston, NY: Edwin Mellen, 1991), 37–46. Other studies that examine the question of hysteria and/or mysticism in *La Regenta* include Stephanie Sieburth, *Reading* La Regenta: *Duplicitous Discourse and the Entropy of Structure* (Amsterdam: John Benjamins, 1990); Beth Wietelmann Bauer, "Novels in Dialogue: *Pepita Jiménez* and *La Regenta*," *Revista de Estudios Hispánicos* 25, no. 2 (May 1991): 104–21; Alison Sinclair, *Dislocations of Desire: Gender, Identity and Strategy in* La Regenta (Chapel Hill: University of North Carolina Dept. of Romance Languages, 1998); Bacon, *Negotiating Sainthood*; DuPont, *Writing Teresa*; Zubiaurre, introduction to *El cura*; Noël Valis, *The Decadent Vision in Leopoldo Alas Clarín: A Study of* La Regenta *and* Su único hijo (Baton Rouge: Louisana University Press, 1981); Valis, "Hysteria."

16. Valis, "Hysteria"; Zubiaurre, introduction to *El cura*; Zubiaurre, introduction to *La Regenta*.

17. The term *histerismo* (hysteria) is used eleven times in *El cura* and once in *La monja*. The term *histérico/a* (hysterical/hysteric) is used nine times in *El cura* and once in *El confesionario*.

18. Saillard, "Ana Ozores," 116, 106.

19. Zubiaurre, introduction to *El cura*, xxxiv.

20. Monlau, *Higiene*, 58.

21. V. Suárez Casañ, *Secretos del lecho conyugal*, vol. 2 of *Conocimientos para la vida privada*, 2nd ed., ed. by Pío Arias Carvajal (Barcelona: Maucci,

[189-?]), 76–77. Although Suárez Casañ's hygiene manual was most likely published shortly after *La Regenta*, the ideas expressed in this text are in keeping with ideas appearing in earlier works, such as Monlau's *Higiene del matrimonio*, and are therefore indicative of the medical theories that were circulating at the time of the publication of Alas's novel.

22. Suárez Casañ, *El amor lesbio*, 77.

23. As we saw in the previous chapter, according to many nineteenth-century doctors, a girl's transition into womanhood was a major cause of hysteria. Other critics have noted that Ana's illness begins when she reaches puberty. See, for example, Labanyi, "Mysticism," 41; Resina, "Ana Ozores's Nerves," 235; and Sinclair, *Dislocations*, 162.

24. Saillard, "Ana Ozores," 103.

25. Kendrea Cherry, "Bowlby & Ainsworth: What Is Attachment Theory?: The Importance of Early Emotional Bonds," Verywellmind, https://www.verywellmind.com/what-is-attachment-theory-2795337.

26. Marleen van Polanen, Cristina Colonnesi, Ruben G. Fukkink, and Louis W. C. Tavecchio, "Is Caregiver Gender Important for Boys and Girls? Gender-Specific Child-Caregiver Interactions and Attachment Relationships," *Early Education and Development* 28, no. 5, https://doi.org/10.1080/10409289.2016.1258928.

27. Kipling D. Williams, "The Pain of Exclusion," *Scientific American Mind* 21, no. 6 (January/February 2011): 30–37.

28. The consequences of maternal neglect are also seen in Visita's abandonment of her own children in order to engage in the frivolous activities of Vetustan society.

29. Jagoe, "Sexo y género," 344.

30. Mainez Fernández, *Teresa de Jesús*, 14; Marie, *Misticismo*, 151–53.

31. Bacon, *Negotiating Sainthood*, 104.

32. For an excellent study of the ways critics from Clarín's time to the present have viewed the question of free will in relation to the novel's protagonist, see Charnon-Deutsch, "Between Agency."

33. Toward the end of the novel, Ana herself acknowledges that in order to be healthy she needs to be like other women (2:420). And, as was noted earlier, her health returns once she begins her affair with Álvaro (2:445).

34. Fernández, *Eduardo López Bago*, 173–75.

35. Yvan Lissorgues, *Clarín político* (Barcelona: Lumen, 1980), 1:246.

36. Alas, 1:245–46.

37. According to Alas, "¡Ser académica! ¿Para qué? ¡Es como si se empeñara en ser guardia civila o de la policía secreta!" (Lissorgues, *Clarín político* 1:244; Become an academic! What for? It's as if she was trying to become a female member of the civil guard or of the secret police!).

38. Clarín writes,

> Es muy fácil no asustarse porque hay en una nación veinte, cien, mil

señoritas bachilleras y doctoras. Hasta ahí puede tener gracia, y sobre todo pimienta.

Pero, figúrese que, como sería natural y justo, todas las mujeres, con posibles, quisieran ser médicas, abogadas, periodistas, ingenieras, catedráticas, etc., etc. . . . como quieren todos los hombres.

¡Oh! ¡cómo se echaría de menos entonces una carrera que debía seguir la mujer! (Lissourges, 1:245)

It is easy not to be frightened by the fact that there are twenty, a hundred, or a thousand young, college-educated women and some with advanced degrees. That much is quaint and above all amusing.

But, imagine that, as would be natural and just, all women, with the means, wanted to be medical doctors, lawyers, journalists, engineers, professors, etc., etc. . . . as all men do.

Oh! How we would then miss having a career that women must follow!

39. Lissorgues, 2:137, 152.
40. Quoted in Carolyn Richmond, "Las ideas de Leopoldo Alas "Clarín" sobre la mujer en sus escritos previos a *La Regenta*," in *Homenaje al Profesor Antonio Vilanova*, ed. by Marta Cristina Carbonell (Barcelona: Anthropos, 1988), 2:526.
41. Laqueur, *Solitary Sex*, 282.
42. Pouillet, *Del onanismo*, 53.
43. Pouillet, *Del onanismo*, 49. It is also "el agradable calorcillo del suave y blando lecho" (the agreeable warmth of the smooth and soft bed) of Saturnino Bermúdez that perverts his imagination and leaves him physically depleted in the morning (Alas, 1:126).
44. Suárez Casañ, *Los vicios solitarios*, 16.
45. The description is included in note 71 of Chapter 3.
46. Jaffe, "In Her Father's Library," 19.
47. Jaffe, 6–7.
48. Jaffe, 19.
49. Lissorgues, *Clarín político* 1:231. Joyce Tolliver argues that "la figura de Emilia Pardo Bazán sería para Clarín como un abominable calco de la literata Ana Ozores y del marimacho Constantino." (The figure of Emilia Pardo Bazán probably was for Clarín an abominable model of the bluestocking Ana and the butch Constantine). Joyce Tolliver, "La voz antifeminista y la amenaza 'andrógina' en el fin de siglo," in *Sexualidad y escritura (1850–2000)*, ed. Raquel Medina and Barbara Zecchi (Barcelona: Anthropos, 2002), 108–9.
50. Lissorgues, *Clarín político*, 1:232.
51. Ruiz Somavilla, "La legitimación," 110.
52. Suárez Casañ, *Enciclopedia médica*, 496.
53. Aldaraca, "El caso de Ana O.," 53–54.
54. Cleminson and Vázquez García, 'Los invisibles,' 67.

55. In *La monja* it is Soledad who is the target of the nuns' envy and depravity, leading to her ostracization and brutal murder. In *La Regenta* it is Ana who ends up ostracized by all of society for doing nothing more than what everyone else did.

56. We know that Visita was Álvaro's lover, and that unlike Ana, she gave in to him right away, and even jumped off her own balcony to be with him. We also know that Fermín despises Visita, and he thinks of her as a "grandísima cualquier cosa" (1:457; a great nobody).

57. "Aquí, aquí, a trabajar todo el mundo—gritaba Visita, chupándose los dedos llenos almíbar" (1:314; Over here, over here, everybody get to work—yelled Visita, licking her fingers, which were covered in syrup).

58. Christine Mathews, "Making the Nuclear Family: Kinship, Homosexuality, and *La Regenta*," *Revista de Estudios Hispánicos* 37, no. 1 (January 2003): 83. The narrator informs us that "Visitación, mientras sentada a los pies de la cama [de Ana] devoraba una buena ración de dulce de conserva, aseguraba con la boca llena que Somoza y la carabina de Ambrosio todo uno." (Alas, *La Regenta*, 2:112; Visitación, as she sat at the foot of [Ana's] bed devouring a large portion of jam, stated with her mouth full that Somoza was useless).

59. Mathews, "Making," 83.

60. James Mandrell, "Estudios gay y lesbianos: La revelación del cuerpo masculino: Una mirada Gay," in *El hispanismo en los Estados Unidos: Discursos críticos/prácticas textuales*, ed. José Manuel del Pino and Francisco La Rubia Prado (Madrid: Visor, 1999), 217.

61. Mathews, "Making," 83.

62. In fact, one of Ana's aunts' greatest fears is that Ana could get a reputation of being an Obdulia (1:217, 227).

63. Lawrence Rich, "Fear and Loathing in Vetusta: Coding, Class, and Gender in Clarín's *La Regenta*," *Revista Canadiense de Estudios Hispánicos* 25, no. 3 (Spring 2001): 511.

64. Rich, "Fear and Loathing," 512.

65. Translation taken from John Rutherford, trans. *La Regenta* (London: Penguin, 2005), 591.

66. Rich, "Fear and Loathing," 508.

67. Mathews, "Making," 83.

68. To the extent that virtue consisted of retaining one's virginity, Paula retained her virtue until she was raped by her future husband, Francisco de Pas, Fermín's father. Nothing ever actually transpired between her and the first priest she worked for despite the latter's sexual advances, advances she used to blackmail him. And after Francisco de Pas raped Paula, he himself was convinced she was a virgin before the rape, and consequently proceeded to marry her (Alas, *La Regenta*, 1:549–51).

69. We learn that "la condición de dormir cerca del *señorito* por si llamaba, se les imponía con una naturalidad edemíaca. Ni las muchachas ni el magistral habían opuesto nunca el menor reparo." (1:405; the require-

ment of sleeping next to the *señorito* in case he called them, was imposed with an Edenic naturalness. Neither the young women nor the canon had ever presented the slightest objection).

70. Translation taken from Rutherford, *La Regenta*, 593. Ana's aunts are also portrayed as witches at a witches' Sabbath as they talk of how to best sell off their niece, like cattle, into marriage (2:230).

71. Leopoldo Alas, "*La evangelista*: Novela de Alfonso Daudet. I," in *Obras completas*, 7 (Oviedo, Spain: Nobel), 289.

72. In a *palique* (chat) published in *La Publicidad* (Publicity) in 1880 Clarín mentions the work, expressing a degree of cynicism when he says: "Créalo el señor Mainez, los médicos pueden decir mucho de lo que le sucedía a Santa Teresa; pero no lo pueden decir todo" (qtd. in Valis, "Hysteria," 333; Mr. Mainez should know that doctors can say a lot about what happened to Santa Teresa; but they cannot say it all). And in an article on the celebration of the *Centenario de Santa Teresa* published in *El progreso* [Progress] in 1882, he again mentions Mainez's work, criticizing the "ruda manera de atacar a la ilustre doctora, figura poética, delicada, que aun sometida al más frío examen de un racionalista, aparece grande, noble, digna de admiración y hasta cariño" (the cruel way of attacking the illustrious doctor, a delicate, poetic figure, who even subjected to a rationalist's coldest scrutiny, appears great, noble, worthy of admiration, and even affection). Leopoldo Alas, "El Centenario de Santa Teresa," in *Obras completas* (Oviedo: Nobel, 2004), 7:149. For more on Alas's review of Mainez's work, see DuPont, *Writing Teresa*, 52–53.

73. Alas acknowledges that Mainez's diagnosis of Santa Teresa as a hysteric, while distasteful, appears to be well founded: "reconocí la justicia de muchas de sus observaciones" ("El Centenario," 7:149; I recognized the accuracy of many of his observations).

74. Lissorgues, *Clarín político*, 1:232.

75. Alas, "El Centenario" 7:151.

76. Valis, "Hysteria," 339.

77. DuPont, *Writing Teresa*, 24.

78. Suggestion of authorial intent does not, however, obviate alternative readings or the fact that any text is necessarily larger than the mind that creates it.

79. Visitación tells Don Álvaro that "Ana, cuando chica, allá en Loreto, tuvo ya, según yo averigüé, arranques así . . . como de loca . . . y vio visiones . . ." (1:333; Ana, when she was young, there in Loreto, already had, according to what I found out, such fits . . . like a crazy woman . . . and had visions . . .).

80. *Edad crítica* is a term employed by nineteenth-century doctors to refer to the onset of menstruation and menopause in women. For example, Francisco de Paula Campá read a speech to the Real Academia de Medicina in 1876 about this topic entitled "Las dos edades críticas de la mujer" (The two critical phases of women).

81. Alas, "La evangelista I," 289.
82. Alas, 290.
83. López Bago, *El confesionario*, 182, 194.
84. Moreover, as Visitación links Ana's hysterical attack with her mystical raptures, Ana's mysticism looks more like hysteria (1:333).
85. Fermín tells Ana that "no es santo, ni es bueno, amiga mía, que al ver a un libertino en la celda de una monja . . . o a la monja en casa del libertino y en sus brazos, usted se dedique a pensar en Dios, con ocasión del abrazo de aquellos sacrílegos amantes" (2:71; it is not saintly, nor is it right, my friend, that upon seeing a libertine in a nun's cell . . . or a nun in the libertine's house and in his arms, you devote yourself to thinking about God, with the embrace of those sacrilegious lovers being the reason).
86. Ciertas funciones de teatro obran de un modo más marcado, aunque acaso menos conocido. En efecto cuando las jóvenes han salido del teatro y vuelto á sus habitaciones bajo la impresión viva aún de la novela que han visto desarrollarse ante sus ojos, se ponen á soñar; con la cabeza sobre la almohada se creen heroínas de todas las comedias, su cerebro delira, aman y son amadas de un ser ideal que crea su deseo. (Pouillet, *Del onanismo*, 55; Certain theatrical performances operate in a more marked way, although perhaps less known. Indeed, when young women have gone out to the theater and returned to their rooms still under the vivid influence of the novel that they have seen acted out before their eyes, they start daydreaming; with their head on the pillow they believe they are the heroines of romantic comedies, their brain becomes delirious, they love and are loved by an ideal being that their desire creates).
87. Pouillet, *Del onanismo*, 75.
88. I have been unable to ascertain what work or author Pouillet is referring to here.
89. In the letter Ana writes: "Si necesita pruebas, si quiere que sufra penitencias, hable, mande, verá como obedezco" (2:194; If you need proof, if you want me to do penance, speak, order me, you will see how I obey). For an illuminating analysis of Ana's masochistic behaviors, specifically as articulated in this letter, see Nuria Godón's *La pasión esclava: Alianzas masoquistas en* La Regenta (West Lafayette, IN: Purdue University Press, 2017).
90. According to Carlos Ozores, "esta *amada* podrá ser la iglesia, pero . . . yo no me fío . . . no me fío . . ." (Alas, 1:208, emphasis in the original; this *beloved* could be the church, but . . . I don't believe it . . . I don't believe it . . .).
91. Marie, *Misticismo*, 170.
92. Valis, Hysteria, 342. Alas appears to have been familiar with Maudsley's work since, as Sobejano notes, he cites him in *La Regenta* (2:377n13).
93. Marie, 170.
94. Alas, 2:442n22.
95. Alas, 2:442n22.
96. Saillard, "Ana Ozores," 91–107.

97. The narrator acknowledges Ana's attempts at imitation: "El espíritu de imitación se apoderaba de la lectora, sin darse ella cuenta de tamaño atrevimiento" (2:191; The spirit of imitation seized the reader, without her realizing the great audacity [in this]).

98. Gonzalo Sobejano, introduction to *La Regenta*, by Leopoldo Alas "Clarín" (Madrid: Clásicos Castalia, 1981, 48.

99. Sobejano, Introduction to *La Regenta*, 45–48.

100. Ana describes the differences in the following way:

> Para lo único que le quedaba un poco de conciencia, fuera de lo presente, era para comparar las delicias que estaba gozando [con don Álvaro] con las que había encontrado en la meditación religiosa. En esta última había un esfuerzo doloroso, una frialdad abstracta, y en rigor algo enfermizo, una exaltación malsana; y en lo que estaba pasando ahora ella era pasiva, no había esfuerzo, no había frialdad, no había más que placer, salud, fuerza, nada de abstracción, nada de tener que figurarse algo ausente, delicia positiva, tangible, inmediata, dicha sin reserva, sin trascender a nada más que a la esperanza de que durase eternamente. (2:424)
>
> *Apart from the present, the only thing for which she had some consciousness left was to compare the delights that she was enjoying [with Don Álvaro] with those that she had discovered in religious meditation. During the latter, there was a painful effort, an abstract coldness, and strictly speaking something sickly, an unhealthy exaltation; and in what she was going through now she was passive, there was no effort, no coldness, there was nothing but pleasure, health, strength, nothing of abstraction, nothing about having to imagine something that was absent, material delight, immediate, tangible happiness without reservations, without transcending to anything other than the hope that it would last eternally.*

101. DuPont also argues that the novel maintains the difference between true and false mysticism (*Writing Teresa*, 65–68).

102. Leopoldo Alas, "Lecturas (Proyecto)," in *Mezclilla*, ed. Antonio Vilanova (Barcelona: Lumen, 1987), 72.

103. Fernández, *Eduardo López Bago*, 61. The biographical information on López Bago is very limited.

104. Yvan Lissorgues, *La pensée philosophique et religieuse de Leopoldo Alas (Clarín): 1875–1901* (Paris: CNRS, 1983), 12.

105. Lissorgues 13–16; Rafael Rodríguez Marín, "Orientaciones para el estudio de los *Relatos breves* de 'Clarín," in *Relatos breves*, by Leopoldo Alas "Clarín" (Madrid: Castalia, 1986), 281.

106. DuPont, *Writing Teresa*, 24.

107. Lissorgues, *La pensée*, 20–21.

108. Lissorgues, 44–45.

109. Francisco Pérez Gutiérrez, *El problema religioso en la generación de 1868* (Madrid: Taurus, 1975), 281.

110. According to Adolfo Posada, "Dejábase llevar, en ocasiones críticas—adolescente aún—por su natural inclinación mística, a extremos que pudieron descentrar su vida. En confidencias ruborosas refería Leopoldo a Rubín—más de una vez—sus arrobamientos, sus exaltaciones, que llegaron a dominarle hasta el punto de producirle verdaderas alucinaciones: sentimental en grado sumo, emotivo, nervioso, estremecíase en la contemplación del mar o del cielo insondable" (He allowed himself, at critical moments—still an adolescent—to be carried away by his natural mystical inclinations, to extremes that could take his life off course. In embarrassing confessions Leopoldo told Rubín—more than once—about his raptures, his exaltations, that came to dominate him to the point of producing veritable hallucinations: sentimental to the maximum degree, emotional, nervous, he would tremble contemplating the ocean or the immeasurable heavens). Adolfo Posada, *Leopoldo Alas "Clarín"* (Oviedo: La Cruz, 1946), 71.

111. Quoted in Saillard, "Ana Ozores," 67.

112. Pérez Gutiérrez, *El problema religioso*, 270, 298–300.

113. Saillard, "Ana Ozores," 67–68.

114. Leopoldo Alas, "Azotacalles de Madrid: La procesión por fuera. La beata." In *Preludios de "Clarín,"* ed. Jean-François Botrel (Oviedo, Spain: Instituto de Estudios Asturianos, 1972), 28.

115. Leopoldo Alas, "Retórica y poética (fragmentos): I. La oratoria sagrada," in *Preludios de "Clarín,"* edited by Jean-François Botrel (Oviedo, Spain: Instituto de Estudios Asturianos, 1972), 42.

116. Leopoldo Alas, "*Gloria* (segunda parte): Novela del Sr. Pérez Galdós," in *Preludios de "Clarín,"* edited by Jean-François Botrel (Oviedo, Spain: Instituto de Estudios Asturianos, 1972), 122–23.

117. Alas seems to be asking himself that very question in the second part of a two-part article published in *El Progreso* entitled "*La evangelista*": "La mujer católica exaltada, tomando por mandatos de Dios sus aprensiones o las de cualquier clérigo imprudente, profanando la doctrina de Jesús con mezcla de superstición y de intolerancia, en fin la beata insufrible, agriada las más veces por decepciones del todo humanas, que ella convierte en fervor de cruel y loco y antipático ascetismo, ¿No podría ofrecer también asunto para una novela muy parecida a la de Alfonso Daudet?" (An exalted Catholic woman, taking her apprehensions or those of an imprudent priest as God's mandate, profaning Jesus's teaching with a mix of superstition and intolerance, in short the insufferable religious fanatic, embittered, usually, by completely human deceptions, which she converts into a fervor of cruel and insane and disagreeable asceticism. Could this not also be the topic of a novel very similar to Alfonse Daudet's novel?). Leopoldo Alas, "*La evangelista*: Novela de Alfonoso Daudet. II," in *Obras completas*, 7:293–97 (Oviedo: Nobel, 2004), 293.

118. Fernández, *Eduardo López Bago y el naturalismo radical*, 187.

119. "Para ellos no hace falta saber inventar; la imaginación sobra; la inspiración es un mito de la psicología vulgar, el genio, una farsa, el verdadero genio es la paciencia; la musa, la asiduidad en el trabajo. Combinad esas dos ideas con un poco de positivismo de boticario o de orador de sección y saldrá un revulsivo infalible." (For them, it is not necessary to know how to create; imagination is enough; inspiration is a myth of vulgar psychology, genius, a farce, true genius is patience; the muse, assiduousness in one's work. Combine these two ideas with a little bit of an apothecary or section speaker's positivism, and you will get an infallible emetic). Leopoldo Alas, "Á muchos y á ninguno," in *Mezclilla* (Madrid: Librería de Fernando Fé, 1889), 175; quoted in Lissorges, "'El naturalismo radical'" 250.

CHAPTER 5

1. Walter T. Pattison, *Emilia Pardo Bazán* (New York: Twayne, 1971), 8.
2. Pattison, *Emilia Pardo Bazán*, 7.
3. Marina Mayoral, "De *Insolación* a *Dulce dueño*: Notas sobre el erotismo en la obra de Emilia Pardo Bazán," in *Eros literario: Actas del coloquio celebrado en la Facultad de Filología de la Universidad Complutense en diciembre de 1988*, ed. Covadonga López Alonso et al. (Madrid: Universidad Complutense de Madrid, 1989), 136; Raquel Medina, "Dulce esclava, dulce histérica: La representación de la mujer en *Dulce dueño* de Emilia Pardo Bazán," *Revista Hispánica Moderna* 51, no. 2 (December 1998): 298.
4. Pilar Faus Sevilla, *Emilia Pardo Bazán: Su época, su vida, su obra* (A Coruña: Fundación Pedro Barrié de la Maza, 2003), 2:445. While Faus notes that Pardo Bazán continued to help the poor through charitable works, she views this as a traditional posture, particularly in light of the growing socialist and anarchist movements in Spain (2:445).
5. Isabel Burdiel, *Emilia Pardo Bazán* (Madrid: Taurus, 2019), 495. Burdiel clarifies, however, that she thinks it is inaccurate to characterize her as "prefascista" (proto-fascist).
6. Denise DuPont, *The Whole Faith: The Catholic Ideal of Emilia Pardo Bazán* (Washington, DC: Catholic University of America Press, 2018), 25.
7. It is important to remember that nineteenth-century liberalism would be conservative by modern-day standards. Most Spanish liberals pushed for a laissez-faire capitalist economy (Carr, *Modern Spain*, 277). It is also important to remember that one of the most important liberal economic reforms of the century, *desamortización*, or disentailment, did not radically redistribute the nation's wealth as it was supposed to (Shubert, *A Social History*, 90; Carr, *Modern Spain*, 4–5).
8. Emilia Pardo Bazán, "La subida de los liberales," *Nuevo Teatro Crítico* 2 (1892): 91.
9. Pardo Bazán, "La subida," 88–89.
10. Pardo Bazán, "La mujer Española," 87.

11. See, for example, Cleminson and Vázquez García, *Hermaphroditism*; Campos Marín, *Monlau, Rubio, Giné*; Campos Marín, Huertas García-Alejo, and Martínez Pérez, *Los ilgeales de la naturaleza*; Vázquez García, *La invención del racismo*.

12. She argues that "el hombre es un ser específicamente uno, compuesto de cuerpo organizado y alma racional y aspirar a estudiarle con solo el auxilio de las ciencias físicas equivaldrá a juzgar de un libro examinando detenidamente la pasta, el papel y el tipo de letra, pero omitiendo leerle. (Man is a specifically unique being, comprised of an organized body and a rational soul, and aspiring to study him only with recourse to the physical sciences may be the equivalent of judging a book by examining carefully the material [from which it is made], the paper, and type of print, without actually reading it). Emilia Pardo Bazán, "Reflexiones científicas contra el darwinismo," in *Obras completas*, ed. Harry L. Kirby Jr. (Madrid: Aguilar, 1973): 3:556.

13. Emilia Pardo Bazán, "Una opinión sobre la mujer: el discurso del Marqués del Busto en la Real Academia de Medicina," *Nuevo Teatro Crítico* 2 (1892): 77.

14. For instance, both Leopoldo Alas and Francisco Giner de los Ríos doubted the veracity of her claims to being a devout Catholic (Pérez Gutiérrez, *El problema religioso*, 346).

15. El sentido de la enseñanza del divino Fundador del cristianismo era este: "De hoy más no habrá entre vosotros amo ni esclavo, hombre ni mujer, sino todos hijos de mi Padre." Pero así como largos siglos, hasta nuestros días, siguió habiendo amos y esclavos, hay todavía entre los cristianos hombres y mujeres, con todo el sentido jerárquico que se atribuye en la sociedad y en la familia á estos dos nombres. (The meaning of the teachings of the divine Founder of Christianity was: "From here on out there will not be any slaves among you, neither man nor woman, but rather you will all be children of my Father." But just as there has continued to be masters and slaves throughout the centuries, until our days, there still are among Christians men and women, with the complete hierarchical meaning that society and the family attribute to these two terms). Emilia Pardo Bazán, "La educación del hombre y de la mujer: Sus relaciones y diferencias. Memoria leída en el congreso pedagógico el día 16 de Octubre de 1892," in *Nuevo Teatro Crítico* 2 (1892): 36–37.

16. She writes, "Me persuadí de que para lo de tejas arriba me convenía la filosofía mística, que sube hacia Dios por medio del amor, para lo de tejas abajo, el criticismo, método prudente que no anda en zancos, pero no expone a caídas" (I became persuaded that in matters of the next world mystical philosophy suited me, since it reached God through the means of love; for matters of this world, cautious methodical criticism that does not walk on stilts, but does not risk falls [suited me best]). Emilia Pardo Bazán, "Apuntes autobiográficos," in *Los pazos de Ulloa* (Barcelona: Daniel Cortezo, 1886), 1:38.

17. Pardo Bazán, "Apuntes," 8.
18. DuPont, *The Whole Faith* 2, 21. Ángles Ezama Gil argues that it is in Pardo Bazán's last three novels, which include *Dulce dueño*, that we see precisely this fusion of religious and artistic values. Ángeles Ezama Gil, "Santidad, heroismo y estética en la narrativa de Emilia Pardo Bazán," in *Emilia Pardo Bazán: Estado de la Cuestión. Simposio, A Coruña 2, 3 y 4 de xuño de 2004*, ed. José Manuel González Herrán, Cristina Patiño Eirín, and Ermitas Penas Varela (Santiago de Compostela: Fundación Caixa Galicia, 2005), 247–48.
19. Si hay una verdad dicha, repetida y trillada, es que la ciencia no nos saca de dudas respecto a la esencia íntima de las cosas. Antaño el hombre pedía a la metafísica la explicación y sistema del mundo; hogaño la metafísica ha caído en descrédito, y por ciencia se entiende el conjunto de las físicas y naturales, que si bien nos ofrecen tesoros de conocimientos relativos, no nos acercan a lo absoluto ni una pulgada más. Sin emprender la apología de la metafísica y de las ciencias teológicas, bien puedo afirmar que las físicas y naturales, no por su atraso, sino por su misma índole, están desquiciadas cuando intentan penetrar en el terreno del gran misterio. (If there is a truth stated, repeated, and well worn, it is that science does not clear up doubts regarding the intimate nature of things. In the past, man looked to metaphysics for the explanation and system of the world; these days metaphysics has fallen into discredit, and science is understood to be the group of natural and physical sciences which, if they do indeed offer treasures of relative knowledge, they do not bring us an inch closer to the absolute. Without undertaking an apology of metaphysics and the theological sciences, I can certainly assert that the physical and natural sciences, not because they are backward, but because of their very character, are off course when they make incursions into the territory of the great mystery). Emilia Pardo Bazán, "La nueva cuestión palpitante," in *Obras completas*, ed. Harry L. Kirby Jr. (Madrid: Aguilar, 1973), 3:1181–82.
20. "La nueva cuestión" 1182.
21. Pardo Bazán, 19–20.
22. Emilia Pardo Bazán, *La cuestión palpitante*, ed. José Manuel González Herrán (Barcelona: Anthropos, 1989), 282.
23. Pardo Bazán, "Una opinion," 79.
24. This section is a slightly modified version of an analysis published by the same title in *Decimonónica* in 2012: "Reinterpreting Hysteria under Patriarchy in Emilia Pardo Bazán's 'La novia fiel' and 'Error de diagnóstico,'" *Decimonónica* 9, no.1 (2012): 92–106, http://www.decimononica. org/wp-content/uploads/2013/01/Smith_9.1.pdf.
25. Gabriela Pozzi, "Madres histéricas, médicos y la sexualidad en tres cuentos fntásticos de Emilia Pardo Bazán," *Letras Femeninas* 26, nos. 1–2 (Spring-Fall 2000): 157–69; Robin Ragan, "Another Look at Nucha's Hysteria: Pardo Bazán's Response to the Medical Field of Late Nineteenth-Century Spain," *Letras Femeninas* 30, no. 1 (Summer 2004): 141.

26. Colleen McAlister, "Una enfermedad social: La histeria y los roles de género en *Doña Milagros* (1894), de Emilia Pardo Bazán," *Decimonónica* 17, no. 1 (Winter 2020): 50–64.

27. See Susan McKenna, *Crafting the Female Subject: Narrative Innovation in the Short Fiction of Emilia Pardo Bazán* (Washington, DC: Catholic University of America Press, 2009); Joyce Tolliver, "Knowledge, Desire and Syntactic Empathy in Pardo Bazán's 'La novia fiel,'" *Hispania* 72, no. 4 (December 1989): 909–18.

28. Carmen Bravo-Villasante also identifies Amelia's "illness" as hysteria. Carmen Bravo-Villasante, *Vida y obra de Emilia Pardo Bazán* (Madrid: Revista de Occidente, 1962), 201–2.

29. The narrator tells us that she "mostrábase llena de rarezas y caprichos, ya riendo a carcajadas, ya encerrada en hosco silencio. Su salud se alteró también; advertía desgana invencible, insomnios crueles que la obligaban a pasarse la noche levantada, porque decía que la cama, con el desvelo, le parecía su sepulcro; además sufría aflicciones al corazón y ataques nerviosos" (she displayed all sorts of eccentricities and whims, either laughing hysterically or shutting herself off in a sullen silence. Her health changed as well; she showed a lack of enthusiasm, terrible insomnia that forced her to spend many of her nights upright, because she said that the bed, with her sleeplessness, felt like her grave; also she suffered afflictions of the heart and nervous attacks). Emilia Pardo Bazán, "La novia fiel," in *Emilia Pardo Bazán: Cuentos completos*, ed. Juan Paredes Núñez (A Coruña: Fundación Pedro Barrie de la Maza, Conde de Fenosa, 1990): 1:306.

30. According to Elaine Showalter, "the two defining characteristics" of nineteenth-century hysteria were "the seizure, and the *globus hystericus*, or sensation of choking." Elaine Showalter, *The Female Malady: Women, Madness and English Culture: 1830–1980*. New York: Penguin, 1985, 130. She also mentions that at the height of the hysterical attack "the victim alternately sobbed and laughed" (*The Female Malady*, 130).

31. Catherine Jagoe summarizes these descriptions as follows: "un período prodromal llamado el 'aura' histérica, caracterizado por la melancolía, la jaqueca, las risas o el llanto [. . .] y la sensación de una bola en la garganta sofocando a la víctima. Todo esto desembocaba en convulsiones epileptoides, con pérdida de conocimiento, gritos guturales, espuma en la boca, espasmos y delirio" ("Sexo y género," 339–40; a prodomal period called the hysterical "aura," characterized by melancholy, headaches, laughter or tears [. . .] and the sensation of a ball in one's throat suffocating the victim. All of this led to epileptic convulsions, with the loss of consciousness, guttural cries, foaming at the mouth, spasms, and delirium).

32. Also, as we saw in Chapter 2, the medical doctor Baltasar de Viguera made the point of underscoring the similarities between the two phenomena, stressing that the only difference is that one is "physiological," in other words, "normal," and the other is "pathological" (*Fisiología*, 2:84–85).

33. Showalter, for example, argues that "It was simpler to blame sexual

frustration, to continue to see hysterical women as lovelorn Ophelias, than to investigate women's intellectual frustration, lack of mobility or needs for autonomy and control" (*The Female Malady*, 131).

34. Maines, *The Technology of Orgasm*, 3.
35. Maines, 3.
36. Viguera, *Fisiología*, 2:85–86.
37. Viguera, 96.
38. Hizo mencion de la confricacion para rechazarla por inmoral" (Pulido Fernández, *Anales*, 79; He mentioned massage only to reject it as immoral).
39. This passage is also important in the way it shows how, in Pardo Bazán's view, priests played a role in women's subjugation by promoting the status quo in terms of gender roles in society. Joyce Tolliver, *Cigar Smoke and Violet Water: Gendered Discourse in the Stories of Emilia Pardo Bazán* (Lewisburg, PA: Bucknell University Press, 1998), 16. It is clear that while the Galician author would find arguments in Catholicism to bolster her demands for equality for women, this did not necessarily mean that she viewed the clergy, or the Church of her day as a whole, as an ally in this fight.
40. "¡Si no le dejo . . ., le imito! ¡Yo también . . .!" (1:307; If I don't break up with him . . ., I will imitate him! Me too . . .!).
41. Pardo Bazán, *El lirismo*, 270.
42. For an insightful and thorough analysis of this passage see Tolliver, "Knowledge," 911–12.
43. Tolliver, "Knowledge," 915.
44. Dianne Hunter, "Hysteria, Psychoanalysis, and Feminism: The Case of Anna O.," *Feminist Studies* 9, no. 3 (Autumn 1983): 485.
45. Hélène Cixous, "Castration or Decapitation?," trans. Annette Kuhn, *Signs* 7, no. 1, (Autumn 1981): 49.
46. Juliet Mitchell, "Femininity, Narrative and Psychoanalysis," in *Feminist Literary Theory: Reader*, ed. Mary Eagleton (Oxford, UK: Basil Blackwell, 1986), 101.
47. Cixous, "Castration," 49.
48. McKenna, *Crafting*, 56–57.
49. Emilia Pardo Bazán, "Error de diagnóstico," in *Emilia Pardo Bazán: Cuentos completos*, ed. Juan Paredes Núñez (A Coruña: Fundación Pedro Barrie de la Maza, Conde de Fenosa, 1990), 4:75.
50. The mother exclaims, "¡Por amor de Dios, le pido a usted que la mire despacio!" (4:75; For the love of God, I beg you to examine her carefully). The narrator tells us that the doctor "procedía así por acceder al deseo de la madre; pero su opinión estaba formada" (4:75; proceeded in this way to please her mother; but his mind was already made up).
51. Micale, *Approaching*, 72.
52. Laura Otis, "Science and Signification in the Early Writings of Emilia Pardo Bazán," *Revista de Estudios Hispánicos* 29, no.1 (January 1995): 81.
53. Otis, "Science," 81.
54. Pardo Bazán, "La nueva cuestión palpitante," 3:1181–82. Full quote pro-

vided in note 19 in this chapter, in the discussion on Pardo Bazán's views on science.

55. At this time, before the existence of antibiotics, surgery would be the only possible treatment, and still the mortality rate was high. Even just fifty years ago, the mortality rate after surgery was greater than 50 percent. Medscape, s.v. "Lung Abscess Surgery," by Shabir Bhimji, updated March 3, 2020, https://emedicine.medscape.com/article/428135-overview.

56. The girl tells that doctor that "Desde que está usted aquí, ya me siento mejor" (4:76; Now that you are here, I feel much better).

57. Fernández, *Eduardo López Bago*, 71, 191; Lissorgues, "El naturalismo radical," n. pag.

58. Pardo Bazán, "La educación," 20–21.

59. Smith-Rosenberg, *Disorderly Conduct*, 215.

60. This section is a slightly modified version of an essay published by the same title, Jennifer Smith, "Women, Mysticism and Alternative Technologies of the Self in Selected Writings of Emilia Pardo Bazán," *Revista de Estudios Hispánicos* 45, no. 1 (March 2011): 155–75.

61. Elaine Pagels, *The Gnostic Gospels* (New York: Vintage, 1989), xx. Here I use the term orthodox Christianity to refer to all forms of Christianity that accept the New Testament as the official canon of the faith and reject the gnostic gospels as heresy. This includes almost all forms of contemporary Christianity.

62. Pagels, xx.

63. Elaine Pagels, *Beyond Belief: The Secret Gospel of Thomas* (New York: Random House, 2003), 75.

64. Foucault uses the term *technologies of the self* to refer to practices that "permit individuals to effect by their own means, or with the help of others, a certain number of operations on their own bodies and souls, thought, conduct, and way of being, so as to transform themselves in order to attain a certain state of happiness, purity, wisdom, perfection, or immortality." Michel Foucault, "Technologies of the Self," in *Ethics: Subjectivity and Truth*, ed. Paul Rabinow, trans. Robert Hurley et al., The Essential Works of Foucault: 1954–1984, vol. 1, (New York: New Press, 1997), 225. Some examples are forms of self-examination such as confession for Christians, or reading, writing and meditation for the Stoics. Such practices should lead, in turn, to changes in behavior in the service of self-improvement.

65. In *Sacred Realism: Religion and the Imagination in Modern Spanish Narrative*, Noël Valis asserts that Foucault views religion primarily as a repressive instrument of power and that this reductive understanding has made Foucauldian theory ill equipped to engage the question of faith. Noël Valis, *Sacred Realism: Religion and the Imagination in Modern Spanish Narrative* (New Haven, CT: Yale University Press, 2010), 5–6. Nevertheless, as Ivan Strenski has pointed out in "Religion, Power, and Final Foucault," such interpretations of Foucault are based on his earlier

work. Ivan Strenski, "Religion, Power, and Final Foucault," *Journal of the American Academy of Religion* 66, no. 2 (Summer 1998): 345. His later work, mainly the second and third volumes of the *History of Sexuality*, which include the essay cited here ("Technologies of the Self") recants some of his earlier ideas and actually engages with questions of asceticism and self-discipline (Strenski, "Religion," 351).

66. Foucault, "Technologies," 246.
67. Foucault, 246.
68. Pagels, *The Gnostic Gospels*, 131.
69. Emilia Pardo Bazán, *El lirismo en la poesía fiancesa* (Madrid: Pueyo, 1923). The third volume of *La literatura francesa moderna* was completed in 1914. Pardo Bazán had planned a fourth volume on French *décadence*, which she never wrote. However, in 1916 she taught a course on French lyricism that dealt extensively with the lyrical sources of *décadence*. The notes for this course were compiled and published posthumously in 1923 with the title *El lirismo en la poesía francesa*. Hereafter I will use the abbreviation *El lirismo* when referring to this text.
70. For a list of the main hagiographic writings of Emilia Pardo Bazán see Ángeles Ezama Gil, "Santidad," 233.
71. Emilia Pardo Bazán, "El porvenir de la literatura después de la guerra," in *Obras completas*, ed. Harry L. Kirby Jr. (Madrid: Aguilar, 1973), 3:1549.
72. Beginning in the second century AD, as Christianity became institutionalized, a group of Christian leaders attempted to strengthen the fledgling and diverse religion, still a marginalized heresy under the Roman Empire, by creating "a single church they called catholic, which means 'universal'" (Pagels, *Beyond Belief*, 80).
73. "el ser humano tanto vive cuanto se educa" (Pardo Bazán, "La educación," 16; a human being's life is only as large as their education).
74. "la educación masculina se inspira en el postulado optimista, ó sea la fe en la perfectibilidad de la naturaleza humana" (19; men's education arose from an optimistic hypothesis, that is to say, from faith in the perfectibility of human nature).
75. "Iguálense las condiciones, y libre evolución hará los demás" (44; Let the conditions be equal, and unhindered evolution will take care of the rest).
76. "La gran obra progresiva del Cristianismo, en este particular, fue emancipar la conciencia de la mujer, afirmar su personalidad y su libertad moral, de la cual se deriva necesariamente la libertad práctica" (36; The great progressive work of Christianity, on this matter, was to emancipate women's conscience, to affirm her personality and moral freedom, from which practical freedoms necessarily derive).
77. Phoebe Porter Medina, "A Vision of Decadence in the Last Three Novels of Emilia Pardo Bazán." PhD diss., Brown University, 1985, 244.
78. Marina Mayoral, introduction to *Dulce dueño*, by Emilia Pardo Bazán, ed. Marina Mayoral (Madrid: Castalia, 1989), 39.
79. David Henn, "Continuity, Change and the Decadent Phenomenon in

Pardo Bazán's Late Fiction," *Neophilologus* 78, no. 3 (July 1994): 398.

80. Lou Charnon-Deutsch, *Narratives of Desire: Nineteenth-Century Spanish Fiction by Women* (University Park: Pennsylvania State University Press, 1994), 176, 178. In a more recent article on the novel, and in light of subsequent feminist readings of the novel, Charnon-Deutsch argues that even if the novel challenges masculine hegemony, the nuptial imagery ultimately reinscribes it. Lou Charnon-Deutsch, "'Tenía corazón': *Dulce dueño* de Emilia Pardo Bazán," *Arbor*, 182, no. 719 (2006): 325–36.

81. Raquel Medina, "Dulce esclava, dulce histérica: La representación de la mujer en *Dulce dueño* de Emilia Pardo Bazán," *Revista Hispánica Moderna* 51, no. 2 (December 1998): 302.

82. Susan Kirkpatrick, "Gender and Modernist Discourse: Emilia Pardo Bazán's *Dulce dueño*," in *Modernism and Its Margins: Reinscribing Cultural Modernity from Spain and Latin America*, ed. by Anthony L. Geist and José B. Monleón (New York: Garland, 1999), 134; Susan Kirkpatrick, *Mujer, modernismo y vanguardia en España (1898–1931)* (Madrid: Cátedra, 2003), 125.

83. Maryellen Bieder, "Intertextualizing Genre: Ambiguity as Narrative Strategy in Emilia Pardo Bazán," in *Intertextual Pursuits: Literary Mediations in Modern Spanish Narrative*, ed. Jeanne P. Brownlow and John W. Kronik (Lewisburg, PA: Bucknell University Press, 1998), 55–75.

84. Maryellen Bieder, "Emilia Pardo Bazán y la emergencia del discurso feminista," in *Breve historia feminista de la literatura española*, ed. Iris M. Zavala (Barcelona: Anthropos, 1998), 5:96.

85. Maryellen Bieder, "Divina y perversa: La mujer decadente en *Dulce dueño* de Emilia Pardo Bazán," in *Perversas y divinas: La representación de la mujer en las literaturas hispánicas: El fin de siglo y/o el fin de milenio actual*, ed. Carme Riera, Meri Torras and Isabel Clúa (Valencia: Ediciones ExCultura, 2002), 15.

86. Pau Pitarch Fernández, "Las armas del martirio: Una lectura del misticismo en *Dulce dueño* (1911) de Emilia Pardo Bazán," in *La hija de Eva: Historia, tradición y simbología*, ed. Inés Calero Secall and Virginia Aifaro Bech (Málaga, Spain: CEDMA, 2006), 194.

87. Carmen Pereira-Muro, "Mimetismo, misticismo y la cuestión de la escritura femenina en *Dulce Dueño* de Emilia Pardo Bazán," *La tribuna* 4 (2006): 153–80.

88. Bacon, *Negotiating Sainthood.*

89. Cristina Sánchez-Conejero, "*Dulce dueño*, de Emilia Pardo Bazán: Una novela posmodernamente anticanónica," *Crítica hispánica*, 50, nos. 1–2 (2008): 161.

90. Elizabeth Smith Rousselle and Joseph Drexler-Dreis, "Lina soy yo: Mysticism as Subversion and Identity for the Modern Woman Writer in Emilia Pardo Bazán's *Dulce dueño*," *Hispanófila* 166 (September 2012): 58. Rousselle more recently took on an analysis of the novel to argue that, while mysticism offers Lina an effective road to happiness, she suffers more social consequences than Nazarín, the eponymous mystical hero of

Galdós's novel. Elizabeth Smith Rousselle, "The Saint and the Hysteric: Mysticism in *Nazarín* and *Dulce dueño*," in *Modernity and Epistemology in Nineteenth-Century Spain: Fringe Discourses*, ed. Ryan A. Davis and Alicia Cerezo Paredes (Lanham, MD: Lexington Books, 2017), 131. See also chapter 6 of Elizabeth Smith Rousselle, *Gender and Modernity in Spanish Literature: 1789–1920* (New York: Palgrave MacMillan, 2014).

91. Eilene Powell, "Sadomasoquismo sagrado y la hagiografía irónica en *Dulce dueño* de Emilia Pardo Bazán," in *Sexualidades periféricas: Consolidaciones literarias y fílmicas en la España de fin de siglo XIX y fin de milenio*, ed. Nuria Godón and Michael J. Horswell (Madrid: Fundamentos, 2016), 116.

92. Brooks, *Body Work*, 34.

93. Catherine Jagoe, "La misión de la mujer." In *La mujer en los discursos de género: Textos y contextos en el siglo XIX*, ed. Catherine Jagoe, Alda Blanco, and Cristina Enríquez de Salamanca (Barcelona: Icaria, 1998), 23–24.

94. Cristina Enriquez de Salamanca, "La mujer en el discurso legal del liberalismo español," in *La mujer en los discursos de género: Textos y contextos en el siglo XIX*, ed. Catherine Jagoe, Alda Blanco, and Cristina Enriquez de Salamanca (Barcelona: Icaria, 1998), 236. This law did not apply in Catalonia ("La mujer," 236–37).

95. Enríquez de Salamanca, 240.

96. Enriquez de Salamanca, 224, 236.

97. Catherine Jagoe, Alda Blanco, and Cristina Enríquez de Salamanca, eds., *La mujer en los discursos de género: Textos y contextos en el siglo XIX* (Barcelona: Icaria, 1998), 268.

98. Emilia Pardo Bazán, *Dulce dueño*, ed. Marina Mayoral (Madrid: Castalia, 1989), 136.

99. Decadent writers such as Charles Baudelaire and Joris-Karl Huysmans greatly admired Wagner's compositions. Ellis Hanson, *Decadence and Catholicism* (Cambridge, MA: Harvard University Press, 1997), 29. Many of the themes peculiar to Wagner's operas, such as the preoccupation with feminine evil, sin, and redemption, and a passionate and mystical conception of love, occur frequently in decadent texts. (*Decadence and Catholicism*, 31). For more on the importance of Wagner's operas in *Dulce dueño*, see Carmen Pereira-Muro, "Relecturas femeninas del modernismo: El teatro de Wilde y las óperas de Strauss y Wagner en *Dulce Dueño*," in *Actas del IV Simposio Emilia Pardo Bazán y las artes del espectáculo* (A Coruña, Spain: Fundación Caixa Galicia, 2008).

100. Juana Inés de la Cruz, "Villancico a Caterina," in *The Defiant Muse: Hispanic Feminist Poems from the Middle Ages to the Present. A Bilingual Anthology*, ed. Angel Flores and Kate Flores (New York: CUNY, 1986): 24, lines 9–12.

101. Juana Inés de la Cruz. "Carol to Catherine," in *The Defiant Muse: Hispanic Feminist Poems from the Middle Ages to the Present. A Bilingual Anthology*, ed. Angel Flores and Kate Flores (New York: CUNY, 1986), 25, lines 9–12.

102. Natalie Underberg, "Sor Juana's Villancicos: Context, Gender, and Genre," *Western Folklore* 60, no. 4 (Autumn 2001): 311, 299.

103. Ezama Gil, "Santidad," 248, 251.
104. Bacon, *Negotiating Sainthood*, 170.
105. See, for example, Charnon-Deutsch, *Narratives*, 176; Charnon-Deutsch, "'Tenía corazón,'" 335; Kirkpatrick, "Gender," 134; Kirkpatrick, *Mujer*, 125; and Medina, "Dulce esclava," 302.
106. Mayoral, Introduction to *Dulce dueño*, 39.
107. Mayoral, 21.

CONCLUSION

1.   Valis, *Sacred Realism*, 32–33.
2.   John B. Gabel and Charles B. Wheeler, *The Bible as Literature: An Introduction*, 2nd ed., (Oxford, UK: Oxford University Press, 1990), 258.
3.   For a recent analysis and reconciliation of the two instincts see Sarah Coakley's *God, Sexuality, and the Self* (Cambridge, UK: Cambridge University Press, 2013).
4.   Sharon Begley and Anne Underwood, "Religion and the Brain," *Newsweek.* US ed., May 7, 2001, *Newsweek Archives*, May 10, 2005, http://msnbc.msn.com/id/3668484/site/newsweek.
5.   Begley and Underwood.
6.   Sokal and Bricmont's book was originally published in French in 1997 as *Impostures intellectuelles* (Intellectual imposters).
7.   Richard Dawkins, *A Devil's Chaplain: Reflections on Hope, Lies, Science and Love* (Boston: Houghton Mifflin, 2004), 14.
8.   Dawkins, 14–15.
9.   Bloodletting appears to date back to 2500 BC. Douglas Starr, *Blood: An Epic History of Medicine and Commerce* (New York: Alfred A. Knopf, 1998), 17–18.
10. Pardo Bazán, "La nueva cuestión," 1182.

BIBLIOGRAPHY

Alas, Leopoldo. "Á muchos y á ninguno." In *Mezclilla*, 167–99. Madrid: Librería de Fernando Fé, 1889.

———. "Azotacalles de Madrid: La procesión por fuera. La beata." In *Preludios de "Clarín,"* edited by Jean-François Botrel, 26–28. Oviedo: Instituto de Estudios Asturianos, 1972.

———. "El Centenario de Santa Teresa." In *Obras completas*, 7:148–51. Oviedo, Spain: Nobel, 2004.

———. "*La evangelista*: Novela de Alfonso Daudet. I." In *Obras completas*, 7:288–92. Oviedo, Spain: Nobel, 2007.

———. "*La evangelista*: Novela de Alfonoso Daudet. II." In *Obras completas*, 7:293–97. Oviedo, Spain: Nobel, 2004.

———. "*Gloria* (segunda parte). Novela del Sr. Pérez Galdós." In *Preludios de "Clarín,"* edited by Jean-François Botrel, 120–24. Oviedo, Spain: Instituto de Estudios Asturianos, 1972.

———. "Lecturas (Proyecto)." In *Mezclilla*, edited by Antonio Vilanova, 43–73. Barcelona: Lumen, 1987.

———. *Mezclilla*. Edited by Antonio Vilanova. Barcelona: Lumen, 1987.

———. *Obras completas*. 12 vols. Edited by Jean-François Botrel and Yvan Lissorgues. Oviedo, Spain: Nobel, 2002–2009.

———. *Preludios de "Clarín."* Edited by Jean-François Botrel. Oviedo, Spain: Instituto de Estudios Asturianos, 1972.

———. *La Regenta*. 2 vols. Edited by Gonzalo Sobejano. Madrid: Clásicos Castalia, 1981.

———. "Retórica y poética (fragmentos): I. La oratoria sagrada." In *Preludios de "Clarín,"* edited by Jean-François Botrel, 41–42. Oviedo, Spain: Instituto de Estudios Asturianos, 1972.

_____. *Solos de Clarín*. 4th ed. Madrid: Librería de Fernando Fe, 1891.

Aldaraca, Bridget A. *El ángel del hogar: Galdós and the Ideology of Domesticity in Spain*. Chapel Hill: North Carolina Studies in the Romance Languages and Literatures, 1991.

_____. "El caso de Ana O.: Histeria y sexualidad en *La Regenta*." *Asclepio* 42 (1990): 51–61.

_____. "The Medical Construction of the Feminine Subject in Nineteenth-Century Spain." In *Cultural and Historical Grounding for Hispanic and Luso-Brazilian Feminist Literary Criticism*, edited by Hernan Vidal, 395–413. Minneapolis, MN: Institute for the Study of Ideologies and Literature, 1989.

Alvarez Peláez, Raquel. "La mujer española y el control de natalidad en los comienzos del siglo XX." *Asclepio* 42 (1990): 175–200.

Álvarez, Tomás. *Santa Teresa a contraluz: La santa ante la crítica*. Burgos, Spain: Monte Carmelo, 2004.

Amezcúa, Efigenio. "Cien años de temática sexual en España, 1850–1950: Repertorio y análisis. Contribución al estudio de materiales para una historia de la sexología." *Revista de Sexología* 48 (1991): 1–197.

"Auguste Marie. Mysticisme et folie. Partie I. Extrait des 'Archives de Neurologie,' (Paris)." *Histoire et folie*. Accessed August 26, 2019. http://www.histoiredelafolie.fr/psychiatrie-neurologie/auguste-marie-mysticisme-et-folie-partie-1-extrait-des-archives-de-neurologie-paris-deuxieme-serie-tome-vii-n40-avril-1899-pp-257-278.

Bacon, Kathy. *Negotiating Sainthood: Distinction*, Cursilería *and Saintliness in Spanish Novels*. London: Legenda, 2007.

Balbo, Eduardo A. "El concepto de perversión en la psiquiatría dinámica." *Asclepio* 42, no. 2 (1990): 101–9.

Bauer, Beth Wietelmann. "Novels in Dialogue: *Pepita Jiménez* and *La Regenta*." *Revista de Estudios Hispánicos* 25, no. 2 (May 1991): 104–21.

Bayo, Ciro. *Higiene sexual del soltero*. Madrid: A. Marzo, n.d.

Begley, Sharon, and Anne Underwood. "Religion and the Brain." *Newsweek*. U.S. ed. May 7, 2001, *Newsweek Archives*, May 10, 2005, http://msnbc.msn.com/id/ 3668484/site/newsweek.

Berceo, Gonzalo de. *Milagros de Nuestra Señora*. Madrid: Clásicos Castalia, 2006.

Bernard, Claude. *Introduction à l'étude de la médecine expérimentale*. Paris: J.B. Baillière et fils, 1865.

Beizer, Janet. *Ventriloquized Bodies: Narratives of Hysteria in Nineteenth-Century France*. Ithaca, NY: Cornell University Press, 1993.

Bieder, Maryellen. "Divina y perversa: La mujer decadente en *Dulce dueño* de Emilia Pardo Bazán." In *Perversas y divinas: La representación de la mujer en las literaturas hispánicas: El fin de siglo y/o el fin de milenio actual*, edited by Carme Riera, Meri Torras and Isabel Clúa, 7–19. Valencia: Ediciones ExCultura, 2002.

———. "Emilia Pardo Bazán y la emergencia del discurso feminista." In *Breve historia feminista de la literatura española*, edited by Iris M. Zavala, 5:75–110. Barcelona: Anthropos, 1998.

———. "Intertextualizing Genre: Ambiguity as Narrative Strategy in Emilia Pardo Bazán." In *Intertextual Pursuits: Literary Mediations in Modern Spanish Narrative*, edited by Jeanne P. Brownlow and John W. Kronik, 55–75. Lewisburg, PA: Bucknell University Press, 1998.

Bienville, M. D. T. *Nymphomania, or a Dissertation Concerning the* Furor Uterinus. Translated by Edward Sloane Wilmot. London: Pater-nofter Row, 1775.

———. *La nymphomanie, ou, Traité de la fureur utérine*. Paris: Office de Librairie, 1886.

Bly, Peter. "The Physician in the Narratives of Galdós and Clarín," In *Imagined Truths: Realism in Modern Spanish Literature and Culture*, edited by Mary L. Coffey and Margot Versteeg, 111–143. Toronto: University of Toronto Press, 2019.

Borderies-Guereña, Josette. "El discurso higiénico como conformador de la mentalidad femenina (1864–1915)." In *Mujeres y hombres en la formacion del pensamiento occidental*, edited by Virginia Maquieira D'Angelo et al, 2:299–309. Madrid: Universidad Autónoma de Madrid, 1989.

Bosco Sanromán, Juan. "Anteriores centenarios de la muerte de Santa Teresa." In *Pérfil histórico de Santa Teresa*, edited by Teófanes Egido Martínez, 2nd ed., 173–95. Madrid, Editorial de Espiritualidad, 1981.

Bourneville, D. M., and P. Régnard. *Iconographie photographique de la Salpêtrière*. Versailles: Imprimerie Cerf et Fils, 1878. *Archives.org*. https://archive. org/details/iconographiephoooregngoog/page/n8.

Bravo-Villasante, Carmen. *Vida y obra de Emilia Pardo Bazán*. Madrid: Revista de Occidente, 1962.

Brooks, Peter. *Body Work: Objects of Desire in Modern Narrative*. Cambridge, MA: Harvard University Press, 1993.

Burdiel, Isabel. "*Los Borbones en pelota*: La pornografía política en la crisis del reinado isabelino." In *Los Borbones en pelota*, edited and introduced by Isabel Burdiel, 42–74. Zaragoza, Spain: Institución Fernando "El Católico," 2012.

———. "El descenso de los reyes y la nación moral: A propósito de los *Borbones en pelota*." In *Los Borbones en pelota*, edited and introduced by Isabel Burdiel, 7–15. Zaragoza: Institución Fernando "El Católico," 2012.

———. *Emilia Pardo Bazán*. Madrid: Taurus, 2019.

Busto, Andrés del. "Problemas morales y sociales que resuelve el estudio médico de la mujer." In *Discursos leídos en la solemne sesión inaugural del año de 1892 de la Real Academia de Medicina*, 4–141. Madrid: Enrique Teodoro, 1892.

Butler, Judith. *Bodies That Matter: On the Discursive Limits of "Sex."* London: Routledge, 1993.

Cadden, Joan. *Meanings of Sex Difference in the Middle Ages: Medicine, Science, and Culture.* Cambridge, UK: Cambridge University Press, 1993.

Campá, Francisco de Paula. "Las dos edades críticas de la vida de la mujer." In *Discursos en la Real Academia de Medicina*. Valencia, Spain: Ferrer de Orga, 1876.

Campos Marín, Ricardo. *Monlau, Rubio, Giné: Curar y gobernar: Medicina y liberalismo en la España del siglo XIX*. Madrid: Nivola, 2003.

Campos Marín, Ricardo, Rafael Huertas García-Alejo, and José Martínez Pérez. *Los ilgeales de la naturaleza: Medicina y degeneracionismo en la España de la Restuaración (1876–1923)*. Madrid: Consejo Superior de Investigaciones Científicas, 2000.

Carr, Raymond. *Modern Spain: 1875–1980*. Oxford, UK: Oxford University Press, 1980.

Carroy-Thirard, Jacqueline. "Possession, extase, hystérie au 19ᵉ siècle." *Psychanalyse à l'université* 5, no. 19 (June 1980): 499–515.

Casco Solís, Juan. "La higiene sexual en el proceso de institucionalización de la sanidad pública." *Asclepio* 2, no. 2 (1990): 223–52.

Castellanos, Jesús, Isabel Jiménez Lucena, and María José Ruiz Somavilla. "La ciencia médica en el siglo XIX como instrumento de reafirmación ideológica: la defensa de la desigualdad de la mujer a través de la patología femenina." In *La mujer en Andalucia: Actas del I encuentro interdisciplinar de estudios de la mujer*, edited by Pilar Ballarín and Teresa Orti, 2:879–88. Granada: Universidad de Granada, 1990.

Castro, Rosalía de. Prologue to *La hija del mar*, by Rosalía de Castro. Biblioteca Virtual Miguel de Cervantes. Accessed August 28, 2019. http://www.cervantesvirtual.com/obra-visor/la-hija-del-mar—1/html/feed8910–82b1–11df-acc7–002185ce6064_2.html.

Charnon-Deutsch, Lou. "Between Agency and Determinism: A Critical Review of Clarín Studies." *Hispanic Review* 76, no. 2 (Spring 2008): 135–53.

———. *Fictions of the Feminine in the Nineteenth-Century Spanish Press*. University Park: Pennsylvania State University Press, 2000.

———. *Narratives of Desire: Nineteenth-Century Spanish Fiction by Women*. University Park: Pennsylvania State University Press, 1994.

———. "'Tenía corazón': *Dulce dueño* de Emilia Pardo Bazán." *Arbor*, 182, no. 719 (2006): 325–36.

Cherry, Kendra. "Bowlby & Ainsworth: What Is Attachment Theory?: The Importance of Early Emotional Bonds." Verywellmind. https://www.verywellmind.com/what-is-attachment-theory-2795337.

Cixous, Hélène. "Castration or Decapitation?" Translated by Annette Kuhn. *Signs* 7, no. 1, (Autumn 1981): 41–55.

Cleminson, Richard. *Anarchism, Science, and Sex: Eugenics in Eastern Spain, 1900–1937*. New York: Lang, 2000.

Cleminson, Richard, and Teresa Fuentes Peris. "'La mala vida': Source and Focus of Degeneration, Degeneracy and Decline." *Journal of Spanish Cultural Studies* 10, no. 4 (December 2009): 385–97. https://doi.org/10.1080/14636200903400173.

Cleminson, Richard, and Francisco Vázquez García. *Hermaphroditism, Medical Science and Sexual Identity in Spain, 1850–1960*. Cardiff: University of Wales Press, 2009.

Cleminson, Richard, and Francisco Vázquez García. *'Los invisibles': A History of Male Homosexuality in Spain: 1850–1940*. Cardiff: University of Wales Press, 2007.

Coakley, Sarah. *God, Sexuality, and the Self*. Cambridge, UK: Cambridge University Press, 2013.

Coronado, Carolina. *Jarilla: Novela original, Los genios gemelos*. Badajoz, Spain: Dip. Prov. De Badajoz, 2001.

Cortejarena y Aldebó, Francisco de. *Memoria presentada a la Academia de Medicina de Madrid: ¿Son hoy mas frecuentes que en otros tiempos las enfermedades de la matriz?* Madrid: T. Fortanet, 1869.

Cruz, Jesús. *The Rise of Middle-Class Culture in Nineteenth-Century Spain*. Baton Rouge: Louisiana State University Press, 2011.

Cruz, Juana Inés de la. "Carol to Catherine." In *The Defiant Muse: Hispanic Feminist Poems from the Middle Ages to the Present. A Bilingual Anthology*, edited by Angel Flores and Kate Flores, 25. New York: CUNY, 1986.

———. "Villancico a Caterina." In *The Defiant Muse: Hispanic Feminist Poems from the Middle Ages to the Present. A Bilingual Anthology*, edited by Angel Flores and Kate Flores, 24. New York: CUNY, 1986.

Cuesta y Ckerner, Juan. *Enfermedades de las mujeres: Extracto de las asignaturas que tienen que estudiar los cirujanos de segunda clase que aspiran al título de Facultativo habilitados por medio de estudios privados*. Madrid, Tomas Alonso, 1868.

Daston, Lorraine, and Katherine Park. "The Hermaphrodite and the Orders of Nature: Sexual Ambiguity in Early Modern France." In *Premodern Sexualities*, edited by Louise Fradenburg and Carla Freccero, 117–36. New York: Routledge, 1996.

Dawkins, Richard. *A Devil's Chaplain: Reflections on Hope, Lies, Science and Love*. Boston: Houghton Mifflin, 2004.

Deveaux, Monique. "Feminism and Empowerment: A Critical Reading of Foucault." *Feminist Studies* 20, no. 2 (Summer 1994): 223–47, http://www.jstor.org/stable/3178151.

Diderot, Denis. *The Nun*. Translated by Russel Goulbourne. Oxford, UK: Oxford University Press, 2008.

DuPont, Denise. "Decadent Naturalism: Eduardo López Bago's Response to Emile Zola." *Excavatio* 23, nos. 1–2 (2008): 47–60.

_____. "Teresa de Jesús and the Creation of Gender Communities in Eduardo López Bago's *El Cura* Trilogy." *Revista de Estudios Hispánicos* 41, no. 3 (October 2007): 345–61.

_____. *Writing Teresa: The Saint from Avila at the fin-de-siglo*. Lewisburg, PA: Bucknell University Press, 2011.

_____. *The Whole Faith: The Catholic Ideal of Emilia Pardo Bazán*. Washington, DC: Catholic University of America Press, 2018.

Durán, Manuel. *Luis de León*. New York: Twayne, 1971.

Enriquez de Salamanca, Cristina. "La mujer en el discurso legal del liberalismo español." In *La mujer en los discursos de género: Textos y contextos en el siglo XIX*, edited by Catherine Jagoe, Alda Blanco, and Cristina Enriquez de Salamanca, 219–52. Barcelona: Icaria, 1998.

Ezama Gil, Ángeles. "Ana Ozores y el modelo teresiano: Ejemplaridad y escritura literaria." In *Leopoldo Alas, un clásico contemporáneo (1901–2001): Actas del congreso celebrado en Oviedo (12–16 de noviembre de 2001)*, edited by Araceli Iravedra Valea, Elena de Lorenzo Álvarez, and Álvaro Ruiz de la Peña, 2:775–90. Oviedo, Spain: Universidad de Oviedo, 2002.

_____. "Santidad, heroismo y estética en la narrativa de Emilia Pardo Bazán." In *Emilia Pardo Bazán: Estado de la Cuestión. Simposio, A Coruña 2, 3 y 4 de xuño de 2004*, edited by José Manuel González Herrán, Cristina Patiño Eirín, and Ermitas Penas Varela, 233–58. Santiago de Compostela, Spain: Fundación Caixa Galicia, 2005.

Faus Sevilla, Pilar. *Emilia Pardo Bazán: Su época, su vida, su obra*. 2 vols. A Coruña, Spain: Fundación Pedro Barrié de la Maza, 2003.

Fernández, Pura. *Eduardo López Bago y el naturalismo radical: La novela y el mercado en el siglo XIX*. Amsterdam: Rodopi, 1995.

_____. *Mujer pública y vida privada: Del arte eunuco a la novela lupanaria*. London: Tamesis, 2008.

_____. "*Scientia sexualis* y saber psiquiátrico en la novela naturalista decimonónica." *Asclepio* 9, no. 1 (1997): 227–44. http://dx.doi.org/10.3989/asclepio.1997.v49.i1.389.

Ferreras, Juan Ignacio. Introduction to *El Cura (Caso de incesto): Novela médico social*, by Eduardo López Bago, 7–21. Edited by Juan Ignacio Ferreras. Madrid: Vosa, 1996.

Filosofía en español, s.v. "Eduardo Ovejero Maury." Accessed August 28, 2019. http://www.filosofia.org/ave/001/a444.htm.

Fisher, Dominique D. "Should Feminists Forget Foucault?" *Studies in 20th Century Literature* 22, no. 1 (January 1998): 1–18. https://doi.org/10.4148/2334-4415.1440.

Flecha García, Consuelo. "La mujer en los discursos médicos del siglo XIX." In *Las mujeres en Andalucia: Actas del 2° encuentro interdisciplinar de estudios de la mujer en Andalucia*, 1:189–202. Málaga, Spain: Diputación Provincial de Malaga, 1993.

Flores, Angel, and Kate Flores, eds. *The Defiant Muse: Hispanic Feminist Poems from the Middle Ages to the Present: A Bilingual Anthology*. New York: CUNY, 1986.

Foucault, Michel. *History of Sexuality. Volume 1: An Introduction*. Translated by Robert Hurley. New York: Random House, 1978.

———. "Technologies of the Self." In *Ethics: Subjectivity and Truth*, Edited by Paul Rabinow, translated by Robert Hurley et al. of The Essential Works of Foucault: 1954–1984, vol. 1. New York: New Press, 1997.

Freud, Sigmund. "Femininity." In *New Introductory Lectures on Psychoanalysis*, edited and translated by James Strachey, 112–35. New York: Norton, 1965.

Gabel, John B., and Charles B. Wheeler. *The Bible as Literature: An Introduction*. 2nd ed. Oxford, UK: Oxford University Press, 1990.

García Guerrero, Isaac. "The Perverted Doctor Bago: The Paradox of Modernity in Eduardo López Bago's *El cura*." In *Perversiones decimonónicas: Literatura y parafilia en el siglo XIX*, edited by Jorge Avilés, 291–307. Valencia: Albatros, 2018.

Gilfoil, Anne. "Doctor vs. Priest: Urban Planning and Reform in Vetusta." *Decimonónica* 6, no. 1 (Winter 2009): 34–45, http://www.decimononica.org/wp-content/uploads/2013/01/Gilfoil_6.1.pdf.

Giné y Partagas, Juan. *Curso elemental de higien eprivada y publica*. 4 vols. 4th ed. Barcelona: Juan y Antonio Bastinos, 1880.

Godón, Nuria. *La pasión esclava: Alianzas masoquistas en La Regenta*. West Lafayette, IN: Purdue University Press, 2017.

———. "Las poseídas: Cuadros histéricos de la mística en el imaginario decimonónico." In *Baroque Projections: Images and Texts in Dialog with the Early Modern Hispanic World*, edited by Frédéric Conrod and Michael Horswell, 109–32. Newark, DE: Juan de la Cuesta, 2016.

Godón, Nuria, and Michael J. Horswell, eds. *Sexualidades periféricas: Consolidaciones literarias y fílmicas en la España de fin de siglo XIX y fin de milenio*. Madrid: Editorial Fundamentos, 2016.

Goode, Joshua. *Impurity of Blood: Defining Race in Spain: 1879–1939*. Baton Rouge: Louisiana State University Press, 2009.

Goldstein, Jan. "The Hysteria Diagnosis and Politics of Anticlericalism in Late Nineteenth-Century Spain." *Journal of Modern History* 54, no. 2 (June 1982): 209–39.

González, Arturo, and Miguel Diéguez. *Sor Patrocinio*. Madrid: Nacional, 1981.

Graus, Andrea. "Mysticism in the Courtroom in 19th-Century Europe." *History of the Human Sciences* 31, no. 3 (March 2018): 21–40. https://doi.org/10.1177/0952695118761499.

————. "'Wonder Nuns': Sor Patrocinio, the Politics of the Supernatural, and Republican Caricature." *Journal of Religious History* 42, no. 4 (November 2018): 568–90. https://doi.org/10.1111/1467-9809.12544.

Groneman, Carol. "Nymphomania: The Historical Construction of Female Sexuality." *Signs* 19, no. 2 (Winter 1994): 337–67.

————. *Nymphomania: A History*. New York: Norton, 2000.

Gross, Paul R., and Norman Levitt. *Higher Superstition: The Academic Left and Its Quarrels with Science*. Baltimore: Johns Hopkins University Press, 1994.

Guereña, Jean-Louis. Introduction to *La sexualidad en la España contemporánea: 1800–1930*, 11–22. Edited by Jean-Louis Guereña. Cádiz: Universidad de Cádiz, 2011.

Hahn, G. S. J. "Les phénomènes hystériques et les révélations de Sainte Thérèse." *La revue des questions scientifiques* 13–14 (1883): 5–77; 39–84.

Halberstam, Judith. *Female Masculinity*. Durham, NC: Duke University Press, 1998.

Hamilton, Alastair. *Heresy and Mysticism in Sixteenth-Century Spain: The "Alumbrados."* Toronto: University of Toronto Press, 1992.

Hanson, Ellis. *Decadence and Catholicism*. Cambridge, MA: Harvard University Press, 1997.

Henn, David. "Continuity, Change and the Decadent Phenomenon in Pardo Bazán's Late Fiction." *Neophilologus* 78, no. 3 (July 1994): 395–406.

Holler, Jacqueline. "More Sins than the Queen of England: Marina de San Miguel before the Mexican Inquisition." In *Women in the Inquisition: Spain and the New World*, edited by Mary E. Giles, 209–28. Baltimore, MD: Johns Hopkins University Press, 1999.

————, ed. and trans. "The Spiritual and Physical Ecstasies of a Sixteenth-Century *Beata*: Marina de San Miguel Confesses before the Mexican Inquisition." In *Colonial Lives: Documents on Latin American History, 1550–1850*, edited by Richard Boyer and Geoffrey Spurling, 77–100. Oxford, UK: Oxford University Press, 2000.

Huerga, Álvaro. *Historia de los Alumbrados*. 5 vols. Madrid, Fundación Universitaria Española, 1978–1994.

Huertas García Alejo, Rafael. "El concepto de 'perversion' sexual en la medicina positivista." *Asclepio* 42, no. 1 (1990): 89–99.

Hunter, Dianne. "Hysteria, Psychoanalysis, and Feminism: The Case of Anna O." *Feminist Studies* 9, no. 3 (Autumn 1983): 464–88.

Huysmans, Joris-Karl. *Là-bas*. Paris: Plon, 1960.

Irigaray, Luce. *Speculum of the Other Woman*. Translated by Gillian C. Gill. Ithaca: Cornell University Press, 1985.

Jaffe, Catherine. "In Her Father's Library: Women's Reading in *La Regenta*." *Revista de Estudios Hispánicos* 39, no. 1 (January 2005): 3–25.

Jagoe, Catherine. "La misión de la mujer." In *La mujer en los discursos de género: Textos y contextos en el siglo XIX*, edited by Catherine Jagoe, Alda Blanco, and Cristina Enríquez de Salamanca, 21–53. Barcelona: Icaria, 1998.

———. "Sexo y género en la medicina del siglo XIX." In *La mujer en los discursos de género: Textos y contextos en el siglo XIX*, edited by Catherine Jagoe, Alda Blanco, and Cristina Enríquez de Salamanca, 305–67. Barcelona: Icaria, 1998.

Jagoe, Catherine, Alda Blanco, and Cristina Enríquez de Salamanca, eds. *La mujer en los discursos de género: Textos y contextos en el siglo XIX*. Barcelona: Icaria, 1998.

Jantzen, Grace M. *Power, Gender and Christian Mysticism*. Cambridge, UK: Cambridge University Press, 1995.

King, Angela. "The Prisoner of Gender: Foucault and the Disciplining of the Female Body," *Journal of International Women's Studies* 5, no. 2 (March 2004): 29–39. https://vc.bridgew.edu/jiws/vol5/iss2/4.

Kirkpatrick, Susan. "Gender and Modernist Discourse: Emilia Pardo Bazán's *Dulce dueño*." In *Modernism and Its Margins: Reinscribing Cultural Modernity from Spain and Latin America*, edited by Anthony L. Geist and José B. Monleón, 117–39. New York: Garland, 1999.

———. *Mujer, modernismo y vanguardia en España (1898–1931)*. Madrid: Cátedra, 2003.

———. *Las Románticas: Women Writers and Subjectivity in Spain*. Berkeley: University of California Press, 1989.

Koertge, Noretta, ed. *A House Built on Sand: Exposing Postmodernist Myths about Science*. Oxford, UK: Oxford University Press, 1998.

Krafft-Ebing, Richard von. *Psychopathia Sexualis*. Translated by Franklin S. Klaf. New York: Stein and Day, 1965.

Labanyi, Jo. *Gender and Modernization in the Spanish Realist Novel*. Oxford, UK: Oxford University Press, 2000.

———. "Mysticism and Hysteria in *La Regenta*: The Problem of Female Identity." In *Feminist Readings on Spanish and Latin American Literature*, edited by Lisa P. Condé and Stephen Hart, 37–46. Lewiston, NY: Edwin Mellen, 1991.

Laqueur, Thomas W. *Making Sex: Body and Gender from the Greeks to Freud.* Cambridge, MA: Harvard University Press, 1990.

_____. *Solitary Sex: A Cultural History of Masturbation.* Brooklyn, NY: Zone Books, 2003.

Lea, Henry Charles. *A History of the Inquisition of Spain.* 4 vols. New York: Macmillan, 1906–1907. Library of Iberian Resources Online, https://libro.uca.edu/title.htm.

Lissorgues, Yvan. *Clarín político.* 2 vols. Barcelona: Lumen, 1980.

_____. "'El naturalismo radical': Eduardo López Bago (y Alejandro Sawa)." *Biblioteca Virtual Miguel de Cervantes,* http://www.cervantesvirtual.com/nd/ark:/59851/bmcrv128.

_____. *La pensée philosophique et religieuse de Leopoldo Alas (Clarín): 1875–1901.* Paris: CNRS, 1983.

Lombroso, Cesare. *The Female Offender.* London: T. Fisher Unwin, 1895.

_____. *Man of Genius.* London: Walter Scott, 1895.

López-Bago, Eduardo. *El confesionario (Satiriasis): Novela médico-social.* Madrid: Juan Muñoz y Compañía, 1885.

_____. *El cura (Caso de incesto): Novela médico-social.* Madrid: Juan Muñoz Sánchez, 1885.

_____. *La monja: Novela médico-social.* Madrid: Mariano Núñez Samper, 1904.

_____. *El preso: Novela médico-social.* Madrid: José Góngora, 1880. *Biblioteca Digital Hispánica. Biblioteca Nacional de España.* http://bdh-rd.bne.es/viewer.vm?pid=d-3488426.

_____. *La pálida: Novela médico-social (Segunda parte de La Prostituta).* 6th ed. Madrid: Juan Múñoz, 1885.

_____. *La prostituta: Novela médico-social.* Madrid: Juan Muñoz, 1900.

_____. "Vosotros y yo." In *El cura (Caso de incesto): Novela médico-social,* by Eduardo López Bago, 259–91. Madrid: Juan Muñoz Sánchez, 1885.

Maines, Rachel P. *The Technology of Orgasm: "Hysteria," the Vibrator, and Women's Sexual Satisfaction.* Baltimore, MD: Johns Hopkins University Press, 1999.

Mainez Fernández, Ramón León. *Teresa de Jesús ante la crítica.* Madrid: Aurelio J. Alaria, 1880.

Malthus, Thomas Robert. *An Essay on the Principle of Population.* Edited by Philip Appleman. New York: Norton, 1976.

Mandrell, James. "Estudios gay y lesbianos: La revelación del cuerpo masculino: Una mirada Gay." In *El hispanismo en los Estados Unidos: Discursos críticos/prácticas textuales,* edited by José Manuel del Pino and Francisco La Rubia Prado, 211–30. Madrid: Visor, 1999.

Mannarelli, María Emma. *Hechiceras, beatas y expósitas: Mujeres y poder inquisitorial en Lima*. Lima, Congreso del Perú, 1998.

Marie, A. *Misticismo y locura: Estudio de psicología normal y patológica comparadas*. Translated by Eduardo Ovejero. Madrid: España Moderna, [1907?].

Marín Hernández, David, and Fernando José Hidalgo Moreno. "La recepción de Diderot en la España del XIX: La traducción de *La religiosa* de Ángel Rodríguez Chaves." *Hispania Nova* 14 (2006): 269–90. https://e-revistas.uc3m.es/index.php/HISPNOV/article/view/2976.

Martínez, José. "Sexualidad y orden social: La visión médica en la España del primer tercio del siglo XIX." *Asclepio* 2, no. 2 (1990): 119–35. http://hdl.handle.net/10261/26237.

Mathews, Christine. "Making the Nuclear Family: Kinship, Homosexuality, and *La Regenta*." *Revista de Estudios Hispánicos* 37, no. 1 (January 2003): 75–102.

Mautner, Thomas. "Comte." In *Dictionary of Philosophy*, 102–3. New York: Penguin, 1997.

———. "Positivism." In *Dictionary of Philosophy*, 437–38. New York: Penguin, 1997.

Mayoral, Marina. "De *Insolación* a *Dulce dueño*: Notas sobre el erotismo en la obra de Emilia Pardo Bazán." In *Eros literario: Actas del coloquio celebrado en la Facultad de Filología de la Universidad Complutense en diciembre de 1988*, edited by Covadonga López Alonso, et al, 127–36. Madrid: Universidad Complutense de Madrid, 1989.

———. Introduction to *Dulce dueño*, by Emilia Pardo Bazán, 7–44. Edited by Marina Mayoral. Madrid: Castalia, 1989.

Mazzoni, Cristina. *Saint Hysteria: Neurosis, Mysticism and Gender in European Culture*. Ithaca, NY: Cornell University Press, 1996.

McAlister, Colleen. "Una enfermedad social: La histeria y los roles de género en *Doña Milagros* (1894), de Emilia Pardo Bazán." *Decimonónica* 17, no. 1 (Winter 2020): 50–64.

McKenna, Susan. *Crafting the Female Subject: Narrative Innovation in the Short Fiction of Emilia Pardo Bazán*. Washington, DC: Catholic University of America Press, 2009.

McKinney, Collin. "'Enemigos de la virilidad': Sex, Masturbation, and Celibacy in Nineteenth-Century Spain." *Prisma Social* 13 (December 2014–May 2015): 72–108. http://www.isdfundacion.org/publicaciones/revista/numeros/13/secciones/tematica/t_03_enemigos_virilidad.html.

Medina, Phoebe Porter. "A Vision of Decadence in the Last Three Novels of Emilia Pardo Bazán." PhD diss., Brown University, 1985.

Medina, Raquel. "Dulce esclava, dulce histérica: La representación de la mujer en *Dulce dueño* de Emilia Pardo Bazán." *Revista Hispánica Moderna* 51, no. 2 (December 1998): 291–303.

Micale, Mark S. *Approaching Hysteria: Disease and Its Interpretations*. Princeton, NJ: Princeton University Press, 1995.

Michelet, Jules. *Du prêtre, de la femme et de la famille*. 4th ed. Paris: Comptoir des Imprimeurs-Unis, 1845.

————. *La sorcière*. Illustrations by Martin Van Maele. Paris: J. Chevrel, 1911.

————. *La Sorcière: The Witch of the Middle Ages*. Translated by L. J. Trotter. London: Simpkin Marshall, 1863.

Merskey, Harold, and Susan J. Merskey. "Hysteria or 'Suffocation of the Mother.'" *History of Medicine* 148, no. 3 (February 1993): 399–405.

Mill, John Stuart. *"On Liberty" and Other Essays*. Edited by John Gray. Oxford, UK: Oxford University Press, 1998.

Mitchell, Juliet. "Femininity, Narrative and Psychoanalysis." In *Feminist Literary Theory: Reader*, edited by Mary Eagleton, 100–103. Oxford: Basil Blackwell, 1986.

Mollow, Anna. "Chriphystemologies: What Disability Theory Needs to Know about Hysteria." *Journal of Literary & Cultural Disability Studies* 8, no. 1 (2014): 185–201. https://www.muse.jhu.edu/article/548850.

Monlau, Pedro Felipe. *Higiene del matrimonio o el libro de los casados*. 2nd ed. Madrid: M. Rivadeneyra, 1858.

Morros Mestres, Bienvenido. "La histeria de Paulina Porreño en *La Fontana de oro* de Galdós," *Bulletin Hispanique* 110, no. 1 (June 2008): 333–70, https://doi.org/10.4000/bulletinhispanique.664.

Oleza, Juan. Introduction to *La Regenta*, by Leopoldo Alas Clarín, 1:9–13. Madrid: Cátedra, 1989.

Otis, Laura. "Science and Signification in the Early Writings of Emilia Pardo Bazán." *Revista de Estudios Hispánicos* 29, no.1 (January 1995): 73–106.

Pagels, Elaine. *Beyond Belief: The Secret Gospel of Thomas*. New York: Random House, 2003.

————. *The Gnostic Gospels*. New York: Vintage, 1989.

Palacios Alcalde, María. "Las beatas ante la Inquisición." In *Hispania Sacra* 40, no. 81 (1988): 107–31.

Pardo Bazán, Emilia. "Apuntes autobiográficos," in *Los pazos de Ulloa*, 1:5–92. Barcelona: Daniel Cortezo, 1886.

————. *Cuentos completos*. 4 vols. Edited by Juan Paredes Núñez. A Coruña: Fundación Pedro Barrie de la Maza, Conde de Fenosa, 1990.

————. *La cuestión palpitante*. 1883. Edited by José Manuel González Herrán. Barcelona: Anthropos, 1989.

————. *Doña Milagros*. In vol. 3 of *Obras completas*, 571–776. Edited by Darío Villanueva and José Manuel González Herrán. Madrid: Fundación José Antonio de Castro, 1999.

_____. *Dulce dueño*. Edited by Marina Mayoral. Madrid: Castalia, 1989.

_____. "La educación del hombre y de la mujer: sus relaciones y diferencias. Memoria leída en el congreso pedagógico el día 16 de Octubre de 1892." *Nuevo Teatro Crítico* 2 (1892): 14–82.

_____. "Error de diagnóstico." In *Emilia Pardo Bazán: Cuentos completos*, edited by Juan Paredes Núñez, 4:74–77. A Coruña: Fundación Pedro Barrie de la Maza, Conde de Fenosa, 1990.

_____. *El lirismo en la poesía fiancesa*. Madrid: Pueyo, [1923?].

_____. "La mujer española." In *La mujer española y otros escritos*, edited by Guadalupe Gómez Ferrer, 83–116. Madrid: Cátedra, 1999.

_____. "La novia fiel." In *Emilia Pardo Bazán: Cuentos completos*, edited by Juan Paredes Núñez, 1:304–07. A Coruña, Spain: Fundación Pedro Barrie de la Maza, Conde de Fenosa, 1990.

_____. "La nueva cuestión palpitante." In *Obras completas*, edited by Harry L. Kirby, Jr, 3:1157–95. Madrid: Aguilar, 1973.

_____. *Obras completas*. 3 vols. Edited by Harry L. Kirby Jr. Madrid: Aguilar, 1973.

_____. "Una opinión sobre la mujer: El discurso del Marqués del Busto en la Real Academia de Medicina." *Nuevo Teatro Crítico* 2 (1892): 71–84.

_____. "El porvenir de la literatura después de la guerra." In *Obras completas*, edited by Harry L. Kirby Jr, 3:1543–51. Madrid: Aguilar, 1973.

_____. *La Quimera*. 1905. Edited by Marina Mayoral. Madrid: Cátedra, 2007.

_____. "Reflexiones científicas contra el darwinismo." In *Obras completas*, edited by Harry L. Kirby Jr, 3:537–70. Madrid: Aguilar, 1973.

_____. *San Francisco de Asís*. Mexico City: Porrúa, 1994.

_____. "La subida de los liberales." *Nuevo Teatro Crítico* 2 (1892): 83–90.

Parker, Robert Dale. *How to Interpret Literature: Critical Theory for Literary and Cultural Studies*. 3rd ed. New York: Oxford University Press, 2015.

Pattison, Walter T. *Emilia Pardo Bazán*. New York: Twayne, 1971.

Payne, Stanely G. *Spanish Catholicism: An Historical Overview*. Madison: University of Wisconsin Press, 1984.

Péladan, Joséphin. *Le vice suprême*. 1884. Paris: Éditions des Autres, 1979.

Perales y Gutiérrez, Arturo. *El supernaturalismo de Santa Teresa y la filosofía médica, ó, Sea los éxtasis, raptos y enfermedades de la Santa ante las ciencias médicas*. Madrid: Librería Católica de Gregorio del Amo, 1894.

Peratoner, Amancio. *Fisiología de la noche de bodas: Misterios del lecho conyugal*. Barcelona: N. Curriols, 1892.

Pereira-Muro, Carmen. "Mimetismo, misticismo y la cuestión de la escritura femenina en *Dulce Dueño* de Emilia Pardo Bazán." *La Tribuna* 4 (2006): 153–80.

_____. "Relecturas femeninas del modernismo: El teatro de Wilde y las óperas de Strauss y Wagner en *Dulce Dueño*." In *Actas del IV Simposio Emilia Pardo Bazán y las artes del espectáculo*. A Coruña, Spain: Fundación Caixa Galicia, 2008.

Pérez Galdós, Benito. *La familia de Léon Roch*. Edited by Íñigo Sánchez Llama. Madrid: Cátedra, 2003.

_____. *La Fontana de Oro*. 1870. Madrid: Alianza Editorial, 1970.

_____. *Halma*. Salamanca: Almar, 1970.

_____. *La loca de la casa: Novela dialogada en cuatro jornadas*. 1892. Madrid: Sucesores de Hernando, 1915.

_____. *Nazarín*. 1907. Madrid: Alianza, 1984.

Pérez Gutiérrez, Francisco. *El problema religioso en la generación de 1868*. Madrid: Taurus, 1975.

Pitarch Fernández, Pau. "Las armas del martirio. Una lectura del misticismo en *Dulce dueño* (1911) de Emilia Pardo Bazán." In *Las hijas de Eva: Historia, tradición y simbología*, edited by Inés Calero Secall and Virginia Aifaro Bech, 183–95. Málaga: CEDMA, 2006.

Polanen, Marleen van, Cristina Colonnesi, Ruben G. Fukkink, and Louis W. C. Tavecchio. "Is Caregiver Gender Important for Boys and Girls? Gender-Specific Child-Caregiver Interactions and Attachment Relationships." *Early Education and Development* 28, no. 5: 559–71. https://doi.org/10.1080/1 0409289.2016.1258928.

Pouillet, Thesée. *Del onanismo en la mujer (Placeres ilícitos)*. Madrid: A. Pérez, 1883.

Posada, Adolfo. *Leopoldo Alas "Clarín."* Oviedo, Spain: La Cruz, 1946.

Pozzi, Gabriela. "Madres histéricas, médicos y la sexualidad en tres cuentos fntásticos de Emilia Pardo Bazán." *Letras Femeninas* 26, nos. 1–2 (Spring-Fall 2000): 157–69.

Powell, Eilene. "Sadomasoquismo sagrado y la hagiografía irónica en *Dulce dueño* de Emilia Pardo Bazán." In *Sexualidades periféricas: consolidaciones literarias y fílmicas en la España de fin de siglo XIX y fin de milenio*, edited by Nuria Godón and Michael J. Horswell, 91–120. Madrid: Fundamentos, 2016.

Pulido Fernández, Ángel. *Anales de la Sociedad Ginecológica Española* 2 (1876): 52–54, 74–79, 104–11, 265–67, 321–29.

_____. *Bosquejos medico-sociales para la mujer*. Madrid: Víctor Saiz, 1876.

Radcliff, Pamela Beth. *Modern Spain: 1808 to the Present*. Hoboken, NJ: John Wiley & Sons, 2017.

Ragan, Robin. "Another Look at Nucha's Hysteria: Pardo Bazán's Response to the Medical Field of Late Nineteenth-Century Spain." *Letras Femeninas* 30, no. 1 (Summer 2004): 141–54.

Resina, Joan Ramón. "Ana Ozores's Nerves." *Hispanic Review* 71 (Spring 2003): 229–52.

Reeves, Sharon L. "El anticlericalismo en la novela naturalista española de Eduardo López Bago." In *Ensayos sin frontera (Estudios sobre literatura hispanoamericana)*, edited by Carlos Aguasaco et al, 106–20. New York: Sin Frontera; 2005.

————. "Behind the Convent Walls: Anticlericalism in Eduardo López Bago's *La Monja*." In *Aportaciones eruditas y literarias en homenaje a Gregorio C. Martín*, edited by Juan Fernández Jiménez et al, 223–30. Erie, PA: School of Humanities and Social Sciences, Penn State Erie, the Behrend College, 2016.

Rich, Lawrence, "Fear and Loathing in Vetusta: Coding, Class, and Gender in Clarín's *La Regenta*." *Revista Canadiense de Estudios Hispánicos* 25, no. 3 (Spring 2001): 509–10.

Richet, Charles. "Les démoniaques d'aujourd'hui." *Revue des deux mondes* (1880): 340–72, 552–83, 828–63.

Richmond, Carolyn. "Las ideas de Leopoldo Alas 'Clarín' sobre la mujer en sus escritos previos a *La Regenta*." In *Homenaje al Profesor Antonio Vilanova*, edited by Marta Cristina Carbonell, 2:523–39. Barcelona: Anthropos, 1988.

Rodríguez, Erika. "Crip Time in Fin-de-siècle Spain: Disability, Degeneration, and Eugenics." PhD diss., Washington University of Saint Louis, 2019.

Rodríguez Marín, Rafael. "Orientaciones para el estudio de los *Relatos breves* de 'Clarín." In *Relatos breves*, by Leopoldo Alas "Clarín," 279–92. Madrid: Castalia, 1986.

Rodríguez Ocaña, Esteban. *La constitución de la medicina social como disciplina en España (1882–1923)*. Madrid: Ministerio de Sanidad y Consumo, 1987.

Rousseau, G. S. "Nymphomania, Bienville and the Rise of Erotic Sensibility." In *Sexuality in Eighteenth-Century Britain*, edited by Paul-Gabriel Bouce, 95–119. Manchester, UK: Manchester University Press, 1982.

Rousselle, Elizabeth Smith. "The Saint and the Hysteric: Mysticism in *Nazarín* and *Dulce dueño*." In *Modernity and Epistemology in Nineteenth-Century Spain: Fringe Discourses*, edited by Ryan A. Davis and Alicia Cerezo Paredes, 119–36. Lanham, MD: Lexington Books, 2017.

————. *Gender and Modernity in Spanish Literature: 1789–1920*. New York: Palgrave MacMillan, 2014.

Rousselle, Elizabeth Smith, and Joseph Drexler-Dreis. "Lina soy yo: Mysticism as Subversion and Identity for the Modern Woman Writer in Emilia Pardo Bazán's *Dulce dueño*." *Hispanófila* 166 (September 2012): 57–75.

Ruiz, Juan. *El libro de buen amor*. Madrid: Cátedra, 2006.

Ruiz Somavilla, María José. "La legitimación de la ideología a través de la ciencia: la salud y la enfermedad de la mujer en el *Siglo Médico.*" In *De la Ilustracion al Romanticismo, VII Encuentro: La mujer en los siglos XVIII—XIX*, edited by Cinta Canterla González, 103–14. Cádiz, Spain: Universidad de Cádiz, 1994.

Rutherford, John, trans. *La Regenta*. London: Penguin, 2005.

Saillard, Simone. "Ana Ozores, de la mystique á l'hystérie." *Co-Textes* 18 (1989): 65–131.

Sánchez-Conejero, Cristina. "*Dulce dueño*, de Emilia Pardo Bazán: una novela posmodernamente anticanónica." *Crítica Hispánica*, 50, nos. 1–2 (2008): 161–73.

Sand, George. *Mademoiselle de la Quintinie*. Paris: Calmann-Lévy, 1863.

Sarrión Mora, Adelina. *Sexualidad y confesión: La solicitación ante el Tribunal del Santo Oficio (Siglos XVI–XIX)*. Madrid: Alianza, 1994.

Sawa, Alejandro. *El criadero de curas*. Madrid: Libros de Ballena, 2014.

SEM. *Los Borbones en pelota*, edited and introduced by Isabel Burdiel. Zaragoza: Institución Fernando "El Católico," 2012.

Showalter, Elaine. *The Female Malady: Women, Madness and English Culture: 1830–1980*. New York: Penguin, 1985.

Shubert, Adrian. *A Social History of Modern Spain*. London: Unwin Hyman, 1990.

Sieburth, Stephanie. *Reading* La Regenta: *Duplicitous Discourse and the Entropy of Structure*. Amsterdam: John Benjamins, 1990.

Simón Palmer, María Pilar. "La higiene y la medicina de la mujer española a través de los libros (S.XVI a XIX)." In *La mujer en la historia de Espana (Siglos XVI–XX): Actas de las II jornadas de investigacion interdisciplinaria sobre la mujer*, edited by Cinta Canterla González, 71–84. Madrid: Universidad Autónoma de Madrid, 1982.

Sinclair, Alison. *Dislocations of Desire: Gender, Identity and Strategy in La Regenta*. Chapel Hill: University of North Carolina Dept. of Romance Languages, 1998.

Smith, Jennifer. "Female Masculinity in *La Regenta.*" *Modern Spanish Women as Agents of Change: Essays in Honor of Maryellen Bieder*, edited by Jennifer Smith, 189–204. Lewisburg, PA: Bucknell University Press, 2018.

———. "Reinterpreting Hysteria under Patriarchy in Emilia Pardo Bazán's 'La novia fiel' and 'Error de diagnóstico.'" *Decimonónica* 9, no.1 (2012): 92–106. http://www.decimononica.org/wp-content/uploads/2013/01/Smith_9.1.pdf.

———. "Women and the Deployment of Sexuality in Nineteenth-Century Spain." *Revista de Estudios Hispánicos* 40, no. 1 (January 2006): 145–70.

———. "Women, Mysticism and Alternative Technologies of the Self in Selected Writings of Emilia Pardo Bazán." *Revista de Estudios Hispánicos* 45, no. 1 (March 2011): 155–75.

Smith-Rosenberg, Carroll. *Disorderly Conduct: Visions of Gender in Victorian America.* New York: Knopf, 1985.

Sobejano, Gonzalo. Introduction to *La Regenta,* by Leopoldo Alas "Clarín," 1:5–56. Madrid: Clásicos Castalia, 1981.

Sokal, Alan, and Jean Bricmont. *Fashionable Nonsense: Postmodern Intellectuals' Abuse of Science.* New York, Picador, 1998.

Sprenger, Jacobus, and Heinrich Kramer. *Malleus Maleficarum.* Translated by Montague Summers. London: Folio Society, 1968.

Standley, Arline Reilein. *Auguste Comte.* Boston: Twayne, 1981.

Starr, Douglas. *Blood: An Epic History of Medicine and Commerce.* New York: Alfred A. Knopf, 1998.

Strenski, Ivan. "Religion, Power, and Final Foucault." *Journal of the American Academy of Religion* 66, no. 2 (Summer 1998): 345–67.

Suárez Casañ, V. *El amor lesbio.* Conocimientos para la vida privada, vol. 9. 2nd ed. Edited by Pío Arias Carvajal. Barcelona: Maucci, [189-?].

————. *Enciclopedia médica popular.* 2 vols. Barcelona: M. Maucci, 1894.

————. *Secretos del lecho conyugal.* Conocimientos para la vida privada, vol. 2. 2nd ed. Edited by Pío Arias Carvajal. Barcelona: Maucci, [189-?].

————. *Los vicios solitarios.* Conocimientos para la vida privada, vol. 5. 2nd ed. Edited by Pío Arias Carvajal. Barcelona: Maucci, [189-?].

Sutherland, Erika. "Death in the Bedroom: Eduardo López Bago and His Suspect Syphilitics." *Excavatio* 18, nos. 1–2 (2003): 278–92.

Tambling, Jeremy. *Confession: Sexuality, Sin, the Subject.* Manchester, UK: Manchester University Press, 1990.

Teresa de Jesús, Santa. *Libro de la vida.* Edited by Dámaso Chicharro. 8th ed. Madrid: Cátedra, 1990.

Thulié, H. Prologue to *Misticismo y locura: estudio de psicología normal y patológica comparadas,* 1–7. Translated by Eduardo Ovejero. Madrid: España Moderna, [1907?].

Tolliver, Joyce. *Cigar Smoke and Violet Water: Gendered Discourse in the Stories of Emilia Pardo Bazán.* Lewisburg, PA: Bucknell University Press, 1998.

————. "Knowledge, Desire and Syntactic Empathy in Pardo Bazán's 'La novia fiel.'" *Hispania* 72, no. 4 (December 1989): 909–18.

————. "La voz antifeminista y la amenaza 'andrógina' en el fin de siglo." In *Sexualidad y escritura (1850–2000),* edited by Raquel Medina and Barbara Zecchi, 105–19. Barcelona: Anthropos, 2002.

Tomsich, Maria Giovanna. "Histeria y narración en *La Regenta.*" *Anales de Literatura Española* 5 (1986–87): 494–517.

Tsuchiya, Akiko. "Entre la ciencia y la pornografía: masculinidades abyectas y perversiones femeninas en la serie *El Cura* (1885) de Eduardo López

Bago." In *Sexualidades periféricas: Consolidaciones literarias y fílmicas en la España de fin de siglo XIX y fin de milenio*, edited by Nuria Godón and Michael J. Horswell, 35–62. Madrid: Fundamentos, 2016.

————. *Marginal Subjects: Gender and Deviance in Fin-de-siècle Spain*. Toronto: University of Toronto Press, 2011.

————. "Taming the Deviant Body: Representations of the Prostitute in Nineteenth-century Spain." *Anales Galdosianos* 36 (2001): 255–67.

Underberg, Natalie. "Sor Juana's Villancicos: Context, Gender, and Genre." *Western Folklore* 60, no. 4 (Autumn 2001): 297–316.

Valis, Noël. *The Decadent Vision in Leopoldo Alas Clarín: A Study of* La Regenta *and* Su único hijo. Baton Rouge: Louisiana University Press, 1981.

————. "Hysteria and Historical Context in *La Regenta*." *Revista Hispánica Moderna* 52, no. 2 (December 2000): 325–51.

————. *Sacred Realism: Religion and the Imagination in Modern Spanish Narrative*. New Haven, CT: Yale University Press, 2010.

Vázquez García, Francisco. *La invención del racismo: Nacimiento de la biopolítica en España, 1600–1940*. Madrid: Akal, 2011.

————. "Ninfomanía y construcción simbólica de la femineidad (España, siglos XVIII–XIX)." In *De la ilustracion al romanticismo, VII encuentro: La mujer en los siglos XVIII–XIX*, edited by Cinta Canterla González, 125–35. Universidad de Cadiz, 1994.

————. "Patologización del celibato en la medicina española (1820–1920)." *Asclepio* 70, no. 2 (June-December 2018): 1–12.

Vázquez García, Francisco, and Andrés Moreno Mengíbar. *Sexo y razón: Una genealogia de la moral sexual en España (Siglos XVI–XX)*. Madrid: Akal, 1997.

Vázquez García, Francisco, and José Benito Seoane Cegarra. "España y la cruzada médica contra la masturbación (1800–1900): Elementos para una genealogía." *Hispania* 64, no. 218 (2004): 835–67.

La vida de Lazarillo de Tormes. 4th ed. Madrid: Castalia, 1984.

Viguera, Baltasar de. *La fisiología y patología de la mujer*. 4 vols. Madrid: Ortega, 1827.

Ward, Peter. *The Clean Body: A Modern History*. Montreal: McGill-Queens University Press, 2019.

Weber, Alison. *Teresa of Ávila and the Rhetoric of Femininity*. Princeton, NJ: Princeton University Press, 1990.

Williams, Kipling D. "The Pain of Exclusion." *Scientific American Mind* 21, no. 6 (January/February 2011): 30–37.

Wolters, Nicholas. "Debajo de la sotana: (Re)Dressing Clerical Masculinity in Alas's *La Regenta*." *Revista de Estudios Hispánicos* 53, no. 1 (March 2019): 329–52.

_____. "Unholy Perversions: Clerical Deviance and Precarious Youth in Nakens, Sawa, and López Bago." In *Literatura y parafilia en el siglo XIX*, edited by Jorge Avilés-Diz, 273–89. Madrid: Albatros Ediciones, 2018.

Zahonero, José. *Mi mujer y El cura. Confidencias de un aldeano*. Madrid: Imprenta Popular,1900.

Zamacois, Eduardo. *El misticismo y las perturbaciones del sistema nervioso*. Madrid: Imprenta Popular, 1893.

Zubiaurre, Maite. *Cultures of the Erotic in Spain, 1898–1939*. Nashville, TN: Vanderbilt University Press, 2012.

_____. Introduction to *El cura (Caso de incesto): Novela médico-social*, by Eduardo López Bago, vii–xlvii. Edited by Maite Zubiaurre and Luis Cuesta. Doral, FL: Stockcero, 2013.

_____. Introduction to *La Regenta*, by Leopoldo Alas (Clarín), vii–xliii. Edited by Maite Zubiaurre and Eilene Powell. Doral, FL: Stockcero, 2012.

INDEX

Page numbers in *italic* refer to illustrations